Contents

Preface

The two dominant aspects of MacNeice's outlook that have conditioned his poetry, as I read it, and therefore my emphasis in this study, are, firstly, his deep and abiding awareness of the poet's need for belief, and, secondly, his equally strong and conscious awareness of the need to find the forms, especially the tone of voice, appropriate to the creative expression of this belief. The two are, of course, as MacNeice constantly affirmed, inseparable, each working upon and modifying the other. Thus, while he rejected all current dogmas, he insisted at the same time that 'to shun dogma does not mean to renounce belief',[1] and held strenuously to the end by his faith in the presence of transcendent ultimates that reveal themselves in phenomenal experience in a consistent, but constantly changing, pattern. Out of this arose, almost as a tenet of faith, his abhorrence of static pattern, his insistence on the absolute necessity for renewal—in life as in poetry—but renewal within a shapely, and consciously shaped, pattern.

It is, then, my conviction that these are the twin essentials of MacNeice's outlook and practice, and it is these I have attempted to illustrate. In Chapters 2–4 I am therefore concerned, having initially discussed some aspects of the connection between poetry and belief, to unfold the dominant strands in the pattern of MacNeice's thinking as the kind of questions he consistently asked threw up hints and suggestions that led him more and more firmly into wide, particular ways. In the chapters that follow, I have tried to illustrate the effect of this upon the form of his poetic expression and communication.

I have deliberately limited myself to this attempt to unfold the strands in a pattern of disciplined questioning, avoiding any attempt to define a positive set of beliefs that might seem to emerge: to analysis, that is, rather than synthesis. It was the creative question itself that MacNeice valued, the question being ultimately identifiable with the questioner, and both with the quest that is the end of our living. The synthesis itself lies ahead, probably unknowable.[2] Similarly, although he himself insisted that he had

---

[1] From an article 'The Poet in England Today', in the *New Republic*, 25 March 1940.
[2] See later the parable of Garlon and Galahad, pp. 49–50.

beliefs, and hoped that these emerged in his poetry, he flatly declined to say what '-ism' they illustrated or solution they offered. He remarked, for instance, in his prefatory note to *Autumn Journal*: 'I have certain beliefs which, I hope, emerge in the course of it but which I have refused to abstract from their context.' He also hopes that the poem 'contains some "criticism of life" or implies some standards which are not merely personal'.[1] He is even more downright in his introductory note to *The Dark Tower*:

In an age which precludes the simple and militant faith of a Bunyan, belief (whether consciously formulated or not) still remains a *sine qua non* of the creative writer. I have my beliefs and they permeate *The Dark Tower*. But do not ask me what Ism it illustrates or what Solution it offers.[2]

Nor have I attempted, except incidentally, what is so often (but not always relevantly) expected of the literary critic: to come forcibly to grips with virtues and defects in the writing itself. This is an important task of literary criticism, but it is not the one I have principally set myself here. No doubt this kind of criticism will be made increasingly by others. And I am certainly not concerned to rank Louis MacNeice, whether as a major or minor poet, or as the first, second or third poet of his generation, although I have suggested in my conclusion the lines along which I think the former kind of assessment might be made. I shall be satisfied if I have achieved my more limited objectives, and others see enough of value in my findings to take them further, applying them in different ways, or even to feel that they merit contradiction. Perhaps this is the more necessary as the metaphysical element in MacNeice's poetry has, so far, been so little stressed by critics. Mr. G. S. Fraser, however, remarked: 'Perhaps the submerged nine-tenths, both of his poetry and his personality, is a speculative metaphysician, of an unfashionably ambitious sort.'[3] This is one of the shrewdest comments I have read on MacNeice and his poetry.

---

[1] *C.P.D.*, p. 101.   [2] *D.T.*, p. 22.
[3] *Vision and Rhetoric*, etc., pp. 182–3. (See Bibliog.)

In a more negative sense, I shall be happy if I have helped to dispose of two of the major obstacles that still incredibly stand in the way of a just assessment of MacNeice: (i) that he was one of a group of (political) poets, whose luminary was Somebody Else; (ii) that he did not develop as a poet. Both of these misconceptions have been very damaging to his reputation, but it was the second that especially annoyed him—witness his late comment: 'Poets are always being required—by the critics and by themselves— to "develop". Most critics, however, to perceive such development, need something deeper than a well and wider than a church-door.'[1]

To illustrate my views I have, for various reasons, confined myself almost wholly to published material. In order to reduce footnoting, however, I have generally not given a page reference to any poem included in the last collected poems, where there is an alphabetical index.

W. T. M.
Bergen, 1971

Acknowledgements

I am greatly indebted to MacNeice's friends and acquaintances and I can only say that MacNeice's own generous nature was reflected in theirs. I received far more help, for which I am endlessly grateful, than I can ever record here, and I can only hope that I have recorded it all privately and, where relevant, in my text and footnotes. But I must especially thank those who, from different viewpoints and at different stages, have read and criticized this book, namely Mrs. Hedli MacNeice, Lady Nicholson, Professor Barbara Hardy, Professor Sir Anthony Blunt, Professor E. R. Dodds, Mr. John Hilton, and Mr. Charles Peake. They have freed me from many a blunder and foolish notion. For those

[1] *P.B.S.B.*, no. 28, February 1961.

errors that remain, I have only myself to blame. Some of these critics have even read my script at more than one stage, notably Professor Dodds, without whose ruthless surgery the book would not have reached its present form. And I must also especially thank many librarians on both sides of the Atlantic, the Irish Sea, and the North Sea for their multifarious help.

On this side of the North Sea, I wish to say how grateful I am to Lise, my wife, for her skilled help as a professional librarian, and her non-professional but invaluable help as typist and proof-reader; to Dr. Rolf Karlsen, Professor of English Philology in the Norwegian School of Economics, for his encouragement of my work; and to my Maecenas, the Academic Council of the Norwegian School of Economics, for its generous support of my researches.

For permission to quote extracts from the published works of Louis MacNeice I am indebted to Mrs. Hedli MacNeice and Professor E. R. Dodds and to the following: Faber and Faber Ltd. (*Collected Poems*, ed. E. R. Dodds, the individual collections and plays, and *The Strings are False*); Victor Gollancz Ltd. (*Blind Fireworks*); the Hutchinson Publishing Group Ltd. ('When I Was Twenty-One'); the Longman Group Ltd. (*I Crossed the Minch*); the Master of Marlborough College (*The Marlburian*); the Editor of the *New Statesman* (extracts from the *New Statesman* and the *New Statesman and Nation*); the Editor of *Orpheus* ('Experiences with Images'); Oxford University Press, London (*Modern Poetry*); Oxford University Press, New York (*Modern Poetry* and *The Collected Poems of Louis MacNeice*, ed. E. R. Dodds, © The Estate of Louis MacNeice, 1966); Random House Inc. (for the MacNeice excerpt from *Letters from Iceland*).

For permission to quote from the published works of W. H. Auden, T. S. Eliot, and Ezra Pound I am indebted as follows: to Faber and Faber Ltd. (*About the House, Four Quartets, Letters from Iceland*, and 'Δώρια' in the *Shorter Collected Poems* of Ezra Pound); Harcourt, Brace, Jovanovich Inc. (*Four Quartets*); New Directions Inc. ('Δώρια' in *Personae* © Ezra Pound 1926); Random House Inc. (*About the House* and *Letters from Iceland*). I am also indebted to Mr. Julian Symons and the Editor of *Poetry* for permission to quote from 'Louis MacNeice: the Artist as Everyman'.

For permission to quote from Louis MacNeice's letters I am indebted to Mrs. Hedli MacNeice, Lady Nicholson, Professor Sir Anthony Blunt, Professor and Mrs. E. R. Dodds, and Mr. John Hilton. The letters from MacNeice to Sir Anthony Blunt are now lodged in the Library of King's College, Cambridge (MSS. Misc. Boxes 37 and 38), and I am further indebted to the Librarian for permission to quote from them.

I also owe a particular debt of gratitude to the B.B.C. for permission to study and to quote from scripts by MacNeice in their archives. I also received much valuable help from friends and colleagues of MacNeice in the B.B.C.

List of Abbreviations

Admin.	*The Mad Islands* and *The Administrator*
Aga.	*The Agamemnon*
A.J.	*Autumn Journal*
'A.L.P.'	'An Alphabet of Literary Prejudices' (page references to *The Windmill*: see Bibliog.)
A.S.	*Autumn Sequel*
Astrol.	*Astrology*
B.F.	*Blind Fireworks*
B.P.	*The Burning Perch*
C.C.	*Christopher Columbus*
'C.M.'	'Childhood Memories' (see Bibliog.)
C.P.	*Collected Poems, 1925–1948*
C.P.D.	*Collected Poems* (ed. Professor E. R. Dodds)
C.P.R.H.	*Poems, 1925–1940* (Random House)
D.T.	*The Dark Tower and other radio scripts*
E.C.	*The Earth Compels*
'E.I.'	'Experiences with Images' (page references to *Orpheus*: see Bibliog.)

F.Q.	*Four Quartets*
G.F.	*Goethe's Faust*
H.N.	Holograph notebook, property of the MacNeice Estate
H.S.	*Holes in the Sky*
L.D.	*The Last Ditch*
L.I.	*Letters from Iceland*
M.E.	The MacNeice Estate
Minch	*I Crossed the Minch*
M.P.	*Modern Poetry*
O.G.	*One for the Grave*
O.P.	*Oxford Poetry*
P.	*Poems* (1935)
P.B.S.B.	*The Poetry Book Society Bulletin* (see Bibliog.)
P.P.	*Plant and Phantom*
P.R.H.	*Poems* (Random House, 1937)
R.P.	*A Radio Portrait* (see Bibliog.)
R.W.	*Roundabout Way*
S.A.F.	*The Strings are False*
Sol.	*Solstices*
Spr.	*Springboard*
T.B.O.	*Ten Burnt Offerings*
'Twenty-One'	'When I Was Twenty-One' (page references to *The Saturday Book 21*: see Bibliog.)
Visit.	*Visitations*
V.P.	*Varieties of Parable*
Yeats	*The Poetry of W. B. Yeats*

Initial letters are used for Lady Nicholson (E.N.), Professor Dodds (E.R.D.), Professor Sir Anthony Blunt (A.F.B.), and Mr. John Hilton (J.R.H.).

Some self-evident abbreviations are used for periodicals: for instance *T.L.S.* for the *Times Literary Supplement*, *N.Y.T.B.R.* for the *New York Times Book Review*, *N.S.N.* for the *New Statesman and Nation*, *N.S.* for the *New Statesman*, as *N.S.N.* became after 6 July 1957.

Part I Metaphysician

I Outline of a Biography

Art has been called an autobiographical game, and it was a popular one in the 1930s. As Virginia Woolf put it:

When everything is rocking round one, the only person who remains comparatively stable is oneself. When all faces are changing and obscured, the only face one can see clearly is one's own. So they wrote about themselves—in their plays, in their poems, in their novels. No other ten years can have produced so much autobiography as the ten years between 1930 and 1940. No one, whatever his class or his obscurity, seems to have reached the age of thirty without writing his autobiography. But the leaning-tower writers wrote about themselves honestly, therefore creatively.[1]

The 'leaning-tower writers' ('Day Lewis, Auden, Spender, Isherwood, Louis MacNeice and so on') are 'the sons of well-to-do parents, who could afford to send them to a public school and universities'.[2] These last are the towers 'built of gold and stucco' that conditioned the outlook of MacNeice and the others: 'But the tendency that makes it possible for us to group the names of these writers together, and gives their work a common likeness, was the tendency of the tower they sat on—the tower of middle-class birth and expensive education—to lean.'[3] Virginia Woolf goes on to illustrate some of the group characteristics.

MacNeice himself, discussing in *Modern Poetry* the connection between the poem and the poet, had expressed himself strongly on the difference between general and particular conditioning factors:

However much is known about the poet, the poem remains a thing distinct from him. But poetry being firstly communication, a certain knowledge of the poet's background will help us to understand him, for his language is to some extent personal. It may be true that any contemporary poet is a mouthpiece of the Zeitgeist, but, as mouthpieces alter what you put into them, it is helpful to consider the shape of the mouthpiece itself. I have no patience with those determinist critics whose determinism merely takes account of *general* conditions. . . .[4]

[1] 'The Leaning Tower', in *Folios of New Writing*, ed. John Lehmann, London, Autumn 1940, p. 28.
[2] Ibid., p. 20.   [3] Ibid., p. 21.   [4] Op. cit., p. 89.

Nevertheless, as a writer preoccupied with himself and his personal situation, he does answer Virginia Woolf's description. Indeed, his preoccupation with his own past amounted, in the words of his friend and literary executor, Professor Dodds, 'almost to an obsession'.[1] It should therefore be profitable to begin a study of MacNeice's poetry by trying to distinguish something of 'the mouthpiece itself'—especially as MacNeice has perhaps suffered more than any of the others from this supposed 'tendency that makes it possible for us to group the names of these writers together, and gives their work a common likeness'.

An almost obsessive theme in the poetry of Louis MacNeice is the search for identity and home. With ancestral roots deep in the West of Ireland, born in Belfast, educated in England and living there for most of his adult life, he found himself perpetually puzzled in face of the combination of factors composing the *I am*. This puzzlement is the theme, for example, of the poem 'Day of Renewal', in the collection *Ten Burnt Offerings*:

> Such and such my beginnings, launched and engined
> With such and such a tackle of nerve and gland
> And steered by such and such taboos and values,
> My What and How science might understand
> But neither the first nor last page tells the story
> And that I am remains just that I am.
> The whole, though predetermined to a comma,
> Still keeps its time, its place, its glory.

He recurs frequently to ancestral influences. We find him, for instance, in 'Auden and MacNeice: Their Last Will and Testament', expressing, with an obvious depth of sincerity, his debt to his Irish peasant ancestors, to whom he gives credit for some of his most valued qualities:

> L.   And to my own in particular whose rooms
> Were whitewashed, small, soothed with the smoke of peat,
> Looking out on the Atlantic's gleams and glooms,

Of whom some lie among brambles high remote
Above the yellow falls of Ballysodare
Whose hands were hard with handling cart and boat

I leave the credit for that which may endure
Within myself of peasant vitality and
Of the peasant's sense of humour. . . .[1]

Elsewhere the ancestral associations are more regal, and he is the Irish Celt, conscious of descent from the kings of his race. Thus, in *I Crossed the Minch,* where he is complaining of his bad luck in being brought up among the hybrid Ulster Scots, he takes comfort (though not without a tinge of self-irony) in the reflection that his remote ancestry was otherwise:

I myself was autochthonous, descended from an Irish king—the name MacNeice being derived from Conchubar MacNessa, the villain of the Deirdre saga. (In later years I was told that the derivation was much more probably from Naoise, the hero of the same saga, and since then I have, in defiance of natural history, claimed descent from both of them and in each case by Deirdre.)[2]

In his letters, too, he plays with the ancestral theme, as in a long one written at the age of twenty to Anthony Blunt.[3] Here he sketches, as a *jeu d'esprit*, a genealogical tree that is of more than passing interest:

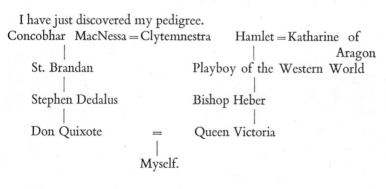

I have just discovered my pedigree.

```
Concobhar  MacNessa = Clytemnestra       Hamlet = Katharine  of
            |                              |               Aragon
    St. Brandan                   Playboy  of  the  Western  World
            |                              |
    Stephen Dedalus                 Bishop Heber
            |                              |
    Don Quixote          =        Queen Victoria
                         |
                      Myself.
```

[1] *L.I.*, p. 237.   [2] Op. cit., p. 26.   [3] From Carrickfergus, 29 March 1927.

Turning to something more like immediate biographical fact,[1] we note that Frederick Louis MacNeice was born in Belfast, on 12 September 1907, in the corner house at 1 Brookhill Avenue, which is still there. He had a sister, Elizabeth, four years older, and a mongol brother, William, two years older. His father, the Rev. John Frederick MacNeice, a clergyman of the Church of Ireland, and at that time Rector of Trinity Church, Belfast, was one-quarter Welsh, through his maternal grandfather, John Howell. Louis's paternal grandfather left County Sligo as a boy, and later became a schoolmaster with the Society for Irish Church Missions. He taught for many years in the school on the island of Omey, some seven miles from Clifden, County Galway, but, when his son was thirteen, left there for Dublin. Here J. F. MacNeice was educated at Trinity College.

Louis's mother, a Clesham, was born in the townland of Killy-mangan, some two miles from Clifden. Clifden itself was a 'new town', which had been founded by one John D'Arcy at the end of the eighteenth century, in a wild and remote district. Hither he had brought the Cleshams, skilled stonemasons, for construction work.[2] The family had at one time been Roman Catholic, but Louis's maternal grandfather had become a Protestant on his marriage to Christina Rosetta Bush, Louis's grandmother, whose father is described in a parish register as a ship's carpenter. She had been an assistant matron in a girls' orphanage, and met her death through returning to help at the height of a scarlet fever epidemic, when Louis's mother was a baby of two.

As for MacNeice's remoter ancestry, it is interesting to note that the credit he gives his assumed peasant ancestors for what may endure within himself 'of peasant vitality and/Of the peasant's sense of humour' is perhaps only in part deserved, at any rate on the MacNeice side. When MacNeice's father read, with pleasure, the reference to the County Sligo ancestors in the 'Last Will and Testament', he remarked to his daughter: 'There

---

[1] It is to MacNeice's sister, Lady Nicholson, that I am largely indebted for my biographical information in the earlier part of this chapter.

[2] Lady Nicholson believes, from enquiries made among very old people in Clifden, that the Cleshams came from Scotland, possibly from the Hebrides, where the name occurs (e.g. as the name of a mountain on Lewis).

is only one mistake in it. The MacNeices were never peasants.'

If, therefore, Louis did inherit the gifts he believed he had from the Irish peasantry, it is much more likely that it was on his mother's side. When the Cleshams reached Connemara they intermarried with the people they found there, marrying into families that had lived in the remote country around Clifden for centuries. From the Clesham side, too, comes a legend of far-off Spanish blood.

J. F. MacNeice left Belfast in January 1909, when Louis was one and a half, to become Rector of Carrickfergus, then a much smaller place. As the previous incumbent, the Rev. George Chamberlain, lay ill for two years at the Rectory, the family occupied a house by the harbour for this time. The main rooms of the house (a tall three-storey one), including the nursery, had fine views of the Lough and its white sails, as well as the very old and impressive Norman castle. It was a rather gloomy house, however, with no garden. The inner harbour was unpleasant at low tide, an expanse of mud and tin cans, and the atmosphere generally was somewhat confined and squalid. (The young Louis called the harbour house 'the Moggy House'.) It was a relief for everyone to move into the Rectory, a fairly new house that had been built for the Rev. Chamberlain, cheerful and sunny, very comfortable for its date, and not typical of Irish rectories of the period. Louis, however, later described it as 'an ordinary little house'.[1]

Unhappily, Mrs. MacNeice was plagued from 1910 by a gynaecological complaint (a uterine fibroid tumour, which occasioned increasingly serious haemorrhages), and her illnesses became more frequent from 1912, when Louis was five. Early in 1913, she visited a specialist in Belfast, who advised a hysterectomy. The operation was performed, and, surgically, was entirely successful. Mrs. MacNeice, however, from the time of her interview with the specialist, suffered from a psychotic depression that never again really lifted. Her condition became so serious that, in August 1913, the family doctor recommended her removal to a private nursing home in Dublin. As her nervous condition

[1] *Zoo*, p. 78.

failed to improve, she was later moved for specialist observation to a Dublin hospital. Here she contracted tuberculosis, from which she died shortly before Christmas 1914. The news was conveyed by their father to the children, who were then ill with measles. This is described by Louis in his autobiography with considerable restraint:

> When our temperatures were falling our father came in one morning, very unlike himself, and told us our mother had died. Elizabeth began to cry but, being unable to cry, I dived down under the clothes and lay at the bottom of the bed where I hoped they would think I was crying. I felt very guilty at being so little moved but decided that when I grew up I would build my mother a monument. And everyone would know that I had built it.[1]

Mrs. MacNeice had always been very fully occupied with parish work, and had consequently required a good deal of house help. The 'Mother's Help' (Miss Craig of *The Strings are False*) played an important part in the children's lives. Her arrival is unsympathetically described by MacNeice:

> One day, however, my mother engaged what was called a Mother's Help. . . . She was small and lean and scrawny, quite unlike Annie, her face was sour and die-hard Puritanical, she had a rasping Northern accent. The daughter of a farmer in County Armagh, she knew all there was to be known about bringing up children; keep them conscious of sin, learn them their sums, keep all the windows shut tight and don't let them run for it is bad for their hearts.[2]

The influence of Miss Craig was counterbalanced by that of Annie, the cook:

> The cook Annie, who was a buxom rosy girl from a farm in County Tyrone, was the only Catholic I knew and therefore my only proof that Catholics were human. She worked very well and fast and filled in her spare time doing Irish crochet work. We would watch the shamrocks and roses growing from her crochet hooks while in a gay

[1] *S.A.F.*, p. 53.
[2] Ibid., p. 41. Lady Nicholson is firmly of the opinion that Louis has expressed in the form of dislike for Miss Craig much of the complicated emotional stress he suffered at the loss of his mother. Miss Craig continued to be a close friend of the family until her death, aged ninety, in May 1963.

warm voice she would tell us about Fivemiletown where she came from and the banshees and fairies and cows of the Clogher valley. They had nice rhymes out there—Lisnaskea for drinking tea, Maguire's Bridge for whisky—and County Tyrone sounded like a land of content. Annie in fact was always contentful except when she had palpitations. And we were content with Annie.[1]

When Annie, who had been their 'bulwark for so long against puritan repression', left in March 1916, she 'was succeeded by Mrs. Knox, a very short little elderly woman with a sharp witch's nose'.[2] Mrs. Knox 'used to have screaming-matches with Miss Craig' and was shortly dismissed, being later reported 'in gaol for working a confidence trick, posing as Lady So-and-so'.[3] When Miss Craig left, she was succeeded by an Englishwoman, Miss Hewitt, who was, apparently, very kind-hearted, and who did her best to bring more order into a household whose ways had slowly deteriorated during nearly four years, when, for practical purposes, it had been without a mistress. Her reforms, however, were resented by the children, and Louis paints an unattractive portrait of her:

This Englishwoman, Miss Hewitt, was very easy game after Miss Craig and Elizabeth and I put on the Wild Irish act for her. Miss Hewitt, who was appalled by the way we raised our hands to protect our faces if ever she spoke the least crossly, soft-pedalled her disciplinary instinct and tried to make the house more genteel. . . . Miss Hewitt considered herself an apostle of light but we thought of her as a heaven-sent ignoramus.[4]

During the time of Mrs. MacNeice's mental illness, the children's father had been distracted with anxiety, and after his wife's death he became sad and withdrawn, having very little contact with the children. In addition to his private pains and anxieties, he was deeply concerned with the bitter political and religious unrest of those years. As one of the very few Church of Ireland ministers who supported Home Rule, he must have been suspect in the eyes of many of his parishioners. This led in 1912 to the expression of a sharp difference of opinion before his

[1] Ibid., p. 41.   [2] Ibid., p. 56.   [3] Ibid.   [4] Ibid., pp. 56–7.

parishioners, and an act of considerable courage. A large company of his parishioners, wishing to travel to Belfast to sign the 'Ulster Covenant', asked the Rector to arrange a special service and give them his blessing before they left. He acceded to their request for a service, but in his sermon gave his reasons for not himself supporting the Covenant. In the years that followed, he never ceased to deplore the increasing violence, or to preach and demonstrate against both its Catholic and its Protestant manifestations. Carson's movement in particular he regarded as lawless and violent, little short of rebellion, and likely to lead to civil war. He did all in his power to combat this ugly and internecine violence, first organizing local people of like mind into a vigilante organization to preserve the peace after dark, and later in a famous series of letters to the press (the Letters of the League of Prayer for Ireland) exhorting leaders of all shades of religious belief to join in opposing violence. The letters appeared in the Dublin and Belfast papers between 21 July 1920, and 23 September 1924.

In April 1917, however, there was a sudden and very welcome improvement in the family relationship: the father remarried. His second wife, Georgina Beatrice Greer, came from one of the wealthiest and best-connected families in the neighbourhood: 'My stepmother's family was the wealthiest family we knew, had made their money in linen and had till fairly recently been Quakers.'[1] The young Louis was 'very angry' and determined to show her what he thought, but his anger quickly evaporated: 'When my stepmother arrived, however, she brought so much comfort and benevolence with her that I dropped my resolution to obstruct.'[2]

Later in the year both Elizabeth and Louis entered English boarding schools. There was no question whatever of the children's being packed off to suit the convenience of their stepmother, with whom Elizabeth and Louis quickly established friendly relations. As Louis records, Elizabeth was now fourteen and her stepmother 'thought it high time she should lose her Northern accent'.[3] Elizabeth, therefore, went to school at Sherborne for the

---

[1] *S.A.F.*, p. 61.   [2] Ibid.   [3] Ibid., p. 62.

Summer Term of 1917, and Louis went to the boys' prep. school in the same Dorset town in September, just after his tenth birthday. Willy, the mongol brother, had gone to an institution in Scotland in the autumn of 1916. He returned for occasional visits, and finally came to live at home permanently about 1923. Hitherto both Louis and his sister had been educated at home by governesses. Their father had interfered very little— only when he became aware that something had gone badly wrong. For instance, 'his humanist feelings were outraged' when he found that the boy had been made to write commonsense essays on The Button and The Pin, 'enumerating the qualities one should look for in each', whereas they had read no Shakespeare beyond Lamb's *Tales*. The children were then in such disgrace that they 'read *Julius Caesar* straight off'.[1] Louis had been writing poems from the age of seven. In *Modern Poetry* he comments on his earliest ode, 'To a Parrot'; and in *Zoo* he quotes the opening lines of his ode 'To a Stuffed Monkey', written when he was eight.[2] A letter to his sister on 23 October 1915 contains a landscape vignette with an effective refrain: 'The water sound/ Gurgles and bubbles around/In a wild country/The cliffs are high/Against the sky/In a wild country/The sun's great ray/Makes hot the traveller's way/In a wild country.' About the time of his ninth birthday, in the autumn of 1916, he began writing his own newspaper.[3]

At Sherborne he immediately fell under the influence of an outstanding headmaster, Littleton Charles Powys, of whom he frequently wrote with affection. He described what seemed to him his strength and limitations in a very sympathetic portrait in *Zoo*, where he concluded that Powys represented

the best (and it is very good) that can come out of that public-school-cum-country-squire attitude, which at its worst is distressingly parochial. Mr. Powys thinks that people bother too much about politics. Love Nature, he says, and your neighbours; then the things beyond the parish boundary or the English Channel will right themselves.[4]

[1] *S.A.F.*, p. 58.   [2] Respectively, pp. 39–40 and p. 69.   [3] *S.A.F.*, p. 58.
[4] Op. cit., p. 222. In the pages that follow, I fill in the background of his schooldays in some little detail, partly because I feel this to be justified on purely biographical grounds;

Louis 'relished being institutionalised', and very soon 'preferred school to home', where he was 'just a child' and 'felt at the mercy of strangers, winced before gutter urchins, crossed the road to avoid the mill-girls'.[1] He 'welcomed even the smells . . . and found even the changing-room much more romantic than the bathroom at home'.[2] His school diary for Monday, 7 January 1918, contains an accomplished and exuberant poem on running a mile race.[3] He entertained his fellow pupils with science fantasies, telling 'a serial story in dormitory which lasted for five terms'.[4] His object being 'to become popular', he played the buffoon (despite a warning from the headmaster), finding the laughter of the boys intoxicating, and 'decided to be generous'.[5] At Sherborne, too, he found deep physical satisfaction in his contacts with the rich yellow sandstone of Dorset, discovering the thrill of collecting fossils under the influence of Littleton Powys, who 'was a lyrical nature-lover and expected us all to collect things'.[6] He also 'studied astronomy which combined the excitement of collecting with the glamour of Church'.[7]

All his pleasure and excitement pour out of him into the weekly letters he wrote home to his family, from the first days of the Winter Term, 1917, to the last days of the Summer Term, 1921.[8] They are filled with delighted reports of games (rugger, cricket, chess, draughts, swimming); with details of reading, meals, class lists and score lists; with his pleasure in natural history (fossils, butterflies); with lively pen and pencil drawings. They all convey the impression of a little boy well contented with his lot.

His last two terms at Sherborne were especially enjoyable, as he had obtained an entrance scholarship to Marlborough College and was marking time. He decided, however, that his days of buffoonery were over, that he would behave differently at Marlborough; he 'had become established as an eccentric and

---

partly because MacNeice himself insists on the importance of the particular environment; and partly because MacNeice was selected as a representative of the typical 1930s poet with a privileged background by Virginia Woolf in her attack on 'the leaning-tower writers'.

[1] *S.A.F.*, p. 67.   [2] Ibid.   [3] The property of Lady Nicholson.
[4] *S.A.F.*, p. 74.   [5] Ibid., p. 66.   [6] Ibid., p. 69.   [7] Ibid., p. 78.
[8] Kept by his stepmother, and now in the possession of Lady Nicholson.

that gets awfully boring'.[1] In the event, he soon acquired a reputation as wit and buffoon that followed him long after his school days. In *Zoo* he records depressing meetings at Lords with Old Boys who laughed whenever he opened his mouth: '. . . this was because at school I had been a professional wit, a role I have long abandoned.'[2]

At Marlborough, as at Sherborne, he was well and happily adjusted to his environment. In various later writings he expressed general satisfaction with the system, admitting only extreme distaste for the inhuman custom of 'basketing'. This last is described in *I Crossed the Minch*[3] and his autobiography:

The wastepaper-basket had another purpose. Once in a while—not more often than once a term—Big Fire decided that someone was undesirable and could therefore provide a Roman holiday. They would seize him, tear off most of his clothes and cover him with house-paint, then put him in the basket and push him round and round the hall. Meanwhile Little Fire, dutifully sitting at their desks, would howl with delight—a perfect exhibition of mass sadism.[4]

It appears again in his radio programme *Return to a School*. Here MacNeice, speaking presumably for himself in the person of Greene, in answer to the Interviewer's insistent question about school community life, 'Did it equip you for life?', makes a comment on the effect of school community life that has an obvious bearing on his later social attitudes: 'Well, sir, I don't really know. It cut me off from most of the community; at the same time it gave me, in a small way, a sort of community sense.'[5] His final attitude may be summed up in a letter home in January 1926, in his last year: 'An article in one paper, written by a man who had collected statistics, says "Marlborough is not a public school, it is a miracle". I should not say so much myself, yet I think it is less cruel to people with minds than any other public school.'

Again he delighted in physical contact with his environment, now the Wiltshire Downs, where he ran with others on 'sweats'

---

[1] S.A.F., p. 78. [2] Op. cit., p. 217. [3] Op. cit., pp. 88–9.
[4] S.A.F., p. 84. [5] Broadcast on the Home Service on 15 October 1954.

when it was too wet for games, or went strenuously cycling with his friend Graham Shepard.[1] Although he says repeatedly he was no athlete, he wrote enthusiastically home to say that he had played rugby for his House (Canning's) and that they had won the House Cup for the first time.[2] Skill in rugby, like skill in Greek grammar, involved the all-important factor of technique. He had begun 'to aspire in all things to a grace that was apparently effortless'.[3]

MacNeice went to Marlborough in September 1921, and had his School Certificate behind him by the end of his third term, when he was still fourteen, after which he specialized.[4] His class marks were excellent and remained so. At the end of his first session he was first in his form, being first in Latin and second in Greek.[5] John Betjeman, in recalling this time, remarked: 'Indeed I envied Louis his brains because he and his life-long friend Graham Shepard . . . used to sit in chairs at the top of the Classical Fifth while their voices were still unbroken and I aged sixteen was near the bottom.'[6] When he returned for his second year, he entered a Classical form, and thereafter had no more Modern Languages, Modern History, Science, or Mathematics.[7] Later, however, he took classes in German with science students: 'In German I have got into an extraordinary set of scientists, where we are reading Hans Andersen's Fairy Tales.'[8]

Fortunately for the young MacNeice, there was a strong, if somewhat recent, highbrow tradition at Marlborough. Bernard Spencer was an exact, and John Betjeman a slightly older, contemporary. Probably the most vitalizing intellectual influence, however, was that of Anthony Blunt, who founded the Anonymous Society, which Louis joined in the autumn of 1924.[9] He wrote home to say that he had heard a paper on Egyptian Art,

[1] *S.A.F.*, pp. 86–8. ('I liked it even when it hailed—hard clean hail whipping the throat and the ears. . . .') In an unpublished poem entitled 'The High Seas' (M.E.), he said: 'The hailstorm and the night express/Furnished my desire to live.' The 'night express' is probably the one on which he is travelling with such excitement in 'Star-Gazer'.

[2] Letter to his family, 12 February 1924. His letters from Marlborough, like those from Sherborne, reflect only his happy acceptance of school life, especially the active, physical pleasures of tennis or squash.

[3] *S.A.F.*, p. 87.   [4] Ibid., p. 82.   [5] Letter to his family, 16 July 1922.

[6] *London Magazine*, December 1963, p. 63.   [7] *S.A.F.*, pp. 82–3.

[8] Letter to his family, 8 June 1924.   [9] *S.A.F.*, p. 95.

and was giving one himself on Northern Fairy Tales and Sagas.[1] In another letter he reports giving a paper to the Anonymous Society on The Plight of the Romantic, and adds the information that 'the other night there was such a silly lecture on architecture. The man evidently rated our intellects very low.'[2] He spoke often at the Debating Society, his contributions generally being noted with appreciation in the school magazine, the *Marlburian*. A characteristic report, for example, of a debate on the motion 'That modern dancing is superior to that of our ancestors' records that:

Mr. MacNeice, in a delightfully entertaining speech, divided dancing into two classes, polite and impolite, of which as usual the impolite is incomparably the better. . . . Some pretty quotations from two great poets, Edith Sitwell and Edward Lear, completed this excellent speech.[3]

Again, a report of the debate on the motion 'That the Victorians were greater than ourselves' records that:

Mr. MacNeice, proposing the motion, brought home to the House intensely the atmosphere of Victorianism. . . . As a last claim to fame, Mr. MacNeice pointed out that the innovation of nonsense as a branch of poetry was due to the Victorians.[4]

The report goes on to record interestingly how 'Mr. Spencer, reading his speech (contrary to the rules) with some fluency, made a violent attack on the snobbery and narrow-mindedness of the Victorians . . .', and concluded by relating that 'Mr. MacNeice gave an example of how a Georgian poet would have written *In Memoriam*'.[5] MacNeice himself lays considerable stress in his *Modern Poetry* on a paper he delivered on Common Sense, where he attacks ' "Common Sense" and, incidentally, Science and the Royal Academy', and says that he has 'learned well the lesson of post-War Anti-Reason', claiming that 'Common Sense is like Jargon: it can only say a thing in one way. Sense is good

[1] Letter to his family, 24 November 1924. The scripts of some of his school and university papers have survived, and are located in the University of Texas library (see Bibliog.).

[2] Letter to his family, November 1925.

[3] *Marlburian*, 10 March 1926.   [4] Ibid., 17 February 1926.

[5] Ibid. It is sad to reflect that MacNeice and Spencer, whose names are linked in this report, died within days of each other in September 1963, in each case tragically and avoidably.

prose and Nonsense is poetry.'[1] Shortly after this (1925), he 'wrote another paper, also on the road to surrealism'.[2]

The *Marlburian*, an extremely good school magazine, provided the young MacNeice with an outlet for his rapidly developing creative instinct and technical skill. He regularly contributed poems and stories (especially parables with a strong vein of satirical fantasy) which show him not only very intelligent and precocious, but already quite clearly a writer.[3] In 1926 he shared the Cotton English Essay Prize. John Betjeman records that Mac-Neice and Spencer 'looked like poets even then. Louis with his dark eyes resembled a startled hare and the wispy Bernard a shy squirrel. Louis was always writing poetry in that thick hand with the strongly marked verticals.'[4] The years 1924–5 were years of most rapid development, when the urge to write was strong.[5]

In his last year at Marlborough (1925–6), he shared a study with Anthony Blunt, which they decorated in style with prints and flowers.[6] As he had secured a Postmastership at Merton before Christmas, he felt himself at liberty to expand, with nothing to do but be fashionable, expound his philosophy of anti-science and anti-religion, indulge the child cult and nihilism, and generally 'outrage the Boy in the Street'.[7] Aestheticism was all: 'The only real values were aesthetic. Moral values were a delusion, and politics and religion a waste of time.'[8] Under the influence of Anthony Blunt, too, he discovered art (especially Cubist) and was converted to a belief in Pure Form.[9]

When MacNeice went up to Oxford in October 1926, the trouble was, as he says, that, having already, before leaving Marlborough, 'caught up with the outside intellectuals' he 'had nothing to move on to'.[10] Besides, on his first visit to Oxford, in December 1925, for his scholarship, he had already decided he

---

[1] Op. cit., p. 53.   [2] Ibid., p. 54.

[3] Some of these are used in illustration *passim*, and they are listed in the Bibliog., as is the script of his entry for the Cotton English Essay, which is now in the University of Texas library.

[4] *London Magazine*, December 1963, p. 63.   [5] *S.A.F.*, p. 94.

[6] 'The study is pretty floral at the moment—tulips, lilac, bluebells, apple-blossom and narcissi.' (Letter home, 20 May 1926.)

[7] *S.A.F.*, p. 97.   [8] Ibid., p. 100.   [9] Ibid., p. 97.   [10] Ibid., p. 99.

was going to have a Pateresque kind of life there, thus effectively
spoiling Oxford for himself in advance, since 'once one starts
expecting things one's own self-consciousness intervenes and
perverts'.[1] That was still his attitude on reaching Oxford. He
would live like a poet and be an ineffectual talker, all mood and
no argument, with self-expression as the ideal: 'Lawrence's
cult of the blood and senses was now tending to take the place
of my child-cult.'[2] Certainly, he 'had not . . . gone to Oxford to
study; that was what grammar-school boys did'.[3] Even if 'the
Oxford Decadence was all but over',[4] it was also true that 'the
absurd old Oxford antithesis of Aesthete and Hearty was still
going strong', and it was 'a point of honour to show which side
one belonged to'.[5] MacNeice showed that he sided with the
Aesthetes:

Although I disliked being stared at, when I first went up to Oxford I
made a point of dressing eccentrically, growing long side-whiskers
and pitching my voice up whenever my opinions were unpopular.
When I got an angry reaction . . . I felt I had scored, even though I
was embarrassed.[6]

He had, as he explains, simply continued the practice of the intellectual minority at school of developing 'elaborate and sometimes paradoxical defence mechanisms'.[7] And the need to do this
at Oxford was even greater, for he was, quite simply, lonely:
'As it was, I spent much of my time at Oxford alone. . . .'[8] Two
of his closest Marlborough friends, John Hilton and Graham
Shepard, were at Oxford, as was John Betjeman, and he soon
became friendly with the poets W. H. Auden,[9] Stephen Spender
and Clere Parsons. Yet he badly missed the company of other
public school boys, who were few in his college, and intellectuals,
who were fewer still.[10]

He continued his classical education by reading for Honour

---

[1] Ibid., p. 231.   [2] *M.P.*, p. 69.   [3] *S.A.F.*, p. 102.
[4] 'Twenty-One', p. 232.   [5] Ibid., p. 235.   [6] Ibid.   [7] Ibid.
[8] Ibid., p. 236.
[9] '. . . W. H. Auden was already in his rooms in Peck, dressed like an untidy bank clerk
and reading in a self-imposed black-out all sorts of technical unaesthetic matter.' (*S.A.F.*,
p. 232.)
[10] Ibid., p. 104.

Mods., but this 'was on the whole repellent', for he 'could not bear niggling over textual commentary'.[1] On the other hand, poetry did matter. He wrote poems for various university magazines, as well as stories of the satirical-fantastic kind he had written for the *Marlburian*, and reviews. He edited the second—and last—number of a very good magazine called *Sir Galahad*, for which John Hilton designed the cover, and *Oxford Poetry, 1929*, jointly with Stephen Spender. In 1929, too, his first collection of poems, *Blind Fireworks*, was published by Gollancz. The Oxford University Dramatic Society attracted him, but he did not join it, or was prevented from joining it by his conviction that 'to get on in the O.U.D.S. it still helped if one were or pretended to be homosexual'.[2] In a letter to Anthony Blunt he said: 'Graham [Shepard] and I are producing *Troilus and Cressida* in modern dress next term.'[3] He was a member of a literary group in his college called the Bodley Society, which held fortnightly meetings, and to which he delivered papers. He refers in a letter to Anthony Blunt to a paper he is giving on Joyce and Modern Poetry,[4] and, jocularly, to another 'on Poetry, with especial reference to Modern English Poetry and myself'.[5] In two other letters he remarks that he 'spoke at a College debate the other night against the Censorship of the Press', and announces that he is 'pregnant with a paper to be called Programme for the New Romantics involving a comparison of Shelley and Nietzsche and a deification of laughter'.[6] In *Modern Poetry* he dwells at some length on other papers given at Oxford. One of the earliest (in his first term) was a paper in which he partially recanted some of the doctrines of his school papers, advocating 'a return to seriousness', although 'seriousness still seems to mean the practice of art'.[7] In 1927 he gave a paper on *Ulysses* and another deploring industrial and commercial vulgarity; and in 1928 he gave a fantasy paper on the theme

---

[1] S.A.F., p. 110.   [2] 'Twenty-One', p. 232.

[3] Dated 9 June 1927. They did not produce it, although it is interesting to note his remark in 'Twenty-One': 'One of my favourite Shakespeare characters was Thersites' (p. 238). See below, p. 41.

[4] 7 February 1927, from Oxford.   [5] Ibid.

[6] Letters to A.F.B. 7 November 1926, from Oxford, and 21 July 1928, from Carrickfergus.

[7] Op. cit., p. 63.

Art is the Gift of the Gab, 'advocating garrulity with a text from Falstaff: "I have a whole school of tongues in this belly of mine"'.[1] His last public gesture before leaving Oxford in 1930 was to deliver a paper entitled We Are the Old, the title being a phrase taken from Gentile's *Mind as Pure Act*, in which he opposed Plato's and Shelley's theories about the nature of poetic inspiration and Croce's insistence that the artistic activity is consummated *before* the work of art, and elaborated his thesis that 'traditionalism is the death of tradition; to keep a tradition alive means constant change and that means change of forms'.[2]

A curious omission from MacNeice's autobiography is any reference to the fact that he played rugby and tennis at Oxford (though not for long). No physical activity more strenuous than walking or canoeing is recorded. Yet he announced to his family in a letter[3] in his first term that he had 'played football for the 2nd time against Balliol 1st XV. They had a blue playing—dreadful.' In the following summer he wrote home[4] to say that he had entered himself for two college Tennis Singles (handicap and non-handicap).

Despite his claim that he had not gone to Oxford to study, and the apparently uncongenial nature of his studies for Honour Mods., he secured his First in 1928,[5] and began reading philosophy for Greats in the summer of 1928. At first he was excited with his new reading: 'I am just getting excited about philosophy . . . and as a consequence am trying to read everyone at once, e.g. Descartes, Spinoza and Berkeley whom I am already plunging in, and Hume and Schopenhauer whom I am trembling on the brink of.'[6] Soon he was even more excited about Nietzsche. In the long vacation of 1928 he accompanied his father on a cruise to Spitzbergen, and *Also Sprach Zarathustra* was in the forefront of his

---

[1] Ibid., p. 67.   [2] *M.P.*, pp. 70–3; *S.A.F.*, p. 127. See below, p. 44.

[3] 9 December 1926. In *Minch* (p. 20) he gives a brief and jocular account of the occasion in March 1938 when he 'went to Birmingham . . . and played rugger for the first time since 1926'.

[4] 6 May 1927.

[5] His announcement of his success to Anthony Blunt was characteristic. He concluded a letter about many other things with the laconic, 'By the way, I now believe in Providence; I got a 1st in Mods.' (From Carrickfergus, Spring 1928.)

[6] Letter to his family, 28 May 1928.

CA

thoughts: '*Also Sprach Zarathustra* is exciting poetry. . . . I worship Nietzsche and I can't abide blonde beasts and husky Uebermensch [*sic*].'[1] Later in the vacation he asked Anthony Blunt, who was to stay with him at Carrickfergus, to bring the German text of *Also Sprach Zarathustra* with him, adding: 'I'm afraid I can't take philosophy seriously yet, being still obsessed by my own little game of stitching words together. Really to be a philosopher you have to really doubt everything and I only pretend to doubt.'[2]

He took philosophy even less seriously on his return to Oxford in the autumn of 1928. For his philosophy tutor, Geoffrey Mure, however, he seems to have had considerable respect. Dr. Mure, a pupil of F. H. Bradley and 'one of Oxford's few remaining neo-Hegelians', held the belief 'that neither logic nor ethics could be separated from metaphysics', and MacNeice 'found his attitude sympathetic' since his own instinct was 'to drag in ultimate reality everywhere'.[3] His tutor sent him to the German Idealists, and, by way of them, to the Italian Idealists. Oxford philosophy was, however, 'in the doldrums', for 'The neo-Hegelian movement which operated so powerfully at the close of the nineteenth century from the strongholds of Balliol and Merton . . . had spent its force.'[4] MacNeice later affirmed that he could not regard philosophy as anything but 'an exquisite engine of destruction'.[5] His friends Graham Shepard and John Hilton were both 'too busy working' and he felt 'more than usually lonely'.[6] He had 'no religion and no exciting personal relationships', was absolutely uninterested in politics ('Political ideas were those which concerned us least'), and was generally tired of university life, as he 'knew all the moves in advance'.[7] He therefore took to calling more and more on Mary Ezra,[8] whom he had met the previous year, and one day later in the autumn 'aided by rum and the Mozart Horn Concerto' he found himself engaged.[9]

---

[1] Letter to A.F.B., 21 July 1928, from Molde, Norway.

[2] 22 August 1928, from Carrickfergus.   [3] *S.A.F.*, p. 125. See below, p. 44.

[4] From an article (*Listener*, 4 November 1965) by Professor A. J. Ayer, who went up to Oxford in 1929, in which he describes the state of Oxford philosophy, his description very much resembling that given by MacNeice in, e.g., *S.A.F.*, pp. 125–6.

[5] *S.A.F.*, p. 113.   [6] Ibid., p. 118.   [7] Ibid., pp. 119–20.

[8] Giovanna Marie Thérèse Babette Ezra ('Mariette' of *S.A.F.*), stepdaughter of an eminent Oxford scholar.   [9] *S.A.F.*, p. 120.

The engagement he did not reveal to his family during the Christmas vacation, and, on his return to Oxford in 1929, he found himself involved in a tense and intricate emotional situation. He had told Mary in a letter about his mongol brother, Willy, and from Mary's violent reaction realized 'what enormous stress certain Jewish families lay upon eugenics'.[1] He was obliged to obtain documentary evidence that the condition was not hereditary, something which proved to be extraordinarily difficult. Under the strain of all this he broke loose, got wildly drunk deliberately, was arrested and found himself in gaol for the night. In consequence, he was all but sent down, only the expectation of his securing a First in Greats influencing the College authorities to reprieve him.[2] The affair could not be concealed from his family, and everything, including the engagement, came to light. His father and stepmother hurried across to Oxford, both sets of parents met, and matters were eventually straightened out.

Mary and Louis spent four weeks of the long vacation in 1929 together on the island of Achill, and another six at Mary's uncle's house at St. Tropez. When he returned to Oxford for his last year, he shared rooms with his friend Adrian Green-Armytage, who had been his companion in many of the escapades of the previous year.[3] He was seeing Mary for a large part of every day, and it proved excessively difficult to find time and energy to concentrate on his reading. In a letter to Anthony Blunt, probably written at this time, he said: 'My philosophy tutor, it seems, remarked the other day that I shall probably land myself with a very poor 2nd. This is much more encouraging than anything they said about me before Mods. (Excuse conceit.)' The conceit was apparently justified: he was awarded his First in Greats. On the last day of term he and Mary were married in the Registry Office at Carfax, in Oxford.

Shortly before his examination he was appointed to a Lectureship in Classics at Birmingham University, and there Mary and he

[1] *S.A.F.*, p. 121. [2] The whole episode is described in *S.A.F.*, pp. 121–2.

[3] 'Last week Adrian and I got into a row (which is now settled) for stealing a replica gargoyle out of the College Sacristy and setting it up in Adrian's room.' Letter to his family, 29 May 1928. The episode is also mentioned in *S.A.F.*, p. 113.

found themselves 'very comfortable living in a converted stables on the south, the genteel, side of Birmingham'.[1] The first months were devoted to buying for the house, which Mary regarded as 'an almost sacred ritual'.[2] He was immersed in domestic life, with little else to occupy his time and energies; his teaching certainly did not. His students depressed him: 'I had to take a course of Plato and intended to teach Plato dynamically . . . [but] An hour of the students' faces punctured my good intentions.'[3] Six years later, a journalist recalled that MacNeice 'could not remember undergraduates' names'.[4] The same journalist (who was, in fact, the writer and critic of later fame, and MacNeice's good friend, Walter Allen) gave an interesting impression thirty years later of MacNeice at that time:

I studied Cicero's *De Officiis* under him. In the drabness of Birmingham and its old University building . . . MacNeice with his striking good looks and his elegant clothes, which managed to suggest at one and the same time the arty and the sporting, was very much an exotic.[5]

His writing suffered badly. Despite the efforts of the Professor of Greek, E. R. Dodds, for whom MacNeice had the profoundest respect, he was unwilling to devote himself to the more orthodox forms of scholarly writing or editing. He had a deep urge to write 'poems expressing doubt or melancholy, an anarchist conception of freedom or nostalgia for the open spaces', but this, he felt, would have been 'disloyal to Mariette'; instead, he was, as he said, disloyal to himself, and 'wrote a novel which purported to be an idyll of domestic felicity'.[6] This was the novel *Roundabout Way*, which Putnam published in 1932, under the pseudonym Louis Malone. It was strongly autobiographical, with full-length portraits of Mary and himself and Anthony Blunt, appropriately touched up. In a letter to Anthony Blunt in October 1932, he remarked: 'Mary contributed a good bit to the girl, and . . . Hogley is the Oxford cultured don, spiced up with my idea of what you might be like if you were two-dimensional and lived in Oxford.' He was not satisfied with the novel, which he called

[1] *S.A.F.*, p. 130.   [2] Ibid.   [3] Ibid., p. 131.
[4] *Birmingham Evening Dispatch*, 20 October 1936.
[5] *Daily Telegraph*, 25 November 1965.   [6] *S.A.F.*, p. 137.

'a negative experiment, an attempt to write a novel according to popular standards "coherent"', but he added, in the same letter, 'I am letting myself go in the next one which will be called *An Everlasting Cold.*'

His letters to Anthony Blunt from the beginning of 1931 are full of similar projects to write novels and plays. He appeared to see the possibility of uniting scholarship with the kind of writing that would give him more satisfaction when he asked Anthony Blunt about the possibility of his doing

> a book in that Hogarth Lectures series on Latin Humour (and of course the lack of it). . . . One could have an amusing and instructive time with the Fathers, who herald the peculiarities of modern Christian Humour (Donne, Swift, etc.). . . . Really I should like to do it very much.[1]

He refers to this again in other letters, saying, for instance, that he was working out his scheme for the book, which, he hoped, would please and reassure 'the blokes here'.[2]

Nor had he by any means stopped writing poetry. Two large notebooks have survived, filled with holograph poems written between 1929 and 1934,[3] some of which appeared in the *Poems* of 1935, while others emerged transformed in later poems. From 1933 his poems were appearing in *The Criterion* and *New Verse*, and we find him in a letter to Anthony Blunt saying that Heinemann's have at length declined his novel (one he had worked and reworked since late undergraduate days), but adding: 'I take it the Spectator never does long poems as I have an Eclogue on Ireland (c 100 lines) which I think should see the light soon.'[4] He refers frequently in letters to the play he is working on and the trouble it is giving him. This is presumably *Station Bell.* It was produced by the Birmingham University Dramatic Society as

[1] From Birmingham, 24 February 1932.

[2] From Birmingham, 6 April 1932. He completed the work. The Introduction and Conclusion are in the Univ. of Texas library (see Bibliog.) and the remainder of the work is the property of M.E.

[3] These are referred to in footnotes as H.N., and are the property of M.E.

[4] Written from Birmingham, 3 March 1934. This is almost certainly the poem ultimately entitled simply 'Valediction', which appeared as 'Valediction: An Eclogue by Louis MacNeice', in *Life and Letters*, vol. 10, April–September 1934, pp. 352–4.

an end-of-term play, and was a satirical comedy set in the Ireland of the future, though the material was highly topical, featuring a dictator and a peculiar brand of Irish Fascism. The only known copies of the play are now in the library of the University of Texas.[1] In a letter later in the year to Anthony Blunt, he says: 'My play is still unfinished—so protean—but I hope it will be done in London by a thing called, I think, the Groups Theatre. I am afraid it wouldn't be allowed in the I.F.S. as De Val. would take it personally. It will look very well on the boards.'[2] Later in 1934 he wrote: 'Old Eliot has at last made me a definite offer to do my poems next season. Tomorrow I am having a BBC audition, so things are looking up.'[3] He was also doing regular reviews for the *Morning Post* (by 1935 he was 'reading 4 novels a week'[4] for this paper), and working on his verse translation of *The Agamemnon*. His literary projects at this stage he sums up in a letter at the beginning of 1934: 'This brings my total of books which I want published 1934–5 up to 5: 1. Poems 2. Novel 3. Play 4. Latin Humour 5. Analytic Autobiography. I have also the most ingenious idea for a new novel.'[5]

In fact, the years 1934–5 (like 1924–5) were years of marked activity and quickening excitement. His son Daniel was born in May 1934, and, as looking after the baby occupied much of Mary's time and energy, he made a flying visit to Ireland in September, to see E. R. Dodds, who was doing research in Dublin. He felt 'born again' as if 'a great wild star of space was smashed in the hot-house window'.[6] Professor Dodds introduced him to Yeats. Altogether it was a liberating experience, and he returned from Dublin 'exhilarated'.[7] Birmingham began to mean more to him. In a letter towards the end of the year he expressed the opinion that he would like to move on in another two or three years, but *not* to Oxford or Cambridge: 'A nausea submerges me at the thought of all these clever people with their pipes.'[8] More

[1] See Bibliog.   [2] From Birmingham, 8 June 1934.
[3] From Birmingham, 10 October 1934. The records of the Midland Region of the B.B.C. show that he made a broadcast in May 1934, and three in 1935 (August, September, December). Unfortunately the scripts have been destroyed.
[4] Letter to A.F.B. from Birmingham, 20 November 1935.
[5] Letter to A.F.B., 3 February 1934.   [6] *S.A.F.*, p. 147.   [7] Ibid., p. 148.
[8] Letter to A.F.B. from Birmingham, 17 November 1934.

of his fellow academics were becoming fast friends, notably Ernst L. Stahl[1] and John Waterhouse.[2] From time to time he would meet W. H. Auden on a visit to his father, Dr. G. A. Auden, the School Medical Officer and Lecturer in Public Health at the university. In a letter to John Hilton, who was considering applying for a lecturing post in philosophy, he said, 'We are all very busy here, lots of books in the making, also a baby (booked for May)';[3] and again, in the summer of 1934, 'Birmingham is now becoming a grand place as there are at least ½ a dozen really good people here (which is more than can be said of almost anywhere).' Outside his circle of academics he had friends whom he deeply admired, such as the sculptor Gordon Herrickx.[4]

This sense of exhilaration and emancipation lasted all through the spring and summer of 1935. He went to Twickenham with Stahl, Stahl's sister and Dodds to watch England play Ireland at rugby, and realized 'what a lot of amusing things one might have been doing before'.[5] In August the MacNeices took a large old farmhouse in the Cotswolds, where 'the sun shone every day' and they 'had a succession of guests'.[6] Among these was Tsalic of *The Strings are False*, 'a Russian Jew from America doing graduate work in Oxford. He had been an American football star and weighed two hundred pounds, had the good looks of a Jewish heavyweight boxer and the charm of a shaggy sheepdog who expects to be laughed at.'[7] Shortly afterwards, Tsalic, who had been invited to stay with them in Birmingham, was seriously injured in a car crash when MacNeice was driving. He convalesced with the MacNeices and then left for London, where shortly after, and quite without warning, Mary went to join him—later explaining that it was because she was 'lonely in her mind'.[8]

Louis was desolate at first, and then appeared to recover from the shock after a week or so, claiming that he 'began to feel free'.[9] In a letter to John Hilton on 26 May, he remarked: 'You

[1] Later Professor of German at Oxford, with whom he collaborated in the translation of Goethe's *Faust*. ('Aloys' in *A.S.*)

[2] A Lecturer in English, who became his close friend (*S.A.F.*, p. 148). He had known MacNeice slightly when he was in his first, and MacNeice his fourth, year at Merton.

[3] From Birmingham, 11 November 1933.   [4] Herrickx is 'Wimbush' of *A.S.*

[5] *S.A.F.*, p. 148.   [6] Ibid., p. 149.   [7] Ibid., pp. 149–50.   [8] Ibid., p. 151.

[9] Ibid., p. 152.

needn't be embarrassed by my situation, which is all right (except financially!).' Those close to him, however, including his sister, Professor Dodds and Mrs. Ann Shepard, felt that, in fact, he was deeply hurt, unhappy and lonely for a very long time afterwards. He initiated divorce proceedings almost at once, and employed a nurse to look after the boy. Early in 1936 he was writing enthusiastically to Anthony Blunt about a visit to Spain at Easter. On this visit he reacted much more strongly to visual impressions and the paintings of El Greco, Zurbaran and Goya in the Prado, than to the Popular Front.[1] Goya especially fascinated him, but not the Goya who was the darling of the Left Wing critics.[2] Shortly after his return he was writing with equal enthusiasm about his projected trip to Iceland with W. H. Auden, his *Agamemnon* and his Venus play:

. . . Dodds wants me to revise Agamemnon some more and then he says it will be rather remarkable. (Eliot is interested in it.) My play about Venus is near done—a draft, I mean . . . Wystan and I are going to introduce cricket to Iceland. . . . Then we are going to go over the lunatic asylum and the leper hospital and climb Hecla. . . . A great life. . . . Tomorrow Wystan and I drive to Stratford to meet Rupert Doone and Robert Medley.[3]

Things were certainly stirring once more. Moreover, as he could not endure being alone in the house, he was out and about in Birmingham, seeing more and more people, including young men like Walter Allen and Reggie Smith.[4]

His days in Birmingham were now numbered, however. In July he accepted an appointment as Lecturer in Greek in Bedford College, University of London, and we find him writing to Anthony Blunt to ask if he knows of flats on the edge of Regent's Park or on Primrose Hill; of a young chap with a First to succeed him at Birmingham; and of a good artist to do the drop curtain

---

[1] See *S.A.F.*, pp. 158–63.

[2] Ibid., p. 160: 'Some Left Wing critics, babbling about "integrity" and "social consciousness" and "realism", have claimed Goya as a great revolutionary.'

[3] Letter to A.F.B. from Birmingham, 24 May 1936. The play is *Out of the Picture*.

[4] The latter is R. D. Smith, the B.B.C. Producer, of whom he writes with affection in *S.A.F.* (p. 154), as he does of Walter Allen (pp. 209–10). Both were lifelong friends of MacNeice. R. D. Smith had been a principal in the student production of *Station Bell*, and Walter Allen had a small part.

for *The Agamemnon*. He says that he is going to Iceland on
4 August and returning early in September, and that *The Rising
Venus* (*Out of the Picture*) was to come out in the spring. He adds
interestingly, 'You saw that Dodds is going to Oxford? . . .
That's really why I'm leaving here. . . . Well, find me somewhere
to lay my head (also heads of Dan, Betsy and the nurse).'[1]

His first London home, sublet to him by Geoffrey Grigson,
was in Keats Grove, Hampstead, where Robert and Sylvia Lynd
were his next-door neighbours. At the Lynds he met one of the
two categories into which he divided literary London, 'the old
gang who were just literary', and he soon met many of 'the new
gang who were all Left'.[2] He was 'delighted to move to London
where there would be so many people to talk to'.[3]

As at Birmingham, his energies and enthusiasms were far from
fully engaged by his academic work. His colleagues in the
Classics Department at Bedford found him 'polite but remote',
and he did not give the impression that he found 'either the classics
in themselves, or the teaching of them, particularly absorbing'.[4]
His 'main interests seemed to be outside, in his own circle of
friends, and in his intellectual and political involvements'.[5]
His liveliness on staff social occasions, however, particularly his
enthusiasm for, and skill in, charades, was much appreciated.[6]
And his growing interest in students at Birmingham during his
last year was reflected in the part he played in student activities.
He helped the Reid Society, for instance, to obtain speakers of the
standing of Spender, Auden, and Isherwood, besides interesting
speakers such as Walter Allen, with reputations yet to make. He
would read and discuss his poems at meetings of student societies,
and contribute to discussions on the political situation.[7] In various

---

[1] Letter from Birmingham, 24 July 1936. (Betsy was the borzoi.)
[2] *S.A.F.*, p. 165.   [3] Ibid.
[4] I quote from a letter kindly written by Mrs. G. Wilkinson, Senior Lecturer in Classics
at Bedford College, which is characteristic of the recollections of his former colleagues.
[5] Ibid.
[6] Mrs. E. A. Serpell, of the Extra-Mural Department of the University of London, then
a student, recollected his playing an I.R.A. agent and a girl student.
[7] Mrs. John Butt records the recollection, by a student friend, of MacNeice's 'treating
as intellectual equals' the audience to whom he read poems at meetings of the Student

ways, therefore, his 'intellectual and political involvements' were, to some degree, reflected in his activities at Bedford.

On 1 November Rupert Doone produced *The Agamemnon*, with stage set and costumes designed by Robert Medley. It was an exciting production, with elaborate masks and the chorus wearing evening dress,[1] which attracted considerable critical attention. The *Sketch* (11 November 1936) remarked on the unusual presence of W. B. Yeats at the first performance: 'Tall, silver-haired, clad in rough tweeds and carrying a hat of large dimensions, he sat in the front row of the stalls and listened with extreme attention.' Yeats said to Professor Dodds on that occasion: 'Dodds, we are assisting at the death of tragedy'— in reference to the production, and not the translation, which he admired. Even more widespread critical notice, in America as well as Britain, was received a year later when the Group finally produced *Out of the Picture*, although the notice was generally much less favourable than for *The Agamemnon*. *Letters from Iceland*, which Faber brought out in July 1937, also received wide notice and mixed acclaim. The Book Society elected it their Book of the Month for July. Louis MacNeice was certainly now a name, and in 1937–8 he accepted commissions for prose works for which he said he 'had no vocation', but which, he thought to himself, he could 'do as well as the next man'.[2] Verse collections followed in rapid succession: *The Earth Compels* (1938), *Autumn Journal* (1939), *The Last Ditch* (1940), *Selected Poems* (1940), *Plant and Phantom* (1941). In 1941, too, appeared *The Poetry of W. B. Yeats*, the first full study of Yeats after his death. In America, where Random House had published his *Poems* in 1937, *Autumn Journal* in 1939, and *Poems 1925–1940* in 1940, he was already having a considerable influence on younger poets.[3]

Christian Movement. He also frequently appeared with students at an organization called New Europe.

[1] The evening dress was not a success, and did not survive the first night.

[2] *S.A.F.*, p. 173. These were, presumably, *I Crossed the Minch* (Longmans, 1938) and *Zoo* (Michael Joseph, 1938).

[3] Horace Gregory, e.g., reviewing the Random House ed. of *H.S.*, remarked:' The young Americans said they were imitating Auden, and then wrote a great number of ballades and villanelles in the manner of MacNeice. . . . This meant that MacNeice's verses were in high fashion. . . .' (*Poetry*, vol. 74, April–Sept., 1949, p. 303.)

The rhythm of his private life had been keeping pace with that of his literary life; he described it as 'a whirl of narcotic engagements—meetings for a drink, political meetings, private views, flirtations, the experimental theatre, the question of my overdraft, the question of Spain'.[1] In November his divorce was made absolute. The year 1937 he described as 'a year of wild sensations',[2] with personal relationships the wildest.

He was, too, almost inevitably, though not extensively, involved in the public movements and gestures of the times. In 1938 he accepted a suggestion that he 'should visit Barcelona in company with some other English writers'; but the others 'falling out or ill', he went by himself.[3] His reactions to the Munich crisis and the preparation for war are, of course, recorded in *Autumn Journal*.[4] Apart from the visit to Spain, the one positive act of participation, recorded in Section XIV, was his work in driving voters to the polls at the Oxford by-election, to support Lindsay, the Lib.-Lab., anti-Munich candidate against the Conservative, Hogg ('. . . leave a blank for Hogg/And put a cross for Lindsay'). His participation in student political discussions has already been mentioned, and he also took a prominent part in a protest march with other members of the university. It was reported thus in the *News Chronicle*:

. . . Professors, lecturers and students of London University marched from the university in a procession 300 strong to protest against the ratification of the Anglo-Italian pact. . . . Mr. Louis MacNeice, poet and lecturer in Greek at the university, told the *News Chronicle*: 'This is the first time that the staff of London University have done anything like this. It shows you how strongly some of us feel about it.'[5]

In the spring of 1939 he had gone to America to lecture, and

---

[1] *S.A.F.*, p. 165. He had been in financial difficulties since Mary left him and he had to provide for a nurse for Dan (of whom he was granted the custody) and a cook/daily help.

[2] Ibid., p. 170.   [3] Ibid., p. 176.

[4] And in *S.A.F.*, pp. 208–10, where he describes the summer of 1939 as 'a steady delirium' (p. 208).

[5] 14 November 1938. I am indebted to Professor K. M. Tillotson for her reliable recollection of such a newspaper report, and to Professor G. Tillotson for looking it out from among his papers. Mrs. E. A. Serpell also kindly lent me 'a faded newspaper photograph of MacNeice on this occasion, looking terribly respectable—macintosh over his arm, and a flag on a long pole over his shoulder'. A thorough search has so far failed to reveal the source.

had met the Impossible She for whom he was always searching,
'someone whom according to fairy story logic I was bound to
meet but according to common sense never. A woman who was
not a destroyer.'[1] The memory of this woman continued to
haunt him on his return to England, and she is poignantly longed
for in two of the poems in *The Last Ditch*. Hope of meeting her
again was probably a strong motivating factor behind an applica-
tion he made in June for a year's leave of absence. The precise
reason was not specified, but it was assumed that he would be
teaching and furthering his studies in America. The leave was
granted but he did not cross to America at once, going instead
with his friend Ernst Stahl to Ireland, from where he suddenly
wrote a letter to the Principal on 11 September tendering his
resignation. The Principal, however, suggested that, as his resignation would not be required until Easter, he should defer and
reconsider it. In December he wrote once more to the Principal,
asking for a letter enabling him to obtain a permit to go to
America, and declaring his firm intention to return in June. The
letter he received, and then the permit.

During the last months of 1939 he remained in Ireland, where
his family 'had taken a beautiful house at the end of Cushendun
bay'.[2] He was badly confused about his own part in the general
situation, as his letters to friends show clearly. He applied at the
same time for the vacant chair of English at Trinity College,
Dublin, and, whilst he was awaiting the result, cast about for
alternatives. The idea of doing propaganda work he rejected, and
thought instead of 'plumping for something brainless. There
must be plenty of people to propagand, so I have no feeling of
guilt in refusing to mortify my mind.'[3] He was depressed by the
fact that 'everyone one meets just thinks from hand to mouth',
and was tempted to solve everything by 'taking the king's shilling
and escaping'.[4] But his mind could not accept any merely escapist
solution: 'It is all very well for everyone to go on saying "Destroy
Hitlerism", but what the hell are they going to construct?'[5] On

---

[1] *S.A.F.*, p. 204. Their meeting is described in the form of a parable on pp. 204–6.
[2] *S.A.F.*, p. 210.   [3] Letter to E.R.D., 24 September 1939.
[4] Letter to E.R.D., 13 October 1939.   [5] Ibid.

went the seesaw, and a month later he was again thinking of active service: 'My conscience is again troubling me about this fool war. I am beginning to think this may be *my* war after all. . . . It might be less soul-destroying to get into something on the sea.'[1] But he seesawed back again: 'I suppose really I ought to hold my hand over the war to see how it evolves. . . .'[2]

He returned to England early in 1940, and crossed almost at once to America, where he lectured at Cornell from February. The months that followed were full of bewildering emotions, and again, as in the summer of 1939, he was reacting strongly both to a public and a private situation. These were the months of the 'phony war' in Europe, compared with which MacNeice, in America, felt himself to be 'on a different planet';[3] and he was still deeply in love with the Impossible She.

He was obviously very happy and excited about his teaching and lecturing in America, writing to his father on 25 May, for instance:

I gave lectures at Harvard, Wellesley, Princeton, Hamilton (a little one by itself in the country) and State College, Pennsylvania. . . . I also took part with Auden and Isherwood in a talk to the League of American Writers in New York. . . . Two or three of my audiences numbered over 300; they seemed, though I say it, pretty appreciative. At Harvard I was made to make gramophone records. . . . You feel a certain warmth in their company which you dont often get in England. I very much want to get back there and see more of them.

Two important consequences of this new feeling of happy assurance he recorded in other letters. On 5 February he wrote to Professor Dodds: 'It is so exciting to find oneself timelessly happy; also I am going to write (at least I hope so) quite new kinds of poems.' This determination he repeated in a letter to Mrs. Dodds on 22 March, and then added a wider affirmation:

Am also (this sounds terribly like Wystan too but it's all right) formulating a new attitude, the basic principle of which is that freedom means Getting Into things and not getting Out of Them; also that one must keep making things which are *not oneself*—e.g. works of art, even

---

[1] Letter to E.R.D., 19 November 1939.   [2] Letter to E.R.D., 5 December 1939.
[3] Colloquy between MacNeice's two selves, Oxford and Ulster, in the broadcast *Return to Atlantis*, 5 July 1953.

personal relationships—which must be dry and not damp. . . . Because it seems high time neither to be passive to flux nor to substitute for it, Marxist-like, a mere algebra of captions.

In a letter written to his father on 16 December, just after his return to England, he said, 'For the last 4 months all my friends over there (both American and British) had been trying to persuade me to change my mind about coming back. However, I thought I was missing History.' He should have returned to England in July, but was prevented by a ruptured appendix and peritonitis, which very nearly cost him his life. The autumn of 1940 he therefore spent convalescing after his operation, and for over a month before his return to England he stayed with W. H. Auden 'in a household on Brooklyn Heights' that was 'a warren of the arts'.[1] He also paid a short visit to Mary and Tsalic.

Shortly after his return to England on 9 December 1940, he appears to have volunteered for service in the Royal Navy, in which his friend Graham Shepard was serving as a Lieutenant R.N.V.R. on North Atlantic convoy duty, but was rejected on grounds of bad eyesight.[2] Instead, he entered the B.B.C. Features Department, on 26 May 1941. He quickly made his mark with his contributions to the dramatic features series *The Stones Cry Out*. The most ambitious of all his wartime programmes was undoubtedly *Alexander Nevsky*, given on the Home Service on 8 December 1941, and conceived on the grand scale. It was prefaced by a recorded introduction by His Excellency the Soviet Ambassador, M. Maisky, and made full use of the B.B.C. Symphony Orchestra, the B.B.C. Chorus and Theatre Chorus, conducted by Sir Adrian Boult, using the music of Prokoviev. The script was based on that of Eisenstein's film. Robert Donat spoke the part of Alexander Nevsky, and the whole programme

---

[1] *S.A.F.*, p. 35.

[2] I have no documentary evidence for this fact, but was assured of its veracity by various people who knew him well at the time, including Mrs. Ann Shepard. Cf. the obituary note in the *Guardian*, 4 September 1963: 'Mr. Laurence Gilliam, Head of Features, Sound, remembered yesterday that MacNeice joined the B.B.C. after he had returned from the U.S. and volunteered for the Navy but had been turned down because of his eyesight.' In the letter to his father just mentioned (16 December 1940), he said, 'I feel very well, but a doctor in Oxford told me I am not technically fit and should probably be rejected by any medical board, so think of trying to crash in on the B.B.C.'

ran for an hour. His first wide fame as a writer for radio, however, came with the publication by Faber in 1944 of his play *Christopher Columbus*, which was first broadcast in the Home Service on 12 October 1942. Many of the other features and plays of those years, in fact, present dramatic portraits of the hero. In 1943 he produced programmes on *The Death of Byron* and *The Death of Marlowe*.[1] It was his declared intention in the dramatic feature, *Sunbeams in his Hat*, 'to correct the popular fallacy which uses the word Tchehov as a synonym for melancholia',[2]—and he presents Chekhov in much the same heroic way as he had presented, for instance, Marlowe. *The Dark Tower*[3] itself was the best and best-known of a series of Morality-Quest plays that he began writing in 1944 with the play *He Had a Date*,[4] an elegy for Graham Shepard, who was drowned at sea in 1942.

MacNeice remained as a producer with the B.B.C. until 30 June 1961, when he left the staff to take up free-lance work, although from 1 July 1961, until his death, he spent half of each year in working for the B.B.C. on what is called a Programme Contract.[5] His range and fertility were remarkable. His next major production was the dramatization of Goethe's *Faust*, *Parts I and II*, suitably abridged (the 12,000 lines are cut to 8,000), but still of considerable length. He worked hard on the translation, together with his old friend Professor Stahl, from the spring of 1949, when, as he explains in his Introduction to the text published by Faber in 1951, the B.B.C. asked him to make a special radio version in honour of Goethe's centenary. Part I (in two instalments) was first broadcast on 30 and 31 October 1949, and Part II (in four instalments) on 10, 13, 17 and 21 November 1949. His radio play *Prisoner's Progress* was awarded the *Premio d'Italia* in 1954, and Faber published in 1964, posthumously, his two radio

[1] Broadcast on the Home Service on, respectively, 10 May and 21 June 1943.

[2] *D.T.*, p. 69. On the same page he makes an interesting distinction between a 'feature' and a 'play', pointing out that while some features 'are as loosely constructed as scrap-books, others come near to the unities and emotional impact of a play'. Clearly it was but a step from features to plays.

[3] First broadcast on the Home Service, 21 January 1946.

[4] The play was re-produced in 1966, by R. D. Smith.

[5] I am much indebted for this and other factual information about MacNeice's service with the B.B.C. to Mr. G. T. M. de M. Morgan of the B.B.C.

plays *The Mad Islands* and *The Administrator*, both Quest plays of different kinds.

This account of some of MacNeice's work for the B.B.C. since 1941 has perhaps run ahead of the rest of the biographical matter, and yet this is not inappropriate, for the MacNeice of the later years seems so characteristically a man of the B.B.C. He was proud of his work and of his colleagues,[1] and some of his closest friends were either colleagues or people with whom he had come into contact at Broadcasting House.[2] His father, who had been consecrated Bishop of Cashel and Waterford in June 1931, and elevated to the see of Down, Connor and Dromore in December 1934, died in April 1942, and his stepmother in 1956. In the summer of 1942 he married Hedli Anderson, the actress and singer for whom W. H. Auden wrote cabaret songs. A daughter, Corinna Brigid, was born in July 1943. Dan had been taken over to Ireland at the outbreak of war, where he stayed partly with his grandparents and partly with a family of relations who had children near his age. After Louis's re-marriage, Dan came back to London to stay with his father and stepmother, with whom he remained until he was eighteen, when he rejoined his mother in the U.S.A. Louis and Hedli ceased to live together after September 1960.

In return for his devoted service, the B.B.C. was generous in granting him leaves of absence so that he could take temporary posts. The B.B.C. also sent him, as Mr. Goronwy Rees remarked, 'as an extremely sharp-eyed observer, to places and scenes he would otherwise not have dreamed of visiting'.[3] Perhaps the most important and best-enjoyed of these interregna was the period from 1 January 1950 to 30 June 1951, for the whole of which time he served the British Council in Athens, as Director of the British Institute from January to September 1950, and as Assistant Representative from then until June 1951. As usual,

---

[1] Among his colleagues in the Features Department of the B.B.C. were the poets W. R. Rodgers, Terence Tiller, Rayner Heppenstall and, later, Anthony Thwaite.

[2] Dylan Thomas, a close friend, was also associated with him in Features. MacNeice made an appropriate casting for him as Agamemnon, the Professor of Rhetoric, in his radio play *Trimalchio's Feast*, first broadcast in December 1948.

[3] *R.P.*, p. 15 of the script in the B.B.C. archives.

he worked wholeheartedly at the job, taking an active part in the intellectual life of Athens, giving public lectures, participating in weekly play-readings, planning literary courses, producing and acting in *The Playboy of the Western World*, and assisting in the planning of an art exhibition. Hedli helped him in his work, giving two concerts.[1]

This was also the time of the sombre yet spirited stocktaking and renewal recorded in the *Ten Burnt Offerings* that he wrote then—one of these apparently confused periods, like the autumn of 1939, when the turbulence and despair were not unmixed with hope, and led, indeed, to the release of new poetic energies, new affirmations. It was, too, a time of strenuous personal involvement, both physical and emotional—symbolized, perhaps, by a climb on Mount Ida with Professor Dodds, who had joined him during the latter part of his stay in Greece, Hedli, and Dan. The climb on this 8,000-foot mountain took two days, the night being spent with their shepherd guides in a cave halfway up. On their return, Louis, along with Hedli, was up all night celebrating Easter with the villagers of Anoyia.[2]

He was in South Africa between 1 August and 16 September 1959, at the invitation of the University of Cape Town, in order to give lectures in the Department of English and elsewhere.[3] He had been in India and Pakistan in 1947, at the time of partition, and was back there again, as well as in Ceylon, at the end of 1955.[4] Mr. Wynford Vaughan-Thomas, who was with him on the first visit, recalled the respect with which Louis was treated by educated Indians, his (Louis's) delight in the muddle and colour, his horror at the massacres following partition in the little village of Shakpura, the vigorous action to help the refugees by 'a Louis who was no longer the detached observer but one deeply and profoundly involved in the human dilemma'.[5] (MacNeice

[1] For most of the information about MacNeice's activities in Athens I am indebted to Mr. R. L. O. Macfarlane of the British Council.

[2] These experiences provided material for *In Search of Anoyia*, Third Programme, 11 December 1951.

[3] The notes for these lectures are extant: see Bibliog.

[4] The two visits are compared and contrasted in the poem 'Return to Lahore'. The first visit resulted in a notably vivid programme, *India at First Sight* (Third Programme, 13 March 1948).   [5] *R.P.*, p. 16.

DA

praises Mr. Vaughan-Thomas, as 'Evans' in Canto X of *Autumn Sequel*, for much the same thing.) He made his third visit to the U.S.A. between 8 February and 14 April 1953, when, at the invitation of the Poetry Center in New York, he gave a series of lectures, concerts, readings, etc., for themselves and other institutions.[1] He was back there again at the end of September in the following year, for three months, to do a joint lecture/recital tour with Hedli; to take up a temporary appointment as lecturer in poetry and drama at the Sarah Lawrence College; to make personal contacts with American writers, with the object of securing scripts for B.B.C. use. Other typical interregna, of longer or shorter duration, were: his stay in Northern Ireland from April to September 1945, to collect material for, and work on, scripts (including *The Dark Tower*), and cultivate local features writers; a ten-day visit to Rome in May 1947, to gather material for a sixty-minute feature, *Portrait of Rome*, in the series *Window on Europe*; a four-week visit to the Gold Coast, from 13 October 1956, to make a documentary film for the Gold Coast Film Unit on Gold Coast Independence, and to collect material for a B.B.C. feature.[2] Much of his time and energy after his departure from the B.B.C. on a Programme Contract[3] was occupied in research for his book *Astrology*, which was published posthumously in 1964.

After translating *Faust*, he was busy writing the long poems in *Ten Burnt Offerings* (1952), and *Autumn Sequel* (1954), and he tells us that when he was writing these he was incapable of writing shorter lyrics.[4] It was not until 1957 that his next collection, *Visitations*, comprising shorter lyrics, appeared. He records that in the spring and early summer of 1960 he 'underwent one of those rare bursts of creativity when the poet is first astonished and then rather alarmed by the way the mill goes on grinding'.[5] This resulted in the lyrics of *Solstices* (1961), followed by his last collection, *The Burning Perch*, in the year of his death.

[1] This visit, too, resulted in the zestful reportage of the programme *Return to Atlantis*.
[2] I am again indebted to Mr. G. T. M. de M. Morgan of the B.B.C. for this information.
[3] On 1 July 1961: see p. 33.   [4] *P.B.S.B.*, no. 14, May 1957.
[5] *P.B.S.B.*, no. 28, February 1961.

As MacNeice was reminded by the poems in *The Burning Perch* of T. S. Eliot's remark about 'the boredom and the horror and the glory', and admitted that in some of them 'the boredom and the horror were impinging very strongly', it is perhaps necessary to note that he himself was surprised at finding so many grim elements in the mood of the poems: 'When I assembled the poems in *The Burning Perch* . . . I was taken aback by the high proportion of sombre pieces, ranging from bleak observations to thumbnail nightmares. . . . All I can say is that I did not set out to write this kind of poem: they happened.'[1] When he made his journey to Yorkshire with the B.B.C. engineers to make the recordings for his last programme, *Persons from Porlock*, he was already enthusiastically planning his next programme, a dramatization of James Hogg's *Memoirs and Confessions of a Justified Sinner*,[2] and he had planned to stay, in the very week of his death, at Dunadry, the lovely home in County Antrim of an old friend, Paddy Falloon.[3] On the day before he left for Yorkshire, he wrote a short letter, in very good spirits, to John Hilton, suggesting that he might like to drive with their old Oxford friend, Sir Moore Crossthwaite, 'down to our Olde Rose Cottage', adding characteristically, 'We also have a Great Dane, nice but a bit oafish.'[4]

Many wondered sadly why he should have accompanied the sound engineers at all when they went underground to record effects for his programme. He had been ill only a short time before, and his journey seemed risky. His main reason was probably his old love of going underground—justified by a characteristic professional desire to check the sound effects. He had written of the earth dwelling at Arnibost: 'Whatever troll lives down there, they have closed his earth. I was disappointed, as I like going under-ground.'[5] His autobiography contains an excited

---

[1] *P.B.S.B.*, no. 38, September 1963.

[2] I have this on the reliable authority of Mr. Denys Hawthorne of the B.B.C., a personal friend of the poet and a leading actor in many of his plays.

[3] Robin Bryans (Robert Harbinson, a friend of the poet's) in *Ulster. A Journey through the Six Counties*, Faber, London, 1964, p. 192.

[4] At the time of his death he was mainly living in, and commuting from, Aldbury, in rural Hertfordshire.

[5] *Minch*, p. 114.

description of a visit with his father and sister to the salt-mines.[1]
One of his favourite books, which may well have suggested aspects
of *Persons from Porlock* to him, was George MacDonald's *The
Princess and the Goblin*, which is full of vivid underground description.[2] After he had caught his severe chill, he refused, true to his
faith in his own physical hardihood, to make any fuss or take
suitable precautions, relying on the warming effects of whisky.
The final tragedy was that the seriousness of his condition was
not immediately apparent, as he suffered from a rare kind of
pneumonia, which is difficult to identify, chiefly because it is
not accompanied by a high temperature, and he did not respond
to any of the antibiotics that were tried. Had he come into
hospital earlier there would have been more time, and a potent
antibiotic might have been found.[3] He died in hospital on 3
September 1963.

[1] *S.A.F.*, pp. 74–5.
[2] I am indebted to Lady Nicholson for suggesting the likely connection with George
MacDonald's book, which features prominently in *V.P.* He had not read it until nine
months or so before his death, but he was deeply impressed by it.

[3] My source of information is again Lady Nicholson, a qualified physician. It was not
known for certain what the form of pneumonia was, but it had many of the characteristics of a virus pneumonia.

2 Poetry and Belief

In an article in 1940, entitled 'Louis MacNeice: the Artist as Everyman',[1] Mr. Julian Symons examined MacNeice's poetry in terms of MacNeice's own view of the poet as the ordinary man. MacNeice had described his ideal poet, in *Modern Poetry*, as 'able-bodied, fond of talking, a reader of the newspapers, capable of pity and laughter, informed in economics, appreciative of women, involved in personal relationships, actively interested in politics, susceptible to physical impressions'.[2] Mr. Symons was, with some reasonable modification, satisfied both with this description and with the related fact that the ordinary man would find some two-thirds of the poems in MacNeice's latest collection, *The Earth Compels*, simple. The remaining poems (notably 'Chess', 'Circus', 'Homage to Clichés', 'Eclogue between the Motherless') he felt the ordinary man would not like, because

> they are written in language which is not too difficult, but too strange for him. Mr. MacNeice differs from his ideal poet in being, first a scholar, and second a literary man who lives, as most scholars and literary men do, a little apart from the run of people. It is the scholar and the literary man who have written Mr. MacNeice's other poems, with their gleaming Bloomsbury wit and sophistication. It has taken some time for the Ordinary Man in Mr. MacNeice to gain the upper hand over the scholar.[3]

He then forecast, with obvious approval, that the ordinary man, having gained the upper hand, was not likely to lose it.

So far, so good. He then went on to enquire how such an attitude might affect the value of the poetry:

> In estimating the worth of Mr. MacNeice's poetic work, then, we have to ask: what is an Ordinary Man, what is his attitude to current events, and how will that attitude affect his poetry?

He answered:

> The Ordinary Man is everybody *except* the violently class-conscious working class and what we still call the 'upper class'. He is at least

[1] In *Poetry*, vol. 56, April–September 1940, pp. 86–94. Mr. Symons repeated this view in his obituary notice in the *Guardian*, 5 September 1963: 'It is MacNeice who appears now as a sort of Everyman of the decade. . . .'

[2] Op. cit., p. 198. [3] Symons, op. cit., p. 88.

three-quarters of the people of England. It is this great 'class'—this class which desires social change, but is terrified by the violent instruments of social change—of which Mr. MacNeice is involuntarily the perfect representative. MacNeice's poems are the expression of this attitude (the Liberal attitude) on a very high level of skill and feeling. The most honest and intelligent adherents of this attitude (like Mr. MacNeice) see themselves as the lost in a changing world. . . . They perfectly realize that 'it is time for some new coinage', but they realize also that *they* are not the new coinage. They are the lost. . . .[1]

On the basis of this approach he suggested that many of Mac-Neice's poems, including some generally acknowledged to be among his best, such as 'An Eclogue for Christmas', 'Eclogue by a Five-barred Gate', 'Turf-Stacks' and 'Snow', are 'unsatisfactory poems' because 'they have no moral basis', because 'his indecision is reflected in his poems'.[2] The nature of his objection he sums up in one word—'belief':

One must be careful nowadays about using the word 'belief': but belief in some external driving force outside himself and his own feelings seems to be what is lacking to make Louis MacNeice a very fine poet. He is wholly self-centred, stuck in a world in which the virtues of the Ordinary Man are the cardinal virtues: generosity, friendliness, physical love.[3]

This is an argument of substance, which becomes no less substantial if we consider how deeply MacNeice himself was disturbed by it, a good fifteen years before this. When he went up to Oxford he was well aware of his lack of any sort of unifying belief, and of the need for this if the poetry he was writing was to have any value:

For me, when I went up to Oxford, anything was of interest and therefore nothing was of interest. . . . The material of literature, more than that of the other arts, is instinct with meaning to start with. For the material of literature is the lives, thoughts, and feelings of men. I had no system which could at the same time unify the world and differentiate its parts significantly. I had no world-view (and any such view is implicitly moral) which could give me a hierarchy, however

---

[1] Symons, op. cit., p. 89.   [2] Ibid., p. 91.   [3] Ibid., pp. 91–2.

approximate, of good and evil. The most that I attained to was a vague epicureanism.

The good poet has a definite attitude to life; most good poets, I fancy, have more than that—they have beliefs (though their beliefs need not be *explicit* in their work). . . .

When I went up to Oxford I felt hampered by this lack of belief. . . .[1]

MacNeice's personal outlook in his earlier Oxford years clearly corresponded to the spirit of the age. Yet he was in revolt against the *Zeitgeist*, and when he edited *Oxford Poetry* with Stephen Spender in 1929 it was dedicated: 'Neither to Poesy nor to the Zeitgeist'.[2] Although he had more than his share of the contemporary cynicism and despair and pessimism, it was only 'despair and disgust in the grand manner'[3] that attracted him, and much of his pessimism was a kind of defence mechanism. Cynicism, too, in its out and out form, he deplored, although it had its place as a grand creative gesture:

P.S. I have also been reading Timon of Athens. I hate your out and out cynics who go on and on like Babel. But he put a roof on his misanthropy—a perfect pediment—

'Timon hath built his everlasting mansion
Upon the beached verge of the salt flood.'[4]

Theories that stressed relativity and denied any reality or substance to the surface of things he was not prepared to accept:

Easily down-cast, over-ridden by scepticism, we are told 'The apple you are eating is mere appearance excepting the pips; *they* are the reality'; and the apple promptly loses its flavour for us. Yet we should have got past judging things by their cores or intestines or origins or atoms. We should say rather: 'No doubt you are right and those things are the real. So much the better for the apparent, the superficial, the conventional. . . . Thank God for Make-Believe.'[5]

[1] *M.P.*, pp. 62–3.

[2] 'I am dedicating it "Neither to Poesy nor to the Zeitgeist". . . .' Letter to A.F.B. from Carrickfergus, 23 July 1929.

[3] 'I had already grown tired of pinprick satire and had no wish to read *Point Counter Point* when it came out in 1928, but despair and disgust in the grand manner enlivened me. I found Donne's Sermons and Jeremy Taylor's *Holy Dying* excellent for reading aloud, and one of my favourite Shakespeare characters was Thersites' ('Twenty-One', p. 238).

[4] Letter to J.R.H., undated, but probably written in 1927.

[5] From 'Our God Bogus' in the second issue of *Sir Galahad*, 14 May 1929. In the same article he rejected the way of the mystics and the salvationists.

Thus to his awareness of the need for a system of belief—
something that would enable him to give due importance to
both core and surface—he added a determination to resist the
Zeitgeist in its despairing and negative aspect. The difficulty of
finding this system remained. Christian dogma was clearly not
the way: 'Having been brought up in a traditionally religious
family, and having, true to my period, reacted violently against
the Christian dogma and, to some extent too, against the Christian
ethic, I felt morally naked and spiritually hungry.'[1] Nor was he
attracted by any of the current socio-political dogmas. Although
he hated the *status quo*, communism had no appeal for MacNeice:

The strongest appeal of the Communist Party was that it demanded
sacrifice; you had to sink your ego. At the moment there seemed to be
a confusion between the state and the community, and I myself was
repelled by the idolisation of the state. . . . I had a certain hankering to
sink my ego, but was repelled by the priggishness of the Comrades
and suspected that their positive programme was vitiated by wishful
thinking and over-simplification. I joined them, however, in their
hatred of the *status quo*, I wanted to smash the aquarium. During
Christmas of 1933 . . . I sat down deliberately and wrote a long poem
called *Eclogue for Christmas*. I wrote it with a kind of cold-blooded
passion and when it was done it surprised me. Was I really as concerned
as all that with the Decline of the West? Did I really feel so desperate?
Apparently I did. Part of me must have been feeling like that for years.[2]

He continued to feel like that for the remainder of the 1930s,
but still refused to follow the way of political ideology. In reply
to the question put to him in 1934, 'Do you take your stand with
any political or politico-economic party or creed?', he said,
'No. In weaker moments I wish I could.'[3] His attitude is the same,
although his tone is more urgent, in a dialogue four years later
with his Guardian Angel, who asks him if it is not about time he
had political opinions and wrote about them:

Me: My sympathies are Left. On paper and in the soul. But not in my
heart or my guts. On paper—yes. I would vote Left any day, sign
manifestoes, answer questionnaires. Ditto, my soul. My soul is all for

[1] 'Twenty-One', pp. 231–2.   [2] *S.A.F.*, p. 146.
[3] Question 5 of 'An Enquiry', in *New Verse*, no. 11, October 1934, pp. 2, 7.

moving towards the classless society. But unlike Plato, what my soul says does not seem to go. There is a lot more to one than soul, you know.[1]

In *Modern Poetry*, moreover, in stressing the distinction between belief and propaganda, he made it quite plain that a poet must, in his opinion, modify any belief, creed, dogma in the light of his own observation:

The distinction must always be maintained between belief and propaganda. It is nonsense to say, as many say nowadays, that all great poetry has in all ages been essentially propaganda. . . . The fact that a poem in which a belief is implicit may convert some whom direct propaganda does not touch, far from proving that that poem is propaganda, only proves that propaganda *can* be beaten on its own ground by something other than itself, so that we can admit that poetry can incidentally have effects like those of propaganda though its proper function is not propagandist.

I have already maintained that major poetry usually implies a belief. Therefore the fact that beliefs are increasing among poets should conduce to a wider, more fertile, and possibly a major poetry. But, *for the poet*, any belief, any creed (and beliefs and creeds tend to be *a priori*) should be compromised with his own individual observation. . . . Shelley was an inferior poet because he did not qualify his dogmas with observation.[2]

Two years later, in reviewing Yeats's *Last Poems and Plays*, he observed: 'It is a lucky thing for the artist that his work usually outruns his ideology.'[3]

MacNeice was not prepared to manufacture any belief, creed or dogma that took him beyond the limits of his personal experience. Within those limits, however, and in the very forefront of his attention during the later Oxford years, was one possible unifying force that might even attain to the status of an external sanction—idealist philosophy. That art would help him to make the synthesis he had no doubt, but this merely begged the question, still leaving him to find the remoter synthesis that should underlie his art. He was disappointed with Croce's statement of the operation of aesthetic activity, to which Croce was not prepared to accord any primacy:

[1] *Minch*, p. 125.   [2] Op. cit., pp. 201–2.   [3] In the *New Republic*, 24 June 1940.

The branch of philosophy most pertinent to my needs was aesthetics but I soon decided that all aestheticians were blind. I was particularly disappointed by Croce. . . . As I understood Croce, he was maintaining that the artistic activity lies almost completely in the vision, the work of art itself being merely an epiphenomenon, a sop to the public. This I considered a blasphemy; the artist does not see the thing completely till he has made it. . . .[1]

Clearly MacNeice does accord primacy to the work of art as the end product of the synthesizing vision and activity, which leaves the understanding of the nature of this vision and activity as the responsibility of another department, or other departments, of philosophy. He was strongly opposed at Oxford to any attitude that pigeon-holed philosophy; he regarded metaphysical enquiry as embracing logic and epistemology (in which he was especially interested), as well as ontology and ethics. This attitude chimed well with that of his tutor, Dr. Geoffrey Mure, who had been a pupil of Bradley.[2] In particular, he was attracted by Bradley's attitude to the absolute, since Bradley's belief that anything at all was a judgement about the universe accorded very well with his own predilection both for the concrete and the ultimate: 'Reading F. H. Bradley's *Logic* I was delighted to find him saying that any judgment about anything whatsoever is a judgment about the Universe. . . .'[3] MacNeice had, however, from his Oxford days to the very end, a decided love-hate attitude towards the absolute. While his logical reason and his unbelief both yearned for an absolute, his common sense and his highly developed individualistic inclination to revolt cried equally loudly to him to deny an absolute—or, at least, any absolute that was either transcendental or in any way resembled a static idea. At Oxford he cast salt on his tutor's tail by referring to Hegel's 'right little,

[1] *S.A.F.*, p. 114.

[2] His close friend of the last two Oxford years, Mr. Adrian Green-Armytage, confirmed (letter to J.R.H. in reply to an enquiry of mine) that MacNeice's reading was both extensive and very eclectic, and that in their joint tutorials with Dr. Geoffrey Mure their discussions were almost always about epistemology. Dr. Mure himself confirmed in a letter to me that he believed MacNeice did a good deal more reading in metaphysics than he would have confessed to. Mr. Green-Armytage recalled MacNeice's allegiance as being equally divided between Hegel's rational optimism and Schopenhauer's pessimistic determinism.

[3] *S.A.F.*, p. 125.

tight little, Absolute',[1] and in a late recollection he commented acidly on the pretensions of the German idealists to a corner in the absolute:

My philosophy tutor . . . had encouraged me to look once—but only once—at the British empiricists and then to turn away to the German idealists, and, although I read these . . . only in translation, their inter-voluted jargon fell upon my ears (repeat 'ears') like an Open Sesame; the cave—excuse me, the club—was very select; the thieves—excuse me, the clubmen—had cornered the Absolute.[2]

MacNeice was possibly trailing his coat or speaking out of sheer exasperation in many such outbursts against the absolute. He does, however, raise a serious practical objection to the postulation of an absolute that very much concerns his search for belief as a poet. To his apparently approving remark about Bradley's attitude, just quoted, he adds the tart rider that the universe is a difficult witness to subpoena: '. . . I tried to suppress the feeling that in that case it becomes impossible to assess a judgment without subpoenaing the Universe (and how difficult it is to get that witness into court).'[3] In other words, the poet requires a more readily accessible standard of right and wrong, for convenient reference here and now, however valid the findings of idealist philosophy may be on a more distant view. This attitude he makes much more clear in a passage in *Modern Poetry*:

F. H. Bradley in his *Logic* states that every judgement is ultimately a judgement about the universe. But this does not mean that one judgement is not more important or more correct than another (in idealist philosophies, so often, we cannot see the trees for the wood). The poet, like the practical man, must presuppose a scale of values. Any odd set of words which anyone uses may, on ultimate analysis, be significant, but the poet cannot wait for this ultimate. And, if he could, why should he bother to be a poet, seeing that the idiots in their institutions, the babies in their prams, can be just as significant without effort.[4]

A basic factor in this dilemma of MacNeice's was that he could not accept any transcendental idea or static absolute, anything

[1] The occasion of the tutorial jibe was recalled independently by both Dr. Mure (letter to myself) and Mr. Green-Armytage (letter to J.R.H. quoted to me).
[2] 'Twenty-One', p. 231.   [3] *S.A.F.*, p. 125.   [4] Op. cit., p. 159.

that created a division between the Many and the One, and so denied to Being the ability to manifest itself in Becoming. This involved him in a rejection of Plato's system as well as Bradley's, and attracted him towards Aristotle:

Aristotle the biologist was anxious to avoid the gulf between Being and Becoming established by Plato the mathematician. His concept of *energeia*—significant and so, in a sense, eternal movement exemplified in the time-world—was an antidote to the static and self-contained heaven of Plato's transcendent Forms.[1]

He was not sufficiently clear in his own mind, however, that Aristotle had, in fact, bridged the gap, although he was attracted by the possibility that the Aristotelian *kinesis* (relative movement) might, in certain circumstances, be identifiable with *energeia* (absolute movement). He was dismayed by Aristotle's supposition of 'a highest grade in which mind thinks only itself. . . . Complete fusion of subject and object; a full stop; death.'[2] Thus he was 'ripe for Marx whose basic thesis, translated into Aristotelian, is that *energeia* can only be achieved by the canalisation and continued control of *kinesis*'.[3] Since Marx was hardly known at Oxford when MacNeice was there, he had recourse, as we have seen, to Gentile.

The attraction, therefore, of Marxist dialectic, in metaphysical terms, must have been strong for MacNeice, as it was for many of his contemporaries in the 1930s:

Those philosophers who, like Schopenhauer, have drawn too sweeping a distinction between the actual and the ideal have thought of the ideal world either as a substitute for the actual or, at best, as something to be abstracted from the actual world by, it may be, the artist, the aesthete, the philosopher, or the mystic. Art in particular has often been regarded recently as an escape from the actual to some transcendent reality on

---

[1] *S.A.F.*, p. 125. Professor Dodds (letter to myself in reply to an enquiry) confirmed this: '. . . I should have said that while the systems of Plato and of F. H. Bradley fascinated him as great imaginative constructions he never really believed in any of them. They conflicted with his sense of the world as "incorrigibly plural" (Snow) and his Aristotelian conviction of the reality of individual things. . . . A similar conflict between his imagination and his empirical common sense underlay, I think, his ambiguous attitude towards religion. . . .'
[2] *S.A.F.*, p. 126.   [3] Ibid.

the pattern of Plato's Forms, whereas Marxist materialism ignores *transcendent* realities and is therefore a good creed for the artist who must move in a concrete world.[1]

In a most revealing dialogue with his Guardian Angel, however, he resisted the urgent demand of one of his conflicting selves to take some form of social or political action. The passage is of central importance to an appreciation of the inflexible strength behind the bantering tone with which he resisted such demands. His Guardian Angel has advised some kind of action, symbolized as walking from London to Reading, but MacNeice cannot see what good it would do. His Guardian Angel is exasperated:

G.A.: You know what you're like? You're like a snowman waiting for the thaw.
Me: There's nothing else a snowman can do.[2]

MacNeice sticks to his point, but, when his Guardian Angel has taken his sorrowing departure, using his wings to fly beyond time and space, he is left to reflect disconsolately on his idealist philosophical interpretation of history, in the light of which he sees the ugly possibilities that the recurrent pattern of history might throw up:

(... I look out of the window and see a Viking longship run up into the harbour. Twenty Norsemen with horned helmets come striding up towards my shack ... I stand in the window unable to turn away. The horned heads move up huge as Molochs. Behind their spears the rain falls on the barren flagstaff and the first tee of the golf-course.)[3]

This is the central dilemma in which the subject confined in relative time and space was placed in relation to the unconfined real, in the metaphysical terms of MacNeice's idealist philosophy, in the late 1930s. Between the subject and the flagstaff and the first tee of the golf course (barren symbols of the temporal), looming through the falling rain (one of his favourite symbols for the Heraclitean endless flow of phenomenal experience),

[1] *M.P.*, pp. 24–5.
[2] *Minch*, p. 135. There seems to be a resemblance to Shelley's melting icicle, although MacNeice disputed Shelley's, as he did Croce's and Plato's, theory of the nature of artistic creation (*M.P.*, p. 70). The dialogue directly underlies his late poem 'The Snow Man'.
[3] Ibid., p. 138.

is the ugly menace of the absolute (all time and all phenomenal experience being, in the Heraclitean metaphysic, perpetually present). The subject, meantime, can do nothing but wait and see, remain stoically in his place in the hope that reasoning insight may supervene—bringing the thaw that will set the frozen water running again in Heraclitean flow.[1]

Perhaps enough has been said to indicate the direction in which MacNeice looked for the shaping or stabilizing attitude that he considered essential to artistic creation. One noteworthy feature of his allegiance to metaphysics must, however, be stressed: the fact that this was another of MacNeice's divided loyalties. He was at some pains to point out on many occasions his lack of trust in any philosophical system. His poems, lectures and articles contain many jibes at philosophers and philosophy, and he left even some of his close friends with the firm impression that he could not abide this discipline, which was neither an art nor a science nor a religion, which often claimed to speak with such certitude, but which left all the important questions unanswered. In his catalogue of influences on his poetry (up to 1938) he included 'a liking (now dead) for metaphysics'.[2] Shortly afterwards, he looked back at his Oxford attitude as a mere stylization to sanction his emotional response to the universe:

As I had no religion and no exciting personal relationships, my approach to ideas was very emotional. Even when it came to metaphysics. Metaphysics for me was not something cold and abstract; it was an account of reality, but an artistic account, not a scientific one. I did not believe that one system of philosophy was truer than another and thought that philosophers themselves were fools in so far as they thought they were getting to the bottom of anything; on the contrary their work was always superstructure, largely a matter of phrases, and these phrases were employed not as the physicist employs them but as the poet employs them; the philosopher's job—to use our favourite word—was stylisation, building a symphony which should sanction his emotional reactions to the universe.[3]

---

[1] The attitude to reality expressed in this dialogue underlies all MacNeice's metaphysical thinking. The imagery, too, recurs strikingly in such poems as 'The North Sea', Canto III of *A.S.*, 'Country Week-End', 'The Pale Panther'.

[2] *M.P.*, p. 89. [3] *S.A.F.*, p. 119.

He did not, therefore, look to philosophy to formalize a structure of beliefs, answers to the unanswerable; to provide a world view, with a hierarchy of good and evil, a valid attitude to ultimate reality. Nor did he look to it to give what religious belief gave to Job—a firm standpoint from which to ask the questions about ultimate reality. He looked to it rather to help him towards a disciplined understanding of the kind of questions to ask. He could thus employ the phrases creatively, 'as the poet employs them'; not as the professional metaphysician in his professional moments would employ them, but as the armature of a poetic outlook. Thus, no matter how many poems originated in a surface impact sharply registered, he can give universality to the best of them.

His innermost conviction, at Oxford and until the end, may well be contained in the ironic parable, 'Garlon and Galahad', which he wrote for the first issue of *Sir Galahad*, the student magazine, the second and final issue of which he himself edited. Here, Sir Galahad, the knightly quester, finds and rejects various illusory systems, realizing that he must quest on until he attains his vision of the ultimate:

Finally he came to the top of Mount Everest, and there sat a bald old man joggling a little case of cardboard and glass, which contained tiny silver balls. 'What are you doing?' asked Galahad. 'I am the oldest person in the world,' he said, 'and I am just arriving at a new synthesis. See here. If I can once get all these little balls all at the same time all into that little hole . . .' 'Goodbye, then,' said Galahad, 'my synthesis lies before me. . . .'[1]

At the same time, MacNeice realizes that Sir Galahad will be struck down, with casual malice prepense, by 'the bad knight, the Knight Invisible', in the very moment of success, when he is about to attain his vision of the Grail:

On then he went through ringing bells and blessed forms, in whistling storms and swinging censers, till he was almost at it, almost got it this time. It. He stood on the last step before It, hand raised to the latch.

---

[1] The paradox of the balls and the hole, or the One and the Many, is, of course, the same as Yeats's in 'A Needle's Eye'. The poem printed next in Yeats's *Collected Poems*, 'Meru', again deals with this theme, in terms of 'Hermits upon Mount Meru or Everest,'.

But Garlon (slipping in from nowhere) hit him in the back and killed him.

The parable recurs continually, and notably in *The Dark Tower* and his other Quest plays. The vitally important thing is the realization that 'my synthesis lies before me', and Garlon or the dragon of *The Dark Tower* cannot ultimately win so long as the Quest continues. And the Quest becomes identifiable with the Question, and both with the Questioner, who comes closer to his synthesis with the Not Self in never ceasing to ask the simple unanswerable questions. In the questioning and in the knowledge that they are unanswerable lie the questioner's pride and belief:

> . . . For himself
> He was not Tom or Dick or Harry,
> Let alone God, he was merely fifty,
> No one and nowhere else, a walking
> Question but no more cheap than any
> Question or quest is cheap. . . .[1]

It was in this belief that he had concluded 'The Stygian Banks':

> . . . Far from perfect
> Presumes perfection *where*? A catechism the drums
> Asseverate day-long, night-long: Glory is what?
> A question! . . .

And that is why he diagnoses the source of all our trouble in the late 'New Jerusalem' quite simply as our failure to go on asking 'the simple unanswerable questions'. The way forward—or back —to faith, for MacNeice, is the way of the unanswerable question, not the unquestionable answer.

[1] 'The Blasphemies'.

3 Appearance and Reality

We have just noticed MacNeice's hostility towards any meta-physical system that postulated or implied a division between the actual world of phenomenal time, space, and experience, and any transcendental principle, where the former was regarded as a mere reflection of the latter, or as a phenomenal creation apart from its creator or prime mover. His hostility was not the less acute—or complex—because he was aware of the apparent existence of a gulf between the two, however much he may have hoped that the gulf was illusory. The awareness of the gulf he expressed (jointly with Auden) in the last lines of their 'Last Will and Testament':

> And to the good who know how wide the gulf, how deep
> Between Ideal and Real, who being good have felt
> The final temptation to withdraw, sit down and weep,
>
> We pray the power to take upon themselves the guilt
> Of human action. . . .[1]

The fact that the gulf exists is a commonplace, although the nature of the gulf has perhaps been viewed differently at different times. This was well expressed by Miss Dilys Powell (in an extension of a remark by Mr. Charles Williams):

Mr. Charles Williams in his interesting study *The English Poetic Mind* declares the work of Shakespeare, Milton and Wordsworth to be rooted in conflict between the ideal and the actual. . . . Certainly most modern poetry is motivated by conflict: discrepancy between the writer's temperament and his convictions, between his experience and his belief. When, however, we come to the new generation, to the work of Mr. Auden, Mr. Day Lewis, Mr. Spender, the nature of the conflict has changed. It has been externalised; it has become a battle, not within the poet, but between poetry and environment. . . .[2]

Dr. C. M. Bowra says much the same thing in reference to T. S. Eliot and the spirit that informs *The Waste Land*

---

[1] *L.I.*, p. 258. It should be noted carefully that the terms 'ideal' and 'real' are used here (and by Dr. Bowra below) to express the antithesis. Elsewhere (e.g. in *A. J.*, XIV, *C.P.D.*, p. 126) MacNeice generally uses the terms (more acceptable, perhaps, to philosophers) 'real' (for 'transcendent(al)') and 'actual' (for 'phenomenal').

[2] Foreword, p. xvi, to *Descent from Parnassus*, by Dilys Powell, London, 1934. (It will be noted that yet a different terminology, 'the ideal and the actual', is used for the antithesis.)

EA

. . . where the conflict passes outside himself to the consciousness of civilized man, and modern civilization is presented as failing in all that it attempts, whether in love or business or religion. If a poet feels this hideous gap between the ideal and the real, he must not gloss over it or attempt to say that all is really well. It is precisely this discord which inspires Eliot. . . .[1]

This conflict MacNeice expresses in a revealing poem that he wrote at Oxford, under an equally revealing pseudonym, John Bogus Rosifer:

PARADISE LOST
(Villanelle)

('. . . *cuncta prospectabam loca, sicubi forte*
conterminis in hortulis candens repperirem rosarium.')

Caught in Apollo's blended dream
On the dim marge of Poesy
My rose-red lips unlock to scream.

My horticultural mind did teem
With roses once and rosemary
Caught in Apollo's blended dream.

Now an unorthodox regime
Has whelmed my soul in lethargy,
My rose-red lips unlock to scream.

The sinister tall gas-works seem
To vitiate my destiny
Caught in Apollo's blended dream. . . .[2]

Here is the dilemma of the consciously Apollonian poet, who traditionally mirrors appearances, aware of his own illusion, but willing to accept the dream of Apollo as conveying a kind of reality to the world of appearance. Yet the illusion now seems impossible to maintain, the conflict having been externalized, and the enemy, the modern environment, too overwhelmingly power-

---

[1] *The Background to Modern Poetry.* An inaugural lecture by C. M. Bowra (then Professor of Poetry), Oxford, 1946, p. 16.

[2] In *Sir Galahad*, vol. 1, no. 1, 21 February 1929. The care that MacNeice habitually gave to his titles has here been bestowed on his pseudonym, which effectively connotes 'one who has gone before, as a false bearer of roses'. Cf. his *persona* in the satirical sequence in the *Marlburian*: 'Apollo on the Old Bath Road'.

ful. As he can no longer reflect only the world of roses and rosemary, but must accept and express the blended dream that includes
the 'sinister tall gas-works', the poet feels that his destiny has been
vitiated. He is sunk in a lethargy out of which there are only two
possible escapes—either to accept the blended dream ('he must
not gloss over it or attempt to say that all is really well') of Apollo,
or transfer his allegiance to Dionysus. MacNeice was strongly
under the influence of Nietzsche precisely at this time, and was
especially struck by Nietzsche's examination in *The Birth of
Tragedy* of the two forces of Apollo and Dionysus, in consequence
of which he was impelled towards Dionysus.[1] On the other hand,
the influence of Eliot and *The Waste Land* spoke powerfully
for the acceptance of his destiny and 'Apollo's blended dream'.[2]
He was even excited about having discovered Eliot's walk at
Oxford and intended to exploit it: 'We discovered T. S. Eliot's
walk at Oxford, where four gasometers stand over the Isis—
"the river sweats oil and tar". There we shall paddle next term
with a large musical box playing silly polkas—"This music stole
by me upon the waters".'[3] In the late 'Memoranda to Horace',
he professes his allegiance to Apollo:

> Though elderly poets profess to be inveterate
> Dionysians, despising Apollonians,
>   I find it, Flaccus, more modest
> To attempt, like you, an appetitive decorum.

Between the early 'Paradise Lost' and the late 'Memoranda to
Horace' lies the whole conflict of the blended dream, with an
allegiance possibly divided between the gods, for the Dionysian
intoxication, as the underlying reality erupts, is strong.[4]

[1] 'I . . . was delighted . . . by Nietzsche's *Birth of Tragedy*, though I knew it to be perverse
and historically upside-down. . . . "Up Dionysus!" became my slogan . . .' (*S.A.F.*,
p. 110).

[2] 'In fact *The Waste Land* did appeal to me; I understood it much better than I did
Prufrock, for instance, in which I completely missed the humour, as I did in much of
Ulysses. . . . *The Waste Land* . . . hit me in the way a person hits one.' ('Twenty-One', p.
237.)

[3] Letter to A.F.B. from Carrickfergus, 29 March 1927.

[4] He deeply admired the Dionysian poet Dylan Thomas, and wrote possibly the most
moving, as well as discriminating, tributes to him in the cantos of *Autumn Sequel* devoted
to him, and in his essay on pp. 85–7 of the collection *Dylan Thomas: The Legend and the
Poet. A Collection of Biographical and Critical Essays*, ed. by E. W. Tedlock, London, 1960.

His deep awareness of the world of appearances as a reflection of another world of realities results in the frequent presence of reflected images in the poems—reflections from mirrors, on glass or on water, reflections cast on walls by fire or any source of light. The theme both of divided and of reflected reality appears already in a very neat-edged little Imagist poem he wrote at school, 'Moon Fishery: A Dialogue', in which an old man stubbornly persists in fishing for the moon's reflection in the water, confident that although his 'willow rod/Is snap't . . ./It will mend again.'[1] Twenty-five years later, the remote ideal is still reflected or intangible:

> Home beyond this life? Or through it? If through, how?
> Through as through glass—or through the nerves and blood?
>
> . . . .
>
> A home from home? But is it a window or mirror
> We see that happiness in or through? . . .

His hope of attaining elusive reality has diminished, however, with his more developed awareness that 'Zion is always future'.[2]

It was a recurrent hope of MacNeice's that, where human reason had failed to find the way, animal instinct would help, but in the later poems animal instinct, too, is operative only in a world of reflected realities:

> Still twice a week the Zoo keeps open late
> Where flanks and shanks, that might be furs or beef
>
> But for the grace of Man, still twitch and wait
> Till the great wilds reconquer Regent's Park—
>
> . . . .
>
> And walls of glass between us and the apes
> Reflect ourselves while shadows hoot and bark
>
> And goats perch high on fabricated capes
> And bears beneath them sleep depolarised
> And night festoons them all with stars and grapes.[3]

The irony of man's artificial and illusory control runs strongly through the lines. In ordering the instinctive lives of the animals,

[1] *Marlburian*, 26 May 1926.   [2] 'Day of Returning'.   [3] *C.P.D.*, p. 333 (*A.S.*, I).

fabricating capes for the goats and depolarizing the bears, smothering them with his gracious protection, man has separated himself from the animals and divided both from the real, deluding himself with a show of tinsel festoons that he is the deviser of some gay festival.[1] As in Plato's myth of the cave, however, the shadows are reflections of what itself is a reflection, and, as in other of MacNeice's poems, the glass walls divide as well as reflect.

In 'Sunday in the Park', where all is meaningless and unreal, 'dark glasses mirror ironies', and the whole poem is a catalogue of reflected ironies. The old men of this poem who 'feel lost/ But stick it out', the refugees who 'forget/Pretences and grow sad', the foreigners who are always asking the time, which no one can tell them, recall the world of Kafka and Beckett, with which MacNeice latterly found himself so much in sympathy:

Beckett's aged and ragged and often crippled soliloquists, senile nostalgia and all . . . are always looking for themselves and so, *ipso facto*, for that which is not themselves. Their quest is metaphysical. They may not be concerned with God but they are concerned with spiritual meaning, even if all they know about this—or almost all—is its absence. . . . Perhaps in Beckett the Original Sin is lack of meaning.[2]

True to his Apollonian sympathies, however, MacNeice does not always find the reflection of reality absurd, a matter for despair. The reflection may well partake of the reality, with which it is one in essence. Thus, the memory of a woman he has loved has left his walls 'Dancing over and over with her shadow'.[3] Here he fuses two of his favourite themes, the instinctively patterned life of a beautiful woman, in harmony with the real, and the concept of life with the rhythmic flow and order of the dance, so that Becoming is equated with Being. The shadow is here the living reality. Again, in 'The Strand', his reflection mirrored in the wet sand of an island holiday place in Ireland recalls his father's reflection mirrored in the same sand sixteen years before. He felt sure that the reflection of his father, 'A square black figure whom the horizon understood', mirrored a reality, and seemed to wonder, by implication, whether his, too, did so.

---

[1] Glitter and gleam here are false and do *not* manifest the real. See p. 56.
[2] *V.P.*, p. 140.   [3] *C.P.D.*, p. 107 (*A.J.*, IV).

On the other hand, the reflections in the sequence 'Entered in the Minutes' represent a purely illusory or ambiguous connection with the real. The business men of the second octet startle him with the phenomenon of 'two strangers talking/The same language for once', but their projection of themselves upon him coincides significantly with his awareness of their reflection on the window pane, which automatically seems to remove their desirable communication to a disconnected plane of unreality. In the fourth octet, 'Didymus', the doubter who refused 'to fall in love with God', spends his life in love with reflections, and consequently the source to which he returns at death is a reflection:

> When he died a swallow seemed to plunge
> Into the reflected, the wrong, sky.[1]

As with the tinsel decorations of the zoo, the flick of the swallows' wings, which would otherwise be tokens of reality,[2] are, for Didymus (Doubting Thomas), mere reflections on the surface of a river that merely runs:

> Accepting only what he could see, a river
> Full of the shadows of swallows' wings
>
> That dipped and skimmed the water; he would not
> Ask where the water ran or why.

A similar reflection of the real appears in 'The Mixer', where the colourless subject has ceased to have any real identity:

> He is only happy in reflected light
> And only real in the range of laughter;
> Behind his eyes are shadows of a night
> In Flanders. . . . .

About the time he wrote this poem, MacNeice was thinking very much in terms of value subsisting in the things made, achieved, by people, with the equation of the real and the actual realized

---

[1] See (p. 172) MacNeice's comment on his wish to stress the 'wrongness'.

[2] 'Whatever it is that jigs and gleams' often manifests the real; it 'Might yet prove heaven this side heaven,//Viz. life. Euripides was right/To say "whatever glints" (or dances)' ('Indian Village'). Cf. his epigraph to *E.C.*, from Euripides' *Hippolytus*, which could be translated: indeed we are obviously sick with love for whatever glints like this throughout the world.

in the value. The mixer is therefore unreal, not only as a reflection of a real principle, but also as a reflection of a phenomenal person who has failed to achieve value, and therefore reality, by his failure in Flanders. Unreal persons, therefore, are the reflections both of actual-and-real persons and of real principles.[1] The imagery of 'Didymus' seems to reappear transposed (and again recalling Plato's cave) in the first poem in the late sequence 'Dark Age Glosses', where the shadows of the revellers on the wall of the dim and smoky interior connote shifting unreality, and the flicker of the swallow's wings a hint of the real beyond.

Often the reflections impress themselves upon him when he is in a trance-like condition, as in the railway journey of 'Business Men', suggesting an Alter Ego or Doppelgänger moving relentlessly on a parallel course to his own, causing him to wonder, perhaps with foreboding, which is the reality. In 'Corner Seat', the questioning subject is glad of the windows that separate him from the cold and the fright of contact with the Other, yet the reflection of self strikes him with equal chill and fright because it seems so isolated and lonely:

> Suspended in a moving night
> The face in the reflected train
> Looks at first sight as self-assured
> As your own face—But look again:
>
> Windows between you and the world
> Keep out the cold, keep out the fright;
> Then why does your reflection seem
> So lonely in the moving night?

The reflection here seems to connote not only the reflected, ideal self, moving separately in another world, but also the horror of solipsism. Another example of his awareness of moving forward in reflection, again with some ambiguity about whether the reflection represents the actual or the real, is in 'Museums', where there is also the element of double illusion, reflection of reflection. The museum, like the learned library, represented for him a slightly disreputable substitute for Becoming, a kind of frozen,

[1] Cf. *S.A.F.*, p. 35: 'Maybe, if I look back, I shall find that my life is not just mine, that it mirrors the lives of the others—or shall I say the Life of the Other?'

fossilized or artificially contrived Being. In 'Museums' the full force of the illusion is emphasized by his being aware of himself moving in reflection along glass cases which themselves contain reflections of reality within them—and the distortion is perhaps further complicated by the cosy self-deception of the subject, reflecting his own inner unreality rather in the manner of 'The Mixer':

> Warmed and cajoled by the silence the cowed cypher revives,
> Mirrors himself in the cases of pots, paces himself by marble lives,
> Makes believe it was he that was the glory that was Rome,
> Soft on his cheek the nimbus of other people's martyrdom. . . .

That MacNeice intended to convey parallel forward movement rather than merely static comparison in reflected unreality is suggested by the MS. alteration from '*measures* himself *against* marble lives' to '*paces* himself *by* marble lives',[1] with its connotation of the simultaneous forward motion of two athletes.

One of MacNeice's most frightening reflection structures is in the late 'Budgie'. The budgerigar of the poem is 'baby blue', and is comfortably adjusted to the 'small blue universe' of his cage (unlike the prowling zoo animals, who have a kind of restless dignity in their confinement), attitudinizing before his mirror, which is cosily 'rimmed with baby pink'. As he twitters to his mirror in confident solipsism the reality of his identity—'I twitter Am'—he is happily unaware that the perch is burning in his weightless cage, suspended in the hostile Other that is infinite space:

> . . . . Beyond
> These wires there might be something different—
> Galaxy on galaxy, star on star,
> Planet on planet, asteroid on asteroid,
> Or even those four far walls of the sitting room—
> But for all this small blue bundle could bother
> Its beak, there is only itself and the universe,
> The small blue universe . . .[2]

[1] In H.N.

[2] The small blue universe where the budgie confidently twitters the reality of its existence and identity strangely recalls the twittering between-world of the third section of *Burnt Norton*, where the false twilight of the London Underground is emblematic of the

MacNeice has described his recurring mood of trance-like terror, 'when everything seems to be unreal, petrified' as he catches his own reflection in a mirror, or notices 'the mysterious gleams of light *glancing* off the mirror'.[1] He says in the same passage that he regards the mirror as 'a symbol of nihilism via solipsism'.[2] Presumably the *glancing* light (MacNeice's own emphasis) connotes, as elsewhere, the presence of the real, while the solipsism of the reflection leads to nihilism because of the awareness of separation from this real in the divided reflection (often the series of reflections). 'Perseus' he himself singles out to illustrate this mood, with the Gorgon's head dominating the poem. The series of mirror reflections, in infinite regression, apart, precluding any possibility of question or act of will, appears in a very early poem, 'This Tournament', and a late one, 'Reflections'. In 'This Tournament' the subject, in trance-like detachment, sees himself and his fate in the determinist terms both of the poised hammer of Thor, 'brooding arithmetician', and the 'phoenix diorama' of his infinitely regressing mirror reflections:

> But I, Banquo, had looked into the mirror,
> Had seen my Karma, my existences
> Been and to be, a phoenix diorama,
> Fountain agape to drink itself for ever
> Till the sun dries it. . . .[3]

The vertiginous catalogue of reflections in the late poem ends with quiet, matter-of-fact finality that makes absolute the separation between self and the reflections that have their real existence, presumably, in the world of things-in-themselves:

> . . . a taxi perhaps will drive in through the bookcase
> Whose books are not for reading and past the fire
> Which gives no warmth and pull up by my desk
> At which I cannot write since I am not lefthanded.

Perhaps his most extended illustration, both of reflection and

world that is neither the lucid daylight nor the fructifying darkness of God: 'Not here/ Not here the darkness, in this twittering world' (*F.Q.*, p. 11). Cf., too, the epigraph from Nietzsche to *P.P.*: '*ein Zwiespalt und Zwitter von Pflanze und von Gespenst*'.

[1] *M.P.*, p. 175. [2] Ibid. [3] *B.F.*, pp. 41–2.

separation, is in the radio play, *The Queen of Air and Darkness*,[1]
where the remote first principle manifesting itself in the phenomenal world is not only the transcendental idea, repellent to Mac-
Neice, but is also itself existent in a world of mere reflection.
Thus it is a source of evil inspiration to its ministers in the phenomenal world. In his introduction to the play, he refers to his
programme as 'a myth, a parable, a study of perverted idealism',
making it plain, however, that, although there are obvious
historical parallels, 'the focus here is on persons rather than on
politics'. Thus he tries to universalize his theme. The remote first
principle, too, has been personified, as in the two poems that,
as he says, suggested the idea—A. E. Housman's poem, from
which he takes his title,[2] and 'The Lady of Shalott'. The dramatic
situation in Tennyson's poem, however, appears to symbolize
only the dilemma of the romantic poet, the paradox of the artist's
dream world: to break out of it is death, and to live in it is death-
in-life. In Housman's poem and MacNeice's play the horror is the
dream world determined by a remote first principle of evil.
In MacNeice's play, moreover, the Queen is blind (perhaps the
culminating evil), expressing her will on the basis of her hand-
maiden's descriptions of what passes in 'the magic mirror which
reflects what occurs in time'. Thus, the first principle in the universe
resembles Schopenhauer's blind will.

A similar treatment at some length of the theme of devotion
to an external idea appears in the extended parable of Cantos
XIV–XVI of *Autumn Sequel*, where the young man spirals out
of the world of Becoming into the timeless realm of false reality,
where the Status Quo lives on in the static reflections of the idea.
Here is

> . . . the Church of Arc-lights where there is much
>
> Too much light and much too much to say
> And too loud speakers to say it . . .

and for some 'aberrant errants' who 'give a miss/To such Utopian
Zions' there is

---

[1] Third Programme, 28 March 1949.
[2] Housman's was his favourite poem for reading aloud. See p. 191.

> . . . the temple of Aesthetic Bliss,
> That blind aquarium of chanting trout
> And quivering fins and suckers. The glass walls
> Reflect the inner lights and squeeze the outer out.[1]

These, and the temptation of the Marxist idea, the young man just manages to resist, spiralling back again from the false darkness of the spirit, illumined by the false light of illusory reality, to actuality and the light of everyday, the world of Becoming, 'Where it is still the Fall'.[2] He has 'found the Ne//Plus Ultra and learnt the worst', but his weakness in looking for the illusory idea is not to be deplored by MacNeice or the reader, who have both served their term 'in similar depths before', but have

> . . . yet regained the sky
> And the give and take of humanity. And yet
> The Quest goes on and we must still ask why
>
> We are alive, though no one man has met
> A full or lucid answer. . . .[3]

A sense of puzzlement at the apprehended presence of a transcendent ultimate appears in such poems as 'Aubade for Infants', 'Donegal Triptych', 'The Riddle' and 'Château Jackson'. In the imagery of the first two, the something is almost palpably there; it seems a matter of simply snapping the blind or drawing the curtain to reveal its presence:

> Snap the blind; I am not blind,
> I must spy what stalks behind
> Wall and window—something large
> Is barging up beyond the down,
> Chirruping, hooting, hot of foot.[4]

The something (which was there at the beginning of time and creation) does not, however, reveal itself, except indirectly:

---

[1] *C.P.D.*, pp. 386–7 (*A.S.*, XIV).   [2] *C.P.D.*, p. 394 (*A.S.*, XVI).
[3] *C.P.D.*, p. 395 (*A.S.*, XVI). The same theme appears in several of the radio plays, notably *Traitors in our Way*. Jerry, the Professor of Physics, in *The Administrator*, similarly refuses to hide his head 'in the pure, pure sand' of the idea. (*Admin.*, p. 76.)
[4] 'Aubade for Infants'.

> ...... Something bright
> Ignites the dumps of sodden cloud,
> Loud and laughing, a fiery face . . .[1]

As these lines recall Blake, so these from 'Donegal Triptych' recall Wordsworth:

> And salute to our bride, Our Bride in the Moon
> Who brings the tides of the world for dowry,
> Lightening our threshold late and soon.
> But never there when we draw the curtain.[2]

In 'The Riddle' the image is again, as in 'Aubade for Infants', the house, with something prowling round and round it, while in 'Château Jackson' it is the Jack that built the house who is elusive. Both of these last poems are examples of the simple nursery-rhyme-riddle material used to suggest the innermost mystery and pose the ultimate questions—the former suggesting the vague menace in the prowling first principle, the latter the almost jocular absurdity of the cumulative creative process, in which only the ultimate questioner matters, as he brings the wheel full circle, uttering

> . . . . . the words
> That tell the truth that ends the quest:
> Where is the Jack that built the house?

MacNeice viewed the gulf between the actual and the real with many differing degrees of intensity. In one mood he merely expresses awareness of the disjunction, as in 'Under the Mountain', where he states bluntly that he belongs in the actual. The technique of visual presentation with shifting perspective states the antithesis simply but starkly—the field, the house, the seashore viewed from above, all irregularities smoothed out, buttoned down; and then viewed from below, with all their confusion and heartache:

---

[1] Ibid. Cf. the 'fiend hid in a cloud' of Blake's 'Infant Sorrow'. (MacNeice instances Blake's image in *M.P.*, p. 93, as 'a concrete intuitive image of the dream-type'.) There is also a strong suggestion of Sir Percevale's words in Tennyson's 'The Holy Grail': 'I saw the fiery face as of a child/That smote itself into the bread' (i.e. into the sacramental wafer). MacNeice's image is both sacramental and non-sacramental: he is not sure what is in the cloud.

[2] The personification is close to Wordsworth's 'This Sea that bares her bosom to the moon', as the 'late and soon' seems a verbal echo from the same sonnet. The attitude, too, is the same as Wordsworth's—we are out of tune with the reality in nature.

And when you get down
The house is a maelstrom of loves and hates where you—
Having got down—belong.[1]

At other times he makes no attempt to conceal his shock or
even horror at the gulf. With an intensity that recalls Hopkins he
cries out in 'Ode' against the awareness of the division between
the actual and the real that leaves him hanging between two iron
spires:

> Not to hang so, O God, between your iron spires!
> The town-dweller like a rabbit in a greengrocer's
> Who was innocent and integral once
> Now, red with slit guts, hangs by the heels
> Hangs by the heels gut-open against the fog
> Between two spires that are not conscious of him.

The horror of separation between the phenomenal thing and the
real thing-in-itself is bleak and extreme in the late 'In Lieu',
where, in the catalogue of things, not one is its essential self:

> Roses with the scent bred out,
> In lieu of which is a long name on a label.
> Dragonflies reverting to grubs,
> Tundra and desert overcrowded,
> And in lieu of a high altar
> Wafers and wine procured by a coin in a slot.

The process of natural evolution towards an end that was implied
in the beginning has been interrupted, and has become a regression
affecting past and future, as well as present, phenomenal time:

> . . . . . . in deep
> Freeze after freeze in lieu of a joint
> Are piled the shrunken heads of the past
> And the offals of unborn children.

And just as the word remains to distinguish the rose, although the
essence is no longer present in existence, so the Word exists, but
the essences it brought into existence are all regressing:

[1] As so often with MacNeice, the thesis of one poem has its antithesis in another, so that
in 'House on a Cliff' the purposeful man inside the house, with its 'ancestral curse-cum-
blessing', is disturbed in his broken sleep by his awareness of the wider rhythms of life
without.

> In lieu therefore of choice
> Thy Will be undone. . . .

In consequence of his horror of separation, MacNeice is fond of connective images: windows or doors in the wall; the gate through the hedge or fence; ladders ascending; webs or structures across the void; bridgeheads into the flux; the customs house at the border. In the false Beyond of the parable of the false idea in *Autumn Sequel*, the young men wander in a static and isolated world, drifting aimlessly 'in defiance//Of everything outside', which state MacNeice rejects on the metaphysical ground that

> . . . Outside and inside shift
> Into each other continually. No sieve,
> Not even the finest in the world, can sift
> Essence from accident. . . .[1]

Similarly, in *The Queen of Air and Darkness* the isolation and *stasis* are absolute:

2nd Handmaid: Here where there is never a draught, where no
    fly buzzes,
    Where no dust settles, where the light never changes,
    But everything is crystal, timeless, frozen.
    And there is no way in—
1st Handmaid: And no way out.
    Slaves of a mirror, the only thing that changes—
    A window into the world of time. . . .
2nd Handmaid: A window? Yes—
    But one which admits no air, no bird will ever
    Fly in through it for there is no way in—
1st Handmaid: And there is no way out. . . .

Adam, however, rejecting his blind and deluded activating idea, did ultimately break into the timeless and frozen place; and increasingly in MacNeice's later poems the window opens to allow the air to flow and the birds to fly between the two worlds.

    The prototype and pattern of all these later poems of free

---

[1] *C.P.D.*, p. 387 (*A.S.*, XIV).

communication, static becoming dynamic, closed becoming open, frozen or stagnant beginning to thaw and flow, is possibly the remarkable school parable story, 'Windows in the Ink'.[1] This is one of a series of stories featuring Mr. Schinabel, a fantasy incarnation of his school worship of un-reason, who asserts the claims of the real world against the phenomenal, the dynamic against the static:

His uncle was a retired business man, insulated in the thick woollen facts of this world. . . . He did not believe in the Abyss; by walling himself in from it he had refuted its claims to existence; there was no Remus from the spiritual world to leap over those walls, cemented as they were with a common sense worthy of that prince of builders, Balbus.

In a very revealing passage, Mr. Schinabel's customary visit to his uncle is described:

All was silent in the house except for the clicking of his uncle's mind from his study. An immutable clicking, the hall-mark of eternity. Like a hen gobbling up the sands of time. Like the absolute getting the better in argument of Einstein.

The situation, however, had altered: his uncle had become aware of the Abyss. He was writing as rapidly as possible, before the ink dried:

While he wrote he spoke, 'In the fresh ink I can see windows and through the windows I can see the gods. I have never seen them before; nor shall I see them when I die; I am clogged with matter of fact. Ah! the windows, the windows, they have the gleam of sunshine.'

In his dread that the ink would dry, he wrote and wrote, threw away the pen, fainted and died. Mr. Schinabel, writing an account of the funeral to a relation, suddenly

noticed a gleam in the freshly-written sentence. In each letter was a little glittering space, a window. One of the windows was thrown open and his uncle looked out. He smiled. 'Not even I', he said, 'could destroy my own personality. I have found the gods.'

[1] *Marlburian*, 10 March 1926.

As well as the themes of communication and personal identity, there is also present here the later recurrent concept of 'whatever glints' and, conceivably, a foreshadowing of MacNeice's later cardinal faith in the value of creative writing.

One of MacNeice's central poems on the communication theme, 'The Window', is discussed later.[1] Here he is optimistic. In his moods of despair, however, the glass walls of modern architecture are not media of communication, but frozen dividing walls: 'Their walls of thin ice dividing greynesses.'[2] Yet the wall can always become a window, miraculously:

> But, as they spoke, their voices
> Faded away while the wall
> Grew nearer so that he heard
> Different voices beyond it,
>
> Singing. And there was light
> Before him as through a window
> That opens on to a garden.
> The first garden. The last.[3]

Similarly, the static world can suddenly become dynamic, the closed and relative experience become the open and timeless. Thus, in 'Order to View' the antithesis is presented in terms of 'a big house, bleak', half remembered, now lifeless, with 'a tarnished/ Arrow over an empty stable' that 'Shifted a little in the tenuous wind'. 'The world was closed', but suddenly the wind gusted:

> And all the curtains flew out of
> The windows; the world was open.

The arrow, blown by the eternal high wind, will now, presumably, point in the direction of dynamic forward movement. Again, in 'The Stygian Banks', in the imagery of the enclosed garden with its high wall, where the wind of relative movement blows, and the tall trees above and beyond are swaying in the upper winds, we have the relative suddenly moving in harmony with the absolute:

---

[1] See pp. 166–7.   [2] 'New Jerusalem'.   [3] 'The Wall'.

> . . . . . . The wind that whitens the cornfield
> And lilts in the telephone wires is tilting the tree-top
> Further and further. . . .[1]

This is the 'real' wind:

> . . . . . A 'real' wind
> Yawns—and flicks a tree-top nonchalantly
> As if to say 'Look, though half in my sleep,
> I can do more than that Other.' So all is well. As it was.[2]

All is well, because, in the garden, we can see the eternal high wind blowing beyond the confining wall:

> . . . . . . Intake of distance.
> What is it that comes in? Can it be that the wall
> Is really a stepping-stone? So that what is beyond it
> (That which as well perhaps could be called what is Not)
> Is the sanction itself of the wall and so of the garden?[3]

The late 'Vistas' also expresses the delighted awareness of a world that had seemed closed suddenly seeming free and open, although the suddenness is seen against the widest background of Being revealing itself to creation in the evolving cosmic cycles, the first two closed, the third slowly opening out, and the fourth dramatically open:

> Emerging from aeons of ocean on to the shore
> The creature found itself in a roadless
> Forest where nothing stretched before
> Its lack of limbs but lack of hope. . . .

The trees gradually part 'to grant it greater scope', so that after another age of forward movement through the forest tunnels the creature emerges on an open plain:

> . . . . Creeping fog and rain
> And deafmute fears are left behind;
> The stuttering grub grows wings and sings
> The tune it never thought to find.

---

[1] *C.P.D.*, p. 261.   [2] *C.P.D.*, p. 262.

[3] *C.P.D.*, p. 263. Cf. Pound's poem 'Δώρια', in *Cathay*, which was favourite reading of MacNeice's at Oxford ('Twenty-One', p. 239): 'Be in me as the eternal moods/Of the bleak wind, and not/As transient things are—gaiety of flowers. . . .'

FA

The Self has now found itself 'in predestined/Freedom', and

> . . . . . . Around, below, above,
> Glinting fish and piping birds
> Deny that earth and truth are only
> Earth, respectively, and words.

Again the glints and the pipings indicate the immanent presence of the real. The gulf has been bridged, and earth and truth and the word form a unity—in absolute contradistinction to such a poem as 'In Lieu', where the word and the thing are divided from each other, and both from truth, where the cosmic cycles move regressively, the dragonflies specifically 'reverting to grubs'.

'Vistas' seems a good illustration of the concept in idealist philosophy sometimes known as 'objective idealism', where ultimate reality is conceived in largely impersonal terms, although this ultimate may be regarded as something that, being higher than individual awareness, includes it in its operation. This attitude gains momentum in MacNeice's poetry, and is frequently expressed in symbols of forward movement, where the subject is simply a passenger, his personal volition limited to hailing the bus or taxi, boarding the ship or plane, or even mounting (or refusing to mount) the wild horse he cannot thereafter control, for it has a will of its own. (Such poems stand in strong symbolic contrast to those in which the subject is, or believes he is, in control—the motor car journeys, for instance, in which he drives gladly along summer lanes, brushing roadside flowers, or where he can scarcely hold the black, rainswept, windswept road, and in which the underlying metaphysical attitude is quite different.) In many of the later poems the subject is conscious of being on a meaningless journey, or carried forward helplessly to a foregone conclusion. The machine has come to a sudden halt because of human or mechanical failure; or the operator has lost contact with the controller. As he believed that Yeats's lines 'The best lack all conviction, while the worst/Are full of passionate intensity' best expressed the mood of the twenty years before the war,[1] so he seems in the later poems to feel with Yeats that 'The falcon

---

[1] In part (ii) of his article 'Broken Windows or Thinking Aloud': see Bibliog.

cannot hear the falconer'. Thus, in 'Half Truth from Cape Town', MacNeice comes 'through the swinging doors of the decades' only to 'Confront a waste of tarmac, a roaring sky'. Ahead of him lies the same pointless journey that lies ahead of all the other travellers, all scurrying with determined lack of purpose:

> In each glib airport between here and you
> As the loudspeaker speaks the ants pour through,
> Some going north into their past and some
> South to this future that may never come,
> But all engrossed to that same point that good
> Ants would die to get to if they could.

The same apparently preordained lack of purpose torments him in 'Solitary Travel', where he feels

> . . . the futility of moving on
> To what, though not a conclusion, stays foregone.

The 'solitary' of the title is important, for in all these poems the traveller is carried in frozen isolation from the other travellers. In some, as in 'Solitary Travel', he tries to communicate:

> . . . the waiters, coffee-coloured or yellow or black,
> All smile, but, should you smile, give nothing back.

In 'Restaurant Car' there is once more the appalled sense of being rushed through a present that races into the past, with the pace of travel wildly accelerating:

> We roughride over the sleepers, finger the menu,
> Avoid our neighbours' eyes and wonder what
>
> Mad country moves beyond the steamed-up window
> So fast into the past we could not keep
> Our feet on it one instant. . . .

Again he feels the longing to communicate:

> Could we, before we stop where all must change,
> Take one first risk and catch our neighbours' eyes?

That all this movement, however hectic, is simply *stasis*, he emphasizes in 'Old Masters Abroad':

> . . . . . . All over the static
> Globe the needle sticks in the groove.

The plane has lost touch altogether with the control tower in 'The Pale Panther', and man, the seeker after knowledge without understanding, is losing his illusion of control—over the atom bomb, or the tiny tractor whose engine has stalled. The stalled engine, symbolic of incompetent, involuntary stoppage, appears again in 'Hold-Up', where the engine of the bus stalled at the lights that 'refused to change', while all movement has frozen outside in nightmare *stasis*, as all inside the bus and immediately outside it watch and listen for a sign. The noises blare, however, from the queue of waiting buses:

> . . . . . for miles behind
> The other buses nudged and blared
> And no one dared to get out. The conductress
> Was dark and lost, refused to change.

The poem is a bleakly punning expression of MacNeice's feelings about the failure of our generation to flow forward, our failure to fulfil the Heraclitean axiom that 'it stays by changing'. It is not only the bewildered conductress, however, who 'refused to change'. The controlling mechanism of the traffic lights has broken down, so that they, too, 'refused to change'. There appears to be no control at any level; not only is the relative forward movement halted, but the whole larger, cosmic rhythm is affected. The pause at the end of the *andante* in 'Slow Movement' has become a full-stop.

In the two contrasting journeys of 'Figure of Eight', MacNeice presents two different faces to the determinist situation. The young man of the first journey is only too eager to co-operate with the objective impulse that, he is confident, is taking him to an exciting journey's end, urging the bus forward, and 'when the lights were changing', jumping and hurrying to the meeting place—where there is no one to meet him. The older man, however, 'in the rear and gloom of a train', cowers as he 'prays/ For some last-minute hitch', the rolling wheels making it 'all too plain/Who will be there to meet him at the station'.

It is Charon who is there to meet the passengers in the poem of that title in the last collection, at the end of a meaningless and unpleasant bus journey. This poem is one of the most powerful in which he expresses his awareness of himself and his generation moving forward together in phenomenal space/time against the background of a showy but empty eternity ('eternity/Gave itself airs in revolving lights'). The temporal journey is a meaningless jog ('we just jogged on'), in which they are vaguely aware through the insulating glass of 'rumours of wars', of denials and betrayals of life ('The lost dog barking . . . his bark . . . as shrill as a cock crowing'). And there is the sad symbol of the request stop at which the bus fails to stop, with the passengers inside looking casually out at the 'crowd of aggressively vacant/Faces' of those whom the bus passes. The conductor alone is active, his hands 'black with money' as he gives and takes in exchange, but he can offer nothing in the way of helpful information beyond the menacing advice to hold on to their tickets, as 'the inspector's/ Mind is black with suspicion'.[1] This is the ultimate journey, the shore of the temporal river Thames, where 'all/The bridges were down', becoming the Stygian banks, where a flashlight reveals the eternal ferryman awaiting them in the gloom.

MacNeice increasingly shows this awareness of himself as a passenger among all the other passengers, moving with his generation.[2] In 'The Taxis', however, there is a significant difference of opinion between MacNeice and the succession of drivers about whether or not he is travelling alone. The 'illusion of Persons' is clearly involved. MacNeice is aware of the illusion, and consequently insists that the ghostly presences of his closest attachments to life are mere illusions. The cabbies think differently.

[1] This is obviously the same attitude as that expressed in the biblical symbol of the temple and the money-changers, with the vague figure of the inspector—temporal judgement or sanctions—replacing Christ, the departed 'man with the whip' ('The Window'). The inspector might also be the last, dread Judge.

[2] Chesterton remarks in his essay 'Lamp Posts': 'The idea of a crowd of human strangers turned into comrades for a journey is full of the oldest pathos and piety of human life. That profound feeling of mortal fraternity and frailty, which tells us we are indeed all in the same boat, is not the less true if expressed in the formula that we are all in the same bus.' (In *The Uses of Diversity*, London, 1920, p. 7.) It is interesting to note MacNeice's English master advising him, in his Report for Easter 1921, to 'avoid G. K. Chesterton and slang in writing'.

In the eyes of the cabbies the ghosts are *real*; the passenger is not travelling alone—and therefore his awareness of illusion is itself illusory. Other people *are* involved, in a real way, in the reality of MacNeice's experience.[1] Another poem in which he conceives of himself as being carried forward alone is the dedicatory poem to *The Burning Perch*, 'To Mary', where he confesses helplessly that 'We must use what transport we can', even if it is the cinder path for walking, or 'the mad-eyed beast' for riding.[2]

In other poems the emphasis shifts from the journey, with the controlling force implied or mentioned with light stress, to the controlling force itself. The attitude here is strongly that of Ecclesiastes, especially the first two chapters, with their theme that wisdom is of no avail, since all has been preordained; that the pattern cannot be changed, nor can what is crooked be made straight. The controlling force is seen to operate now beneficently, now maleficently, now in a manner that simply makes no sense. In his late work *Astrology*, he is markedly unwilling to commit himself. He jibes at the excesses of astrological determinism, and sympathizes with the scepticism of Chaucer, who 'seems to have taken his astrology with a grain of salt (. . . being a typical English empiricist and good-humoured iconoclast)'.[3] Similarly, he expresses disapproval of Pythagoras for the same reason as he had disapproved of Plato:

Like the Babylonians, Pythagoras and his followers saw the universe as a system of correspondences, a unified whole made up of corresponding parts. This is especially clear in Pythagorean astrology. . . . This sort of geometrical perfectionism (which was extended by Pythagoras's followers, and by others, like Plato) imposed a sort of deep-freeze on the universe. . . .[4]

In other places he merely illustrates without comment, as where he refers to the remark of Jung, 'much quoted by modern

[1] In *Zoo* (p. 125) he says: 'The taxi represents Escape.' This poem seems to me one of the profoundest and most intricate of MacNeice's metaphysical enquiries into the illusion and the reality. For the 'illusion of Persons', see pp. 98, 108, 127–8.

[2] In 'Birthright' he refused to mount the mad beast until it was too late.

[3] *Astrol.*, p. 146.

[4] Ibid., p. 114. Cf. the Platonic 'white-out': 'Aristotle never let the transcendental radiance destroy the shapes of the creatures or impose a white-out on everything.' ('Twenty-One', pp. 237–8.)

astrologers', that 'all of us, being born at a given moment and a given place, are invested for life with the qualities of the time of our birth'.[1] On the other hand, he clearly sympathizes with the wish of the astrologers 'to make sense of the universe',[2] and shares their 'sense of mystery, and . . . hankering for harmony'.[3] Both as poet and as one who never ceased to be fascinated by the appearance of sequences, especially in card games, he sympathized with the attitude to 'correspondences':

This grouping of interrelated creatures and objects has the same appeal as certain card games with their sequences, flushes and so on. It all goes back to the basic concept of sympathy. . . . There is sympathy between the parts of the universe, between things celestial and things terrestrial. From this stems a whole system of correspondences. . . .

There is something in this concept of natural correspondences that attracts the mystic in us. And there is an equally strong attraction for the poet in us, or at any rate for the patternmaker.[4]

The concept of men as the 'tin toys of the hawker', who nevertheless keep up 'the pretence of individuality', appears in 'An Eclogue for Christmas', where men are presented as

A. . . . . blind
  To the fact that they are merely the counters of an unknown Mind.
B. A Mind that does not think, if such a thing can be,
  Mechanical Reason, capricious Identity.
  That I could be able to face this domination nor flinch—
A. The tin toys of the hawker move on the pavement inch by inch
  Not knowing that they are wound up; it is better to be so
  Than to be, like us, wound up and while running down to know—
B. But everywhere the pretence of individuality recurs. . . .

And the horror of knowing that he is one of the mechanical toys wound up by the hawker and running down develops strongly, as we have seen, in the late poems, with all their images of congestion, engines stalling, incapable of starting again.

How far the objective will may be beneficent was one of the unanswerables that MacNeice left very much open to the end. Despite his recurrent pessimism, most of the 'visitations' of the

later poems seem to convince him that a beneficent will is operative
—at least upon his own destiny. The train in which he is travelling in
the last canto of *Autumn Sequel* is blessed, carrying inspiriting faces
and sages, as well as Lords of Misrule 'misruling as before':

> . . . . . All that I know
> Is that good will must mean both will and well
>
> And that, crowded or empty, fast or slow,
> This train is getting somewhere. . . .

The twisting gimlet of his fate in 'Donegal Triptych' is being
turned by a beneficent hand, screwing him farther from home
but closer to it with each spiralling twist. The sheer relief, certitude,
and hope is probably at its most intense in the 'Visitations'
sequence, where in the annunciations of the visitors from the
unknown in 'Visitations, I' he feels himself being piped by an
undoubted force of innocence and truth:

> They pipe us yet where birds are flying
> Beyond the ridge to lands unknown
> Where we, once come, could boast when dying
> We had not always lived alone.

Whether the objective will in the universe is beneficent or not,
there remains the problem of the proper exercise of the individual
will, which involves the resolution of its central paradox. At
Oxford he had 'fumbled' with Schopenhauer 'through the dark
night of the Will',[1] and although he had sufficient optimism late in
life to feel that he had fumbled his way through to a personal
adjustment, he was much less sure that his age had resolved the
paradox. The paradox may be stated in many forms, and Mac-
Neice did so state it, but perhaps at its core is the antinomy between
will as 'creative imagination', 'the great instrument of individuality, of freedom', and will as 'determinist tyranny'. MacNeice
states it thus in comparing the paradox of technology with the
paradox of the will:

. . . that is the paradox of technology. It begins with sheer creative
imagination and it ends—at least that is how it looks in 1940—in a brute
and random necessity, negation of human freedom.

[1] 'Twenty-One', p. 231.

Like the paradox of the Will. One supposes the will to be the great instrument of individuality, of freedom, and one lets it rip, then cannot put the drag on, the Will runs away with the lot of us, we have no more choice in the matter than a falling stone. Hence Schopenhauer's view of the Will as determinist tyranny and his opposition to it of *Vorstellung*, the freedom which is freedom from the Will and from narrow personality, the presentation to the mind's eye in a crystal of entities which are not subordinate to any practical purpose. . . .[1]

The paradox might also be expressed as the antinomy between freedom and egotism:

The gospel of the twenties, Self-Expression, taught us that the more you indulge your personality the more you become free; you can trace this back to Shelley but it is wrong. . . . There is an antinomy between Freedom and Egotism.[2]

Nor did it help to express this antinomy in the Christian terms of the Gospels ('. . . not to do mine own will, but the will of him that sent me'),[3] for MacNeice was not prepared to submit himself to the dictates of the Christian or any other external authority. He knew, however, that he had to 'act or be damned',[4] well aware that action would probably, in fact, entail damnation. Thus the paradox as it presented itself to him in the decade after he went down from Oxford seemed to be a paralysing one.

The sheer misery of the awareness of the need for action as he felt it in the later 1930s is expressed in the second verse of 'Passage Steamer', where he voices, in the mood of Ecclesiastes, the futility of beginning, when 'all our beginnings were long since begun'. Yet he is clear that this is the original sin, certain damnation:

> For never to begin
>   Anything new because we know there is nothing
> New, is an academic sophistry—
>   The original sin.[5]

Nevertheless, we continue to repeat the unctuous self-justification of Burns's Holy Willie:

[1] *S.A.F.*, p. 32.   [2] Ibid., p. 144.   [3] John 6:38.
[4] 'A man must act or be damned': *The Queen of Air and Darkness*. The external authority in the case of Adam, who speaks the words, was, of course, evil.
[5] *C.P.D.*, p. 150 (*A.J.*, XXIII).

> We thank thee, Lord, upon our knees
> That we were born in times like these
>
> When with doom tumbling from the sky
> Each of us has an alibi
> For doing nothing. . . .[1]

During the period between about 1937 and 1947 he reminds himself with increasing urgency of the need to act, and yet he is still miserably aware both of indecision and of the appalling consequence of wrong action. His awareness of the price paid by the man who has 'fought for the wrong causes' is given poignant expression in 'Suicide',[2] written in the summer of 1939. The subject, who, in his youth, had gone confidently 'Walking on the crown of the road', failed to find the right causes, and, at the end:

> . . . . . taking a shotgun
> As if for duck went out
> Walking on the crown of the road.

This is the wavering voice of denial, doubting the wisdom of Grettir's bold call to him in Iceland to disregard the eyes and the voices that would dissuade him from going his own way, from holding the open road:

> You cannot argue with the eyes or voice;
> Argument will frustrate you till you die
> But go your own way, give the voice the lie,
> Outstare the inhuman eyes. That is the way.
> Go back to where you came from and do not keep
> Crossing the road to escape them. . . .[3]

Years later he is still telling himself to stop puzzling and 'go ahead and live':

> . . . . It is time
> We left these puzzles and started to be ourselves
> And started to live, is it not?[4]

---

[1] 'Bar-room Matins'. Presumably the parody allusion to 'Holy Willie's Prayer' is intentional.   [2] *P.P.*, p. 46.

[3] *C.P.D.*, p. 46. Auden and MacNeice also made it explicitly clear that man is 'responsible for what he does,/Sole author of his terror and his content': *L.I.*, p. 236 ('Last Will and Testament').

[4] 'Indoor Sports (Crossword Puzzles)'. Cf. 'We need no metaphysics/To sanction what we do . . .' ('London Rain').

Meantime the two voices kept insisting on the need for action and the futility of action. 'The Conscript' is a moving statement of the antinomy of freedom and necessity, or horizontal necessity and vertical aspiration:

> He lives a paradox, lives in a groove
> That runs dead straight to an ordained disaster
> So that in two dimensions he must move
> Like an automaton, yet his inward stalk
> Vertically aspires and makes him his own master.

The conscript

> . . . would, if he could, fly
> In search of a future like a sycamore seed
> But is prevented by his own Necessity,
> His own yet alien. . . .

MacNeice, however, had come out much more confidently in 'A Toast', written slightly earlier, for the possibility that the will might triumph over the future, with luck and skill, when he proposed his toast to

> The will that flings a rope—though hard—
> To catch the future off its guard. . . .

Nevertheless, the voice that cried 'deny, deny, deny' to the subject of 'Schizophrene' refused to desist, and its promptings are recorded in the failure of the will in poems such as 'Flight of the Heart', 'The Death-Wish' and 'The Springboard'. In the first, the evasions of the 'copper tower' and alcohol being rejected, the defeated heart proposes, in despair, an absolute retreat to 'the fore-being of mankind'. Similarly, in 'The Death-Wish', the dead habits are rejected as an evasion, and another ultimate evasion recommends itself, the failure of suicide, 'The way the madman or the meteor fails'. The will to act in self-sacrifice is strong in 'The Springboard', but his 'unbelief' and the 'fright /That kept him crucified among the budding stars' are stronger, so that 'He never made the dive'.

During this period (1937–47) he expresses, in poems such as 'Convoy' and 'This Way Out', his admiration for the purposive and even ruthless exercise of will. The more personal note of confidence in the possibility of exercising effective choice comes through in the two long reflective poems, 'The Stygian Banks' and 'The North Sea', written at the end of the period. In the former, the determinist will is seen, as in 'A Toast', as an opponent who may be outwitted by man's exercise of wit and cunning, 'smuggling in/To a world of foregone conclusions the heresy of choice'.[1] The paradox is now 'the fertilizing paradox'; men are 'heretics all' and 'unlike anything else that breathes in the world' because, despairing, we 'Can choose what we despair of'.[2] Our despair is unlike that of the animals, which is chiefly the exhaustion of the bull dying in the ring, and in it lies the acceptance of the paradox, our willingness 'to recognize the insoluble/And going up with an outstretched hand salute it'.[3] In 'The North Sea' the paradox is strikingly expressed in the image of the muzzle of the pointing gun and the eye of the gun-layer; for 'we the target are the pupil too,/Sighted and sighting',[4] who may, in the very instant of annihilation by absolute necessity, assert our own identity and will. This is precisely the theme of 'Garlon and Galahad'.

This confidence remained with him during the 1950s. The power to exercise will within the limits of necessity, denying the absolute of predetermined destiny, yet admitting the limits it imposes, is expressed in the symbolism of 'The merman under the Plough' and 'The mermaid under the Southern Cross', in the third poem of the 'Visitations' sequence. Both are lost in a solipsism in which they

> Dissect in mirrors their own eyes and lips
> And, to kill time, make wrecks of unknown ships.

Although they will themselves 'across/That emptiness to some less empty goal', their will fails them. Suddenly 'stars apart, grown mindful of their freedom', they both act, divining their way to a meeting upon the Line—which, however, they 'never cross'.

Yet, despite his confidence, he could not stop his ears to the

---

[1] *C.P.D.*, p. 260. [2] Ibid., p. 267. [3] Ibid., p. 261. [4] Ibid., p. 272.

voice of despair and denial. It cried to him in *Autumn Sequel* as the voice of the cock and the parrot; it is equally insistent in *Visitations*, as 'the cold voice' of 'Donegal Triptych', that 'chops and sniggers'. MacNeice simply could not forget or deny that the individual will judges wrongly. He knew, with Eliot, that 'love would be love of the wrong thing',[1] but he could not accept, as Eliot could, the Negative Way. The punning ambiguity in the last line of 'Twelfth Night', written in the middle of 1948. is a poignant acceptance of the inevitable:

> For now the time of gifts is gone—
> .   .   .   .   .   .   we have reached
> Twelfth Night or what you will . . . you will.

The desolation wrought by the fire-raids had been evidence enough that the words of the prophets had been fulfilled:

> Then twangling their bibles with wrath in their nostrils
> From Bonehill Fields came Bunyan and Blake:
> 'Laredo the golden is fallen, is fallen;
> Your flame shall not quench nor your thirst shall not slake'.[2]

The note of prophetic foreboding continued to deepen. In the last analysis, however, as pessimism and resignation fought with rational and dogged optimism, he might still be described, in the terms of 'The Grey Ones', as one who believed that man's chief glory lay in his determination to 'ask the way':

> Crouched beneath a snowbound sky
> Three grey sisters share an eye;
> Before they lose it and forget
> Ask the way to Never Yet. . . .[3]

Although the terrible 'lonely eye' of the sisters

> Skewers the perspectives of the mind
> Till what you wished you fear to find,

---

[1] *F.Q.*, p. 19.   [2] 'The Streets of Laredo'.

[3] The 'three grey sisters' here seem to be a composite image of the Norns of Norse (and the Moirae or Parcae of classical) mythology, and the trolls of the Norse folk tales, who are frequently depicted as sharing one eye. In the fusion he obtains the effects of both destiny and horror.

you must still make your wish, prepared to face the consequences, while the grey sisters

> . . . . . pass the eye
> And check the client next to die . . .

MacNeice compared the paradox of the will to the paradox of technology, and the will that seemed to him to have gone wrong was largely the will that expressed itself in terms of technological control. His distaste for the will of the technocrats is expressed, and often well and strongly expressed, in his earliest printed school stories and poems. Mr. Schinabel, in one of the series of fantasy parables already mentioned, ran away from this world:

As he ran on he became glad that no one was following him. 'Their motives would not be the true motives', he thought, 'fawning for food and flattering for favour and running like a broken-down Ford. In every action they are machines. I am glad they are not with me.' And he ran on.[1]

In 'Homage to Clichés' he opposes

> . . . all this clamour for progress
> This hammering out of new phrases and gadgets. . . .

The familiar paradox of over-production, poverty in the midst of plenty, provides his sardonic wit with much of its material in 'Bagpipe Music'.[2] MacNeice the individualist and liberal poet expresses his fear in 'Epitaph for Liberal Poets' that the end has come for his kind, that they are about to be superseded by the 'tight-lipped technocratic Conquistadores'. Nor had he any faith in the expert. In the poem of that title, 'this ex-professor who had already/Outlived his job of being in the know', who was run over while drunk, appears to be a political economist.[3]

The poem 'The Other Wing' in *Visitations* is a central state-

[1] *Marlburian*, 23 October 1924. The story ends on a note of prophetic pessimism that anticipates the mood of the late poems. He rushed down a steep slope, 'like Apollo descending from heaven', and vanished into a great lake of slime, 'known in the neighbourhood as "The Bottomless Pit" '.

[2] Cf. *Minch*, p. 39: 'The great career in the Hebrides is the dole . . .'; and his conversation on p. 172 with the two coastguards in a disguised herring boat, who told him that 'Unless something were done the fishermen would soon be all on the dole or the parish. . . . It was mathematically impossible for the herring boats to average a profit; only the minority of them could make profits.' [3] *P.P.*, p. 53.

ment of MacNeice's attitude to technological advance. The Lazarus figure of the last two verses appears to be modern technological man in his living grave, awaiting the call to life; the other figure is the Christ child. Lazarus is bound in a 'Mummicose death-dress', while the Christ child is 'Lagged against life'. The centuries unwind 'the swaddling/Bands and the death-bands', allowing the Christ child to grow into life, and Lazarus to grow from death. Technological advance is unwinding ahead of Christian wisdom and must wait for it, as each needs the other. Christ, spiritually warm, is cold and haunted in his foul stable, while Lazarus, who could clean and heat the stable, is spiritually cold and empty. In these symbolical terms, the major theme of the last collection is the full-stop that has ensued because Lazarus has unwound far ahead and must wait for the Christ child to catch up. We may readily note this full-stop, or meaningless relative movement, in such poems as 'Spring Cleaning', 'Another Cold May', 'The Pale Panther', 'New Jerusalem'.

One possible way to resolve the paradox which recommended itself particularly strongly to MacNeice in the 1930s and intermittently thereafter, was acceptance of an instinctive, unreflective, traditional way of life, with roots deep in the wisdom of an ancestral past. Despite his respect for the Hegelian blend of opposites, MacNeice tended at times to regard the way of instinct and the way of reason almost as mutually opposed. He recalls that, while reading Plato for examination purposes at Oxford, he was 'reacting against the view that reason dominates instinct',[1] but, at the same time, as he records in *Modern Poetry*, he came out strongly for mind, and against vague, instinctive profundity in the manner of Whitman or Tolstoy:

To put the unlearned on the same level as the learned, i.e. to reduce both to the level of mere feeling where no elaboration is required, is to assert the vague profundity which is their identity and to neglect their essential surface distinctions. Whitman was proclaiming the same heresy that Tolstoy was preaching in Russia in his book *What is Art?*— trying to be simple, genuine, primitive.[2]

[1] *S.A.F.*, p. 127.
[2] Op. cit., pp. 72–3. He is quoting from his farewell student paper at Oxford, 'We Are the Old'.

Similarly, in the later 1930s, he rejected the way of the natural instinctive man, insisting to his Guardian Angel that he belonged irrevocably to the 'lost intelligentsia'.[1] Later he deplored the flight from reason and integrity of the American intellectuals, who sought for wisdom in truck drivers:

It may be good for an intelligentsia every so often to confess that 'there is no truth in us' but, after the catharsis of such humility, they should remember that there is damn little truth around anywhere, that truth—in the social and political, as in the artistic, sphere—is something which is made, or at least discovered, and that the intellectual has no right to abdicate his post of discoverer or to scrap the necessary instrument of Reason.[2]

This opposition is reflected in the poems. When, however, he celebrates, in poems such as 'The Casualty', 'The Kingdom' and 'The Stygian Banks', the 'high humble company'[3] of those who realized value in their lives, it is not simply a matter of 'the orchestration of instinct' but also of 'the fertilisation of mind', of responding 'Both to the simple lyrics of blood and the architectonic fugues of reason'.[4] Similarly, in 'A Toast', he praises the balance of man's instinct and reason, although he accords the ultimate executive authority to instinct, praised as

> The balance of his body and mind,
> Who keeps a trump behind his brain
> Till instinct flicks it out again. . . .

MacNeice, we saw, praised in the harmonious lives of women he loved a dynamic pattern that was shaped by instinct, so that Becoming and Being were often one, uncomplicated by reflection or act of will. In 'Leaving Barra', his sympathy for the 'easy tempo' of traditional ways is fused with his gratitude to the woman he loves 'for the example/Of living like a fugue and moving', and the fusion gives him the hope that he may

> Wake with the knack of knowledge
> Who as yet have only an inkling.

[1] *Minch*, p. 131.
[2] From an article entitled 'Touching America' in *Horizon*, vol. 3, no. 15, March 1941.
[3] 'The Casualty'.   [4] 'The Kingdom'.

Again, in *Autumn Journal*, the truth of the woman is 'not of a statement but of a dance'; she disproves the proven fact 'that men are automatons', and acts on an instinct that sanctions all she does, knowing

> . . . that truth is nothing in abstraction,
> That action makes both wish and principle come true.[1]

An eloquent expression of his delight in woman's instinctive harmony and equilibrium is 'Flowers in the Interval', the last of his *Ten Burnt Offerings*.[2]

He also took recurrent comfort from the instinctive ways of animals and birds—a comfort from which he characteristically recoiled when he felt that animal instinct, like traditional peasant ways, was not enough. Thus he admired the elephants in 'Circus' ('Tonnage of instinctive/Wisdom in tinsel') and the pigeons in 'The British Museum Reading Room':

> Out on the steps in the sun the pigeons are courting,
> Puffing their ruffs and sweeping their tails or taking
> A sun-bath at their ease . . .

The pigeons he contrasts with the world of book learning within, the 'world of inverted values', and 'the totem poles—the ancient terror—'; as he does again in 'Time for a Smoke', preferring to linger outside 'with pigeons and sparrows'. Yet he gives the lie direct to all this in 'Explorations', where he rejects the apparent freedom of the whale 'butting through scarps of moving marble':

> . . . . . . it is only instinct
> That plots his graph and he,
> Though appearing to us a free and a happy monster, is merely
> An appanage of the sea . . .

and the swallows:

> . . . . . their imputed purpose
> Is a foregone design. . . .

Man, however, is unique, 'the final/Anomaly of the world', his design not foregone:

[1] *C.P.D.*, pp. 122–3 (*A.J.*, XI).
[2] The poem is addressed to Hedli, of whom he remarked to a close friend, the actor Allan McClelland, 'She is the elbow I write with.'

GA

> Our end is our own to be won by our own endeavour
> And held on our own terms.[1]

In the last poems he often seems to be clutching at the straw of instinct as he is overwhelmed in the waves of a wrong exercise of will and a failure of reason. He has lost all confidence in 'Our lonely eminence' in 'Jigsaws, III', which derives

> From the submerged nine-tenths we share
> With all the rest who also run,
> Shuddering through the shuddering main.

That this submerged nine-tenths of instinct is as cold as the 'jagged tops' of our lonely eminence he makes quite clear in 'Icebergs', where, in retrospect, he considers that all we have of life is contained in the 'mere/Ninth or tenth' of white crest above the cold, dark water:

> . . . . . the rest is sheer
> Snub to those who dared suppose
> Icebergs warm below the water.

This failure to communicate at the level of instinct is stressed in several late poems. The men in the park and 'urban enclave' poems of *Solstices* exist in isolation from one another and from nature. For the 'small clerk/Who thinks no one will ever love him' there is only contempt from the creatures of the park: 'Everything mocks', and 'there is no consorting//For him with nature or man . . .'[2] Yet the contact the animals and birds still maintain with their ancient kingdom of free instinct is precarious at best. The 'man-made walk' may open for the dogs 'vistas to a past of packs',[3] but the dachshunds that 'run/Like centipedes' are as lost as the men; and

> Carolina duck and Canada goose forget
> Their world across the water.[4]

Nor can the dog, despite fumbling efforts, communicate even his own vestigial connection with his past:

[1] In his last published poem, 'Thalassa', however, he again asserts the freedom of the narwhal, incorporating (presumably in deliberate self-contradiction) the line 'Butting . . . marble'.

[2] 'The Lake in the Park'.   [3] 'Dogs in the Park'.   [4] 'Sunday in the Park'.

And at the last and sidelong he returns,
Part heretic, part hack, and jumps and crawls
And fumbles to communicate and fails.[1]

Nor do the animals realize the extent to which man's will has perverted their instinctive ways. Even the natural desert environment of the lizard and snake is, in 'Pet Shop', a miniature and man-made desert, where the sand is

. . . . . . littered with rumpled gauze
Discarded by snakes like used bandages;

while

In the next door desert fossilized lizards
Stand in a pose, a pause.

For instinct, as for will, it is a full-stop.

[1] 'Dogs in the Park'.

4 Challenge of the Absolute

The absolute as a lurking menace is the theme of many poems. In the early 'Homage to Clichés' the granite sphinxes and the great two-ton tenor bell are linked with the black panther to form a composite horror image of the absolute, threatening to crush the fragile world of the controlled relative:

> Never is the Bell, Never is the Panther, Never is Rameses
> Oh the cold stone panic of Never—
> The ringers are taking off their coats, the panther crouches
> The granite sceptre is very slightly inclining. . . .

In *Modern Poetry* he explains that these three images connote 'the brute Other, the fate which we cannot influence', and refers to the fact that we cannot peal the tenor bell, but only play chimes upon it, and to the popular belief that the black panther is said to be untamable. He adds: 'The movement of each of these three will be the movement of Fate. . . .'[1] The movement of uncontrollable Fate, already beginning, is connected with the time theme in the person of the 'time-keeper with a watch and a pistol/ Ready to shoot . . .'. In 'Insidiae',[2] written about the same time, the awareness of 'the brute Other' is much more neurotic, the subject of the second of the three movements being a young woman sensitive that

> Each walks within a ring of dancing hands
> That no one sees. . . .

The movement ends with an eerie image of her stepping into this menacing ring of hands:

> Many hands, coming out of the air,
> Like skimming milk
> Stroked ominously her glossed hair.

Something of the same menace lurking behind the caressing calm and quiet he expresses in 'Evening in Connecticut':

> Unreal but still can strike.
> And in defence we cannot call on the evening
> Or the seeming-friendly woods—
> Nature is not to be trusted. . . .

[1] Op. cit., p. 112. [2] *P.*, p. 48.

In the very last poems the menace of the absolute is urgent and omnipresent, with the human race receding and dwindling in 'Budgie', while 'the giant/Reptiles cackle in their graves', and, in 'New Jerusalem'

> Bulldozer, dinosaur, pinheaded diplodocus,
> Champ up forgotten and long-dry water-pipes.

Although MacNeice could not come to terms with the absolute conceived as God, the hope and the possibility tempted him, for it was an obvious way to end the menace and the haunting. In an early letter he actually associates God in a dramatic landscape of the mind with the granite sphinxes of the menacing absolute:

But at present I am rather impressed with God. Do you know a line of Yeats—'And God stands winding his lonely horn'? You find him in a valley sitting on a rock with his hair long and still like icicles and his eyelids half closed like Buddha. And covered with bracken a few yards away is a granite sphinx of the first Egyptians. . . .[1]

It was long before he could dissociate his concept of Christianity from the image of Bilbatrox of *Roundabout Way*, the representative of 'Ulster fanaticism', or purge himself of the image of eighteenth-century Christianity as he described it in Canto XXI of *Autumn Sequel*:

> They each and all of them showed all the expected
> Virtues of Christian gentlemen, paid calls
>
> On those that were well off or well connected,
> Men like themselves of a superior mind
> Who never skimped their duties nor neglected
>
> The chance of what their probity could find
> In the City or Bengal. . . .

Even at the height of his overt Oxford hostility to Christianity, however, he did not cease reading his Bible, and made no bones about the fact; in several of his letters to Anthony Blunt, for instance, he referred to 'Michael's illustrated bible', which he was missing. There was a marked change in his attitude around 1932–3,

[1] To A.F.B. from Carrickfergus, 15 October 1926.

as his sympathy and admiration for his father strengthened. In a review of R. V. Feldman's *The Domain of Selfhood*, in 1935, he remarked: 'Anyone can pick holes in anything that has ever been written about God. But many people would sympathise with Mr. Feldman when he argues that it is more arrogant to dispense with God than to assume him (even when one assumes him in one's own image).'[1] In the early poem 'The Creditor' he expressed his awareness of his 'debts to God' and his futile attempts at evasion:

> . . . . for His mind strays
> Over and under and all ways
> All days and always.

MacNeice had recited this poem at Oxford,[2] to illustrate his conclusion to a paper called 'The Policeman': 'If you really want to know about this deity you must first remember that you cannot do so. You must surrender yourself to the unknowable, which you feel in your bones. If you go trying to pick the marrow out of your own bones, so much the worse for you.' It was not until the bombs were dropping, however, that he could see God clearly as anything like a defence against the menace of the granite sphinx:

> 'The Lord's my shepherd'—familiar words of myth
> Stand up better to bombs than a granite monolith,
> Perhaps there is something in them. . . .[3]

He was sharply aware at this time of the need for a common aim, as he stresses in the two-question refrain of 'Babel': 'Can't we ever, my love, speak in the same language? . . . Have we no aims in common?' His longing erupts in the urgency of the 'Prayer in Mid-Passage', where he addresses God as the harsh Jehovah of the Old Testament, asking Him to unveil Himself, that all might see His 'fierce impersonality'. He implores God to provide a ladder for men

> . . . . . that they may climb
> This time-bound ladder out of time.

---

[1] In the *Criterion*, vol. 14, October 1934–July 1935, pp. 161–2.

[2] To a society at Corpus Christi. I am grateful to J.R.H. for showing me extracts. I do not know if the original exists.   [3] 'Whit Monday'.

He again stresses man's need for unity in God in the urgent concluding line of 'Hands and Eyes': 'Oh would He, were there a God, have mercy on us all?' Yet he seems to imply in the obliquely dramatic 'Place of a Skull' that the first time he really tried to wear the seamless garment of the Christian absolute it failed him:

> . . . . . Why the first time I wore
> That dead man's coat it frayed I cannot say.

In the second of his *Ten Burnt Offerings*, 'Areopagus', written at the time when he was thinking very much in terms of the invisible Kingdom, the dominant theme is the Pauline one of Christian unity, 'members one of another', and there is an implied rebuke to the Athenians and their altar to the Unknown God. Christ is equated with the Furies, who are also the Kindly Ones, ever living even if men forget them, alive to plague or to bless; and the rock, the Areopagus, the Athenian place of judgement beneath which they reside, is equated with the living rock of the Christian faith, the death of mere plurality: 'Their living rock was the death of sea.'[1] The early dichotomy of 'The Creditor' between the firm need for action and the temptation towards 'The peacefulness of the fire-blaze' has been unified in the brightly flaming cross:

> As Christ's dead timber fired by blood
> Was to blossom bright as peach or almond.[2]

In the fourth poem of the collection, 'Didymus', he similarly stresses the simple unity of Thomas's doubting faith against the self-multiplying Indian gods,

> . . . . . who could sprout at pleasure
> All the hands they might need.

This attitude accorded well with the theme of 'visitations': 'That God exists we cannot show',[3] but we have inklings of His real presence in visitations, when, as he asserts in 'Easter Returns',

---

[1] *C.P.D.*, p. 289. Cf. the 'Living granite against dead water' of 'Mahabalipuram'.

[2] *C.P.D.*, p. 289. The difference between the two fires is vital. The earlier fire symbolizes the repose of the quietism he could not accept, while the latter is the steady flame of the Heraclitean fire. See below, pp. 94–5.

[3] 'Jigsaws, V'.

'the myth returns' and 'the stone/Is rolled away once more.'[1]
In the same mood, he seemed prepared to welcome his father's
principles in 'The Truisms'; and in 'Tree Party', where he toasts
so many other finalities of metaphysic and belief, he expresses
in his toast to the Holly his pleasure and surprise that Christianity
has retained so much vitality:

> Your health, Master Holly. Of all the trees
> That decorate parlour walls you please
> Yet who would have thought you had so much blood in you?

The Christian way did not, however, for the greater part
of his own way, offer anything like a continuous answer to the
menace of the absolute. Another way that attracted him, but which
had to be continually combated, at least in the earlier part of his
life, was the way of mysticism. As he remarked in a letter to
Anthony Blunt from Oxford: 'How good it would be to be a
mystic (i.e. not an actor, everyone else is an actor) and be fused
with the universe.'[2] He added, 'but of course I shan't be'. Mysticism
and idealist philosophy seemed to him the two most obvious ways
of being of this world but more than it:

The artist is proud to be of the world but it enrages him to know himself such a small part of it. This latter fact can be glozed over in various
ways—for instance, by an idealist philosophy which makes man the
centre of things and any one man the standard of the whole, or by a
mysticism which allows the individual to overflow himself.[3]

But he was always wary about entering what he described in a
lecture as 'the metaphysical territory that we find in the more
esoteric Hindu scriptures or in the accounts of the Negative Way
given by Christian mystics'.[4] He felt that a creative writer 'cannot
afford to stay long in that territory'.[5] In the same lecture he put
his finger on what was probably his main reason for rejecting the
way of mysticism when he ventured the paradox that Francis
Thomson 'would probably have been better equipped to put over
the claims of the other world' had he not been 'in the vulgar

---

[1] The mood is close to Eliot's in 'East Coker': 'Again, in spite of that, we call this Friday
good.' (*F.Q.*, p. 21.)
[2] 4 June 1928.   [3] *Yeats*, pp. 128–9.
[4] *V.P.*, p. 146. He is discussing Samuel Beckett.   [5] Ibid.

sense, such an "unworldly" or "other-worldly" person'.[1] His practical sense continually asserted itself when he was tempted to annul the menacing absolute by trying to be at one with it: 'So the mystic proper will often take it that he has complete knowledge of everything and is at one with it. But being at one in this mystical sense . . . leaves in practice most of the bars still standing. I am a materialist in this matter. . . .'[2]

Two of his earliest school poems voice the temptation to leave the world, and the need to resist this. In 'The Witch of Widdigo-free', he wishes to escape to the Witch, who sat in the West before and during all creation, and who still 'sits while the whole world slips'; there he, too, would 'sing till the world go west'.[3] But Circe, in the poem of that title, similarly tempted, 'put away the thought of flight' and returned to her 'Brute beasts'—but sadly, from sense of duty.[4] The 'Circe' attitude strengthened, especially in the middle and later 1930s, when the temptation seems to have been strongest. In 'Ode' he announced his refusal to be 'mystic and maudlin', and in 'Leaving Barra' he rejected both 'the self-abnegation of Buddha' and the 'denial of chiaroscuro', while he wrestled successfully in *Autumn Journal* with the temptation to 'equate Being in its purest form/With denial of all appearance', as 'the scent grows warm/For pure Not-Being, Nirvana'.[5] He felt that the 'saint on the pillar', Simeon, 'has stood so long/ That he himself is stone': the dreaded full-stop.[6] In the parable story *The Sixpence that Rolled Away*, the Indian Wise Man comes off no better than the Toy Tin Pilot with his instruments. Like the Yogi of the satirical 'Salute to all Fools', with his slogan of 'Up the Immanent and Transcendent Rope',[7] he is free from the world of Becoming, but his freedom is a delusion: ' "Lost?" said the Indian Wise Man. "Om! Om!" And he waved all his four arms, threw his rope up in the air and sat lost in thought on the top of it.'[8]

Yet he admired especially the story of Buddha, with the white light of wisdom at the back of his mind, and it is probably

[1] Ibid., p. 108.   [2] *Zoo*, p. 123.   [3] *Marlburian*, 11 March 1925.
[4] Ibid., 24 June 1925.   [5] *C.P.D.*, pp. 58, 87, 104.   [6] 'Stylite'.
[7] *D.T.*, p. 193.   [8] Op. cit., p. 14.

Buddha's kind of mystical union that he has in mind when he admits the validity, in 'Coming from Nowhere'[1] and 'Donegal Triptych', of entering solitude

> . . . . . . to find communion
> With other solitary beings, with the whole race of men.[2]

Thus there is an important residual longing, despite all his resistance and denial, for a religious or mystical identification with the One. He was also, however, intermittently attracted by other, more negative and artificial, devices for attaining something like the same end. The most negative of these was the death-wish, *ripae ulterioris amor*, 'something such as Rilke meant by Death, something unknown but comprehensive where everything falls into place'.[3] On his first visit to France he was deeply impressed by Chartres:

The cathedral of Chartres, to me, was a nice breath of life—or was it death?—after Fontainebleau. I don't think I yet knew the phrase 'death-wish'; but that stone should run away from the earth where it belonged, to lose itself not in heaven but in its own inner darkness, stirred something in my own unquarried depths, something which if not a 'death-wish' was at least a wish to escape—the same desire to escape which, outside on the west front, had elongated and emaciated the saints.[4]

True to his instinct to stress both surface and core, however, he adds: 'But a little later, at Versailles, I found the antidote to this, which I had failed to find at Fontainebleau.'

In *Autumn Journal* he admits that he is seduced by 'the quiet hands . . . /Of the god who is god of nothing' and sympathizes with 'the wish to quit, to make the great refusal', but he feels

> . . . . . that such a defeat is also treason,
> That deaths like these are lies.[5]

---

[1] 'Coming from Nowhere' is in *C.P.R.H.*, pp. 269–71. The 'pillared saint' sits and waits on his rock 'Till time erodes /The walls of thought,/The thoughts of self', after which 'he leaves/His rock and with/Deliberate feet/On golden water/Walks the world.' See p. 111.
[2] *C.P.D.*, p. 448. [3] *S.A.F.*, p. 35. [4] Ibid., p. 237.
[5] *C.P.D.*, p. 145 (*A.J.*, XXI). Cf. the bitter dramatic vignette '*Il Piccolo Rifiuto*' where he is completely out of sympathy with the subject, who makes the little refusal.

In 'The Death-Wish', too, he sympathizes with the motives of
those who refuse 'to wait the communal failure', refuse merely

> To save their lives by weighting them with dead
> Habits, hopes, beliefs, anything not alive. . . .

His sympathy is even more apparent in 'The Suicide', where the
'Hidden Ice' theme reappears in the different imagery of the
'manhole under the hollyhocks'. In 'The Revenant', moreover,
there is the clear implication in the symbolic imagery of 'The
yellow eye of a beast of prey' and the 'sea-shell in a quiet room'
that the lovers by their willed death will annul the menace of the
absolute and return to the One:

> The yellow eye of the beast will close,
> The stolen shell return to the sea. . . . [1]

The assaults of the death-wish were, however, feeble in comparison with his love of life.

Alcohol, too, he invested with something of the same mystical,
unifying power, although he was wholly aware both of the pal-
pableness of the illusion and the retrogressiveness of the movement,
and his presentation of this way is generally ironical. In 'Alcohol',
for instance, the 'self-deception' is approved, and he concurs with
Bacchylides, who regarded the 'golden seas of drink' as resolving
all differences. The retrogressive movement, in which all Becoming is reversed to the ultimate of (Not-)Being, is ironically
approved, and God, the absolute, is a 'peeping tom' who is
truculently challenged to peep if he wishes. God has been rejected
along with all the other 'beautiful ideologies', and we have escaped
(again, presumably, ironically) *into* reality by 'The last way out
that leads not out but in'. The subject of 'The Drunkard' likewise
finds the movement of returning from 'the absolute moment'
of his inebriation to be 'Purgatory in reverse', and the whole
imagery of the poem is mock-sacramental:

> God was uttered in words and gulped in gin,
> The barmaid was a Madonna, the adoration
> Of the coalman's breath was myrrh. . . .

[1] The whole song cycle, of which this is the last lyric, was printed in the *Michigan
Quarterly Review*, vol. 4, no. 3, Summer 1965, pp. 174-6.

We noted MacNeice's admiration for the perfectly harmonious lives, patterned by instinct, of women he loved. Woman also represented escape from the temporal and relative. As the drunkard gulped God in gin, the Doctor, in *The Queen of Air and Darkness*, shocked by Adam's reference to 'mere woman', inverts Hamlet's pronouncement to assert that 'Divinity lies in woman— and in man.' The libertine in the poem of that title had tried to evade 'the cosmic disarray' by losing himself in love affairs, but had found himself, like the drunkard, left disillusioned and alone. In Canto XI of *Autumn Sequel*, however, and in the last of his *Ten Burnt Offerings*, as we have just noted, the illusion of timelessness and unification with the absolute through woman remained a very important and valid fiction.

For MacNeice, another possible means towards achieving harmony with the absolute was to burn in life with the steadiness of the Heraclitean fire:

> O fire, my spendthrift,
> May I spend like you, as reckless but
> Giving as good return . . .[1]

The imagery of fire and sun recurs very frequently, from first to last, and it is particularly notable that as man's fire is burning low in the last poems, the watery element dominant, so the sun, too, in Heraclitus' phrase seems no longer to 'know his measures'. In the very early poem, 'Coal and Fire',[2] the flaming coal is identified with the untamable black panther, not as menace, but as perfect, timeless movement. The sun in 'The Pale Panther', with which it is again associated, is, however, pale and feeble, burning low on the horizon. In the confident later cantos of *Autumn Sequel* the flame still burns brightly, and Sir Thomas Browne, 'Whose major object was to understand/The microcosm', is described as 'basking in the ray/Of his invisible sun';[3]

---

[1] *C.P.D.*, p. 144 (*A.J.*, XXI). The theme again recalls Eliot: 'We only live, only suspire/ Consumed by either fire or fire' (*Little Gidding*, *F.Q.*, p. 42, where Eliot's context is a favourite of MacNeice's, the pentecostal fires). In a letter to A.F.B., deploring 'all this scientific approach to reality', he said: 'Heraclitus was much better who said fire was the primary substance. Laughter is the fire rioting and flapping as it goes upwards all the time instead of burrowing. . . .' (From Carrickfergus, 3 August 1928.)

[2] *B.F.*, pp. 45–7. [3] *C.P.D.*, p. 397 (*A.S.*, XVI).

while MacNeice insists that both Browne and Dame Julian of
Norwich were right 'to descry//That life, in spite of all, is a flame
and a pure flame.'[1]

Our purpose has been to illustrate how MacNeice approached
the problem of reality with the attitudes and concepts of metaphysics, and not with any of the 'nostrums/Of science art and
religion' or the 'beautiful ideologies'.[2] This is nowhere more
apparent than in his treatment of this problem of the Many and
the One (and the associated problem of the unity of the surface and
the core of experience), which was, for him, perhaps the central
problem. It is in his treatment of this problem, too, that we see
most clearly his developing awareness of the need for a unifying
principle.

We have already noted his sense of the lack of any system
'which could at the same time unify the world and differentiate
its parts significantly'.[3] At the same time, his love of particulars
was so intense that for long periods, and over many years, he was
content to exist in the 'concrete particular' and was troubled only
intermittently by the problem of the 'concrete universal'.[4] In a
letter to John Hilton in the autumn of 1929, he asserted: 'I agree
with Anaximander that all (specific) existence is an usurpation (or
perhaps it is flying in the face of God). I then specifically exist.
The more specifically the more of an usurper. . . .' In another
letter (autumn 1930), he advocated: 'Lots of lovely particulars; I
suggest keeping generalisations out of it . . .', and in the same
letter, in reply to an enquiry about a suitable gift, he wished for
'one of those things you roll things into or round or up and down—
the high Metaphysicke of the Fair'. The attitude here is the same
as that in his Oxford story in which Sir Galahad bids goodbye
to the old man attempting a synthesis by getting 'all these little
balls all at the same time all into that little hole in the middle'.
The synthesis will have to look after itself. In a letter written
just before he went up to Oxford he had made the same point,
partly anticipating his reading in logic and metaphysics: 'An
abstraction is the rough and ready term that covers a lot of

---

[1] *C.P.D.*, p. 400 (*A.S.*, XVII).   [2] 'Ode'.   [3] *M.P.*, p. 62.
[4] See pp. 96–7.

individual concretes. . . . I don't believe in pure form, I don't believe in pure anything. Anything pure is an abstraction. All concretes are adulterated.'[1] In a letter of the mid-1930s he longs to stop writing and indulge in sensations: 'And then there are all the good things one could be holding in one's hands—cakes of soap, borzoi's ears, raw herrings under the tap. . . .'[2]

The early 'Upon this Beach' indicated the importance of the particular by the very sub-title ('a thought for intending mystics') with which it originally appeared in the first number of *New Verse*, in January 1933. Here the sea is a perpetually crumbling wall: 'the falling wall of the sea/Explodes its drunken marble.' It is the One that is the fiction here, and the 'monstrous fatuity' of the waves, the Many, lies in their supposing that their 'ever-crumbling masonry, cancelling sum', can ever make a unity. Thus the tripper may take heart, enjoy the Many, pay no heed to the One. Similarly, in some of his best lyrics of the middle and later 1930s, such as 'To a Communist', 'The Brandy Glass' and 'Snow', the concrete particular seems to be what is real, while the abstract universal seems to be what does not exist.

MacNeice's attitude here seems so close to Bradley's in his *Principles of Logic* that it might be illuminating to look at Bradley's attempt to distinguish what is real in the concepts 'universal', 'particular', 'abstract', and 'concrete'. The result Bradley established was that:

The *abstract* universal and the *abstract* particular are what does not exist. The *concrete* particular and the *concrete* universal both have reality, and they are different names for the individual.

What is real is the individual; and this individual, though one and the same, has internal differences. You may hence regard it in two opposite ways. So far as it is one against other individuals, it is particular. So far as it is the same throughout its diversity, it is universal. . . . Thus a man is particular by virtue of his limiting and exclusive relations to other phenomena. He is universal because he is one throughout all his different attributes. You may call him particular, or again universal, because, being individual, he actually is both, and you wish to emphasize one aspect or side of his individuality. The individual is

<hr/>

[1] To A.F.B. from Portstewart, 25 September 1926.
[2] To A.F.B. from Birmingham, 20 November 1935.

both a concrete particular and a concrete universal; and, as names
of the whole from different points of view, these both are names of
real existence. . . .

Bradley concludes:

. . . we may go so far as this, that in the end the individual is real, and
that abstract universal and abstract particular are distinctions taken
within that reality, which a mistake has afterwards turned into divisions
and hardened into units. . . . And we may muster courage, perhaps, to
profess that the individual is the identity of universal and particular.[1]

The something 'more than glass between the snow and the huge
roses' in 'Snow' is the uniqueness of the concrete particular, and,
presumably, the absolute metaphysical distinction between the
concrete particular and the abstract universal. In 'The Brandy
Glass', the snow that sifts into the empty dining hall, obliterating
the precious moment and all particular objects, and choking the
revolving doors, is the hostile One obliterating the Many, as the
snow in 'To a Communist' is the unreal abstract universal. That
he apparently wished to stress beyond all doubt the essential
plurality, or particularity, of things is indicated by his heavy
deletion in the MS. of the word 'different', for which he substituted
'various' in the phrase 'the drunkenness of things being various'
in 'Snow'.[2] This theme is repeated in the long poem of metaphysical reflection, 'Plurality' (which is much less effective than
the short, dramatic and emblematic lyrics), where he re-echoes,
perhaps deliberately, the phrasing of 'Snow' in asserting that
'World is not like that'; it is not 'a dead ideal of white/All-
white Universal' or 'a dumb static identity/Of Essence and Existence . . .'.

Similarly, in many other poems of the late 1920s and the
1930s he rejoices in the concrete particular as the flux, surface,
or circumference of experience. It was especially for his ability
to convey this delight in the surface of experience that he was
praised by most critics in the earlier years, including those (notably
in *Scrutiny*) who could find little else to admire, and some of his
best poems of this time do certainly convey this delight. In

[1] Op. cit., London, 1922, 2nd, rev., ed., pp. 186–9.   [2] H.N.

'Thank You',[1] he thanked his 'friendly daemon', close to him as his shadow, for 'the sluice of hearing and seeing'.

The friendly daemon of 'Thank You' is a spirit of natural, instinctive response, and much of MacNeice's celebration of the surface up to the later 1930s is, under this influence, a celebration of the concrete particular. Deepening through these years, however, was a spirit of dissatisfaction with his delight in what he was clearly coming to regard as mere surface, together with an awareness of the transience. In one of his articles in the *Marlburian*,[2] he already saw his generation as 'passed away... immediately to be forgotten, to be wiped with a chalky duster off the blackboard'. And in what must have been one of his first poems after Oxford, 'Sleep', he despaired of his daemon, admitting that he had 'pretended it was a loving/Daemon, mate of my soul.' The uniqueness of days, experiences, persons he finds to be an illusion. The sunset bells 'kill the living/God-of-the-Moment, only god ever.' All particulars pay the inevitable penalty and are merged, not in the permanent, universal One, but in meaningless oblivion. The most hopeless illusion of all seems to be the 'illusion of Persons':

> I remember the illusion of Persons.
> There is no person,
> I live in an empty box full of frauds.[3]

This awareness recurs in the much-quoted lines at the end of 'An Eclogue for Christmas', the prayer to

> . . . Let all these so ephemeral things
> Be somehow permanent like the swallow's tangent wings. . . .

His celebration of the 'ephemeral things' in this poem is a high-water mark of inspiration by his friendly daemon:

On all the traffic-islands stand white globes like moons,
The city's haze is clouded amber that purrs and croons,
And tilting by the noble curve bus after tall bus comes
With an osculation of yellow light, with a glory like chrysanthemums.

---

[1] *E.C.*, p. 51.   [2] 26 July 1926.
[3] *This Quarter*, vol. 4, June 1932, pp. 610–11. The 'empty box full of frauds' may be the well-known illusion box in the National Gallery, painted by S. van Hoogstraaten. See below, pp. 108, 127–8.

Yet he seems to have had difficulty in wishing for their permanence at the end, as his MS. alterations indicate.[1] The first expression he wrote was close to the one he finally used: 'Yet be somehow or other permanent like the swallow's flash of wings.' His intention was therefore to include all the 'lovely particulars' he had cele-brated in the valuable category of 'whatever glints' or gleams or flashes, thereby making them manifestations of the universal. He altered the 'flash of' wings to 'tangent', which still connotes darting movement, and then altered the 'permanent' to 'immortal', again without any change in meaning or connotation. Then, curiously, he altered the whole of the first half, up to the caesura, to 'Be somehow *mortal* . . .'. The prayer would then be that the lovely particulars might die the death of swallows' wings, flying off tangentially from the surface of phenomenal experience. The version he adopted is undoubtedly the better, but the rejected version appears to be a logical development from the thought of the opening lines of the poem, which becomes a nagging worry through it, and an obsession later: that the particulars are not universals. Christmas is 'an evil time'. The 'jaded calendar' is revolving, moving towards a new year and a new spring, with little hope of vital renewal:

> Its nuts need oil, carbon chokes the valves,
> The excess sugar of a diabetic culture
> Rotting the nerve of life and literature. . . .

The beauty of the particulars is 'narcotic and deciduous', their sum a 'vast organism grown out of us', a 'long-pent balloon' near bursting point. Therefore, however exciting the metaphysical concept of their permanence and universality might be, pragmatic common sense would more naturally suggest their *mortality* than their immortality.

Much of *Autumn Journal* is in this spirit:

> . . . . . the woodpigeon starts again denying
> The values of the town
> And a car having crossed the hill accelerates, changes
> Up, having just changed down.[2]

---

[1] H.N.   [2] *C.P.D.*, p. 110 (*A.J.*, V).

The gear-changing has ironical Heraclitean undertones of meaningless change, contrasting with, for example, the delighted undertones of the image in 'Mayfly', where he is happily adjusted to the surface:

> The mayfly flirting and posturing over the water
> Goes up and down in the lift so many times for fun.

Throughout the poems of the later 1940s and the 1950s the neurotic awareness of failure to unify the particulars of experience, to connect surface and core, gathers in intensity. In the dedicatory poem to his *Collected Poems*,[1] he admitted 'having lived, and too much, in the present', being 'content if things would image/ Themselves in their own dazzle'. Now he is

> . . . . . dumbfounded by the volume
> Of angry sound which pours from every turning
> On those who only so lately knew the answers.

In the opening canto of *Autumn Sequel* he is dismayed to reflect how little control he has managed to exercise over the mere inflow of experience in the interval since *Autumn Journal*; while in Canto V he is all but overwhelmed by the Jack of Wrecks in the sea of plurality. The horror of his 'Dreams in Middle Age' is that 'we ourselves remain/Ourselves or less', because

> Our lives are bursting at the seams
> With petty detail. . . . .

And the last two collections, as we have noted in other contexts, are bleak with the awareness of the system choked through mere, and sheer, surface and plurality:

> . . . . . fender to fender
> The cars will never emerge, not even
> Should their owners emerge to claim them, the move
> Is time's, not theirs; elbow to elbow
> Inside the roadhouse drinks are raised
> And downed, and downed, the pawns and drains
> Are blocked, are choked, the move is nil. . . .[2]

---

[1] 'To Hedli'.   [2] 'Another Cold May'.

He emphasizes in 'Spring Cleaning', ironically entitled, that there is no renewal, however much it is needed, as the new season brings 'Blain and dazzle together' and 'the tills ring//The Rites of Spring.' Someone must soon re-join surface and core, 'make all things new'. 'Constant', also ironically entitled, stresses the same theme of mere flux, history as mere particulars:

> . . . . . too much history,
> Tilting, canting, crawling, rotting away,
> Subsiding strata where ghosts like faults, like mites,
> Reminders of stagnation or collapse,
> Emerge into the mist. . . .

The 'Subsiding strata' (recalling the 'crumbling masonry' of 'Upon this Beach') seem far from the ultimate principle embodied in the Santa Sophia mosaic of:

> . . . . . . one
> Who calmly, having other things in mind,
> Bears on his palm the Church of the Holy Wisdom.

Although MacNeice thus felt increasingly that, in metaphysical terms, the concrete particular was not enough, there were various important factors that helped him to hold to his faith in the world as various and the world as surface. In his early article of faith, 'Our God Bogus', he had stubbornly refused to be panicked into a denial of the reality of surface, either by mystical or transcendental philosophies or by the current theories of the physicists. He remarked tartly: 'It is as well to know that a thing has a root, but I suspected it all along. Hence I was not surprised by the discovery into concluding that the root is the only reality.'[1] Thus he had already begun in the earlier poetry to look for the concrete universal, the surface experience that was identifiable with the universal, to try to achieve what he wished for his son in 'Ode', to 'accumulate, corroborate . . ./The blessedness of fact', not attempting to 'falsify the world/By taking it to pieces . . .'. Similarly, in 'Prayer Before Birth' he prays that his child will be neither all core, rigid in system, 'a thing with/One face, a thing', nor all circumference, with her entirety dissipated; that she will

---

[1] *Sir Galahad*, no. 2, 14 May 1929. See also p. 41 above.

be neither a stone nor spilled. In 'Departure Platform',[1] he is anticipating not only a pleasant experience, but also the real hope of contact with what is 'Divined but never known—the evasive universal'. The experience might turn out to be just another futile attempt 'To catch intact what is always in dispersal', but there is just 'the off-chance' of catching it ('the evasive universal'). The 'god of the place' *may* be able to 'fuse his person' with MacNeice's for his companion's enjoyment, 'but whether he could there is nobody can tell us'.

The crux of the whole matter of metaphysical finalities may well be in that admission: 'whether he could there is nobody can tell us'. The same kind of admission was made by F. H. Bradley in the Preface to the first edition (1883) of his *Principles of Logic* (which he did nothing to retract in the Preface to the 1922 re-issue). Here, modestly affirming that his metaphysics were 'really very limited', he said:

This does not mean that, like more gifted writers, I verify in my own shortcomings the necessary defects of the human reason. It means that on all questions, if you push me far enough, at present I end in doubts and perplexities. And on this account at least no lover of metaphysics will judge me hardly.

Thus Bradley, while leaving open the possibility of achieving something like certitude by human reason, admits the difficulties and uncertainties. The evasive universal could be 'divined but never known', and MacNeice became more and more hopeful from the earlier 1940s that he could, in fact, divine its presence.

Such a concrete universal is expressed with every appearance of conviction in 'Meeting Point'[2] with its deliberately ambiguous title, embracing both the meeting of the 'two people with the one pulse' and the intersection of the moment in time and the time-

---

[1] *P.P.*, pp. 17–18, (*L.D.*, p. 20). The stanza containing the explicit reference to 'the evasive universal' he omitted from the *P.P.* version, perhaps because it was too obvious a give-away.

[2] There is a similarity not only between this theme and Eliot's in 'Little Gidding' ('the intersection of the timeless moment'), but also between Eliot's unforgettable fused image 'Ash on an old man's sleeve/Is all the ash the burnt roses leave' (*F.Q.*, p. 37) and MacNeice's 'Her fingers flicked away the ash/That bloomed again in tropic trees.' MacNeice employs his image in an active, Eliot in a passive, movement.

less: '(Somebody stopped the moving stairs)'. Both heart and body 'verify' that the event was real:

> God or whatever means the Good
> Be praised that time can stop like this,
> That what the heart has understood
> Can verify in the body's peace
> God or whatever means the Good.

In poems such as 'The Cromlech', 'Street Scene' and 'The Cyclist', all written in the middle 1940s, he writes with equal certitude, as of a verified reality, of similar points of intersection. The unity of the Many and the One in Hindu mystic philosophy he admired in the rock carvings of the temple at Mahabalipuram. Here, too, the granite of the rock temple defeats the waves of mere flux, and the movement is taken a step further in 'Areopagus', where, true to the hierarchy of Heraclitean physics (where water becomes earth, and earth fire), the 'living rock' of the Furies (and the Church founded on Peter) 'was the death of sea', and 'Christ's dead timber' was 'fired by blood'. In 'Our Sister Water' the Heraclitean movement is reversed, but the stress is still on the unity, for we are identified with this essence ('Such is water, such are we,/World's most variables, constant in our variability') before we return to be immersed in the One of ocean:

> . . . . yet must fall back
> In the end and find our level absolved of earth and breath
> In that bed we were conceived in, born in, the bed of ocean, of death.

'Solstice' provides a kind of anticipatory counter to the later ironical 'Constant', for his old horror of failing to catch the seasons is here stilled in the arrested flux of high midsummer:

> And what was nowhere now was here
> And here was all and all was good. . . .

The most evasive particular of all has become a concrete universal:

> One entrance to one constant song.
> How can midsummer stay so long?[1]

[1] Cf. 'And I realize how now, as every year before,/Once again the gay months have eluded me.' 'August'.

And in the late 'Round the Corner' the gimlet of his fate is still twisting him more deeply into experience, but all his depth, as in 'Donegal Triptych', continues to usurp his surface, the Many remember the One as

> . . . the exiled shell complains or a wind from round the corner
> Carries the smell of wrack or the taste of salt, or a wave
> Touched to steel by the moon twists a gimlet in memory.
> Round the corner is—sooner or later—the sea.

Now the glinting wave actually manifests the presence of the universal, which was not so in 'Donegal Triptych', where, even if it is divined, it is 'never there when we draw the curtain'. There seems no doubt that he had found the real or ideal, as well as the actual, Atlantic he had despairingly hankered for in 'Ode'; had made, in the words of W. H. Auden's 'Postscript' to his memorial poem for MacNeice, 'The Cave of Making', the equation between the 'timeless fictional worlds' and his 'temporal one':

> Timeless fictional worlds
> Of self-evident meaning
> Would not delight
>
> Were not our own
> A temporal one where nothing
> Is what it seems.[1]

It is perhaps not surprising that MacNeice should have come increasingly to identify himself in terms of his Aristotelian function, finding his nature in his creative writing, judging the value of his works and days in terms of his integrity as a writer. Although he did not in his early days ever regard his art as a substitute for belief, he had no doubt about its ability to order the flux and give it reality and permanence. The integrity of the creative imagination was already a theme in his school articles. Mr. Schinabel, in 'The Devil', began his days on a foul buoy upon the sea of flux, but ended by destroying the Devil, embodied as insincere art.[2] At Oxford he admired Virginia Woolf, D. H. Lawrence and James Joyce for serving up the flux 'on golden

---

[1] *About the House*, London, 1966, p. 21.   [2] *Marlburian*, 22 October 1925.

platters', and *Mrs. Dalloway* and *Ulysses* in particular for the 'interweavings of subjective and objective'.[1] Devlin, in *Round-about Way*, reflected at length on the need to write up people's lives, so untrue in their ill-ordered actuality, and MacNeice similarly insisted in a letter home from Oxford that 'one must beat things into shape . . . till . . . an artificial harmony is produced which is more real than an unharmonious reality. . .'.[2] At Oxford, too, he argued that E. E. Cummings's 'insistence on poetry not as something made but as making is a mere corollary of or implicate in Gentile's main thesis that knowledge is not things thought but thinking'.[3]

Despite these sympathies and assertions, however, he lacked confidence in the value of his making in the earlier and middle 1930s. In 'August' he complains that the best he can do to arrest the exciting flux is, like Poussin, to 'make a still-bound fête of us'. Similarly, in 'Nature Morte' he disclaims any virtue in 'the pretentious word' to stabilize 'the light on the sun-fondled trees'; 'the appalling unrest of the soul' still exudes from the still life. Craven (Auden) in the 'Eclogue from Iceland' presumably voices their joint sense of futility at returning home to

> Admire Flaubert, Cézanne—the tortured artists—
> And leaning forward to knock out our pipes
> Into the fire protest that art is good
> And gives a meaning and a slant to life.

His poems between *Autumn Journal* and *Holes in the Sky* indicate both explicitly and implicitly his growing faith in the closeness of the relationship between art and universal reality. He had noted his admiration in *Autumn Journal* for the power of 'these arrogant Old Masters' to affront 'Our own system of values' with their apparently unsound premises, which 'history has refuted', but which still 'cast their shadows on us like asper-sions'.[4] He praised them again in 'Picture Galleries', pointing out that

[1] *S.A.F.*, p. 118; letter to A.F.B. from Carrickfergus, 29 March 1927.
[2] Op. cit., pp. 15–17; letter of 11 June 1927.
[3] *M.P.*, p. 71: quoted from 'We are the Old'.   [4] *C.P.D.*, p. 142 (*A.J.*, XX).

> . . . . viewed as history they remind us of what we always
> Would rather forget—that what we are or prefer is conditioned
> By circumstances, that evil and good
> Are relative to ourselves who are creatures of period. . . .[1]

The same point is made in 'The National Gallery', where he expresses his delight at the return of the Old Masters, so that 'Hundreds of windows are open again on a vital but changeless world . . .'. It is not the shock of sensing 'the appalling unrest of the soul' exuding from the still life he records now, but the fact that 'a still life lives' and there is now air 'Blowing from times unconfined to Then, from places further and fuller than There' to 'Purge our particular time-bound unliving lives . . .'. He wishes to identify himself and the value of his making with this timeless, unifying creation in such poems as the final section of *Autumn Journal*, where the synthesizing mind of the poet strives to reconcile all the warring opposites in himself and humanity in the long prayer for a harmonious organism, and the 'Elegy for Minor Poets', at the end of this period, where he praises the minor poets (seeming to include himself) with 'the Great' for transcending their limitations of time, place, and gifts. His faith in poetry as the act of making he explicitly advanced once more at this time in an article in which, recalling that 'poet' is derived from the Greek word for 'maker', he asserts that the poet is more than one who reflects or records impressions: 'Does he live in a world of chaos? All right. Perhaps he can do nothing about it as a man, he can do something about it as a poet.'[2]

This faith is strong in the ambiguously titled 'Suite for Recorders', and is omnipresent in *Autumn Sequel*. In the sixth poem of the 'Visitations' sequence his good daemon is, by clear implication, his Muse:

> The world one millimetre beyond him—
> Is it the Muse?
> The soul untold light years inside him—
> Is it the Muse?

In 'Déjà Vu', deliberately taking 'this selfsame pencil' and writing,

[1] *P.P.*, p. 26.   [2] 'English Poetry Today', in the *Listener*, 2 September 1948.

he illustrates his conviction that art perpetuates the timeless moment. And in 'Memoranda to Horace' he wonders whether Horace's (and his own) art has, in fact, been more permanent than their mayfly moods of personal harmonious adjustment, whether they have 'raised a monument/Weaker and less of note than a mayfly'; but he concludes that Horace's 'image,/"More lasting than bronze" will do . . .'.

It is of basic significance that his strengthening faith in himself as poet should keep pace with his conviction that as a man, thinking and sensing and acting as other men, he could achieve a meaningful condition of being. He had somewhat overstated his case in his much-quoted definition of a poet as an ordinary man in *Modern Poetry*, where he stressed the Wordsworthian 'a man speaking to men' in his opening lines.[1] He affirmed this bluntly in 'A Statement' in *New Verse* at the same time: 'I think that the poet is only an extension—or, if you prefer it, a concentration—of the ordinary man . . .'.[2] And, in Section XXI of *Autumn Journal*, where he is preoccupied with the theme of value in living, he asserts that 'each individual . . ./Would be fighting a losing battle' unless he could live 'A life beyond the self but self-completing', and advances his concept of 'life as collective creation', which became central to his attitude in the 1940s and 1950s.

This was the beginning of the period of widening friendships, communication, growing familiarity with the concrete universal as connection with his friends who were realizing value in their lives. They would soon include colleagues such as 'Harrap . . . whose words were hard to follow/But not his values'; 'Devlin the double bluffer or bluffly witty', who 'has been the rounds' of that rare and enduring England that 'still is with us'; and 'blandly bulking Herriot who could swallow/Every jack sprat and oyster in this city'.[3] This attitude he voiced explicitly in an article at the end of 1947:

Since 1939 we seem to have become more humane; we have also become—in the widest sense of the word—more religious. Those

[1] See p. 39 above. [2] Nos. 31 and 32, Autumn 1938.
[3] *C.P.D.*, pp. 357, 364 (*A.S.*, VI, VIII). 'Harrap' was E. A. (Archie) Harding, 'Devlin' was Francis (Jack) Dillon, and 'Herriot' was Laurence Duval Gilliam, Head of Features.

writers who have plumped for an established religion have probably handicapped themselves, but what is a fact, and something to be glad of, is that many others have regained a sense of value, i.e. of the value of people and things in themselves, of ends as distinct from means.[1]

He seems more than willing to forget what he had forcefully reminded himself in 'Sleep' he must 'remember to forget': his knowledge of manifold illusion, especially the 'illusion of Persons'.[2] The sheer peace and relief of communication, contact, he expressed in 'The Window':

> Communication. Alchemy.
> Here is profit where was loss
> And what was dross is golden,
> Those are friends who once were foreign
> And gentler shines the face of doom. . . .

The same mood dominates his blessing in the last canto of *Autumn Sequel* to all his friends, and to the friends to whom they, too, reach out:

> . . . and to all
> Their others cherishing whom their selves aspire
>
> To something more than selfhood . . .

The 'wall/Of isolation' has crumbled, the light has broken in, and the journey has value and reality. This was the faith that sustained him through two decades, despite his moments of despair.

In 'The Kingdom' he celebrated those who, 'as being themselves, are apart from not each other/But from such as being false are merely other', those who 'are humble/And proud at once, working within their limits/And yet transcending them'. Similarly, in 'The Trolls' (written after an air-raid, April 1941), he had answered the demons of destruction by asserting:

> . . . the value
> Of every organism, act and moment
> Is, thanks to death, unique.

---

[1] 'The English Literary Scene', in the *N.Y.T.B.R.*, 28 September 1947.
[2] See pp. 96–8, 127–8.

Fifteen years later, in the fourth part of the title poem of *Visitations*, he reasserted this uniqueness, and in 'The Suicide', in the last collection, he denied that death could destroy the 'Something that was intact' that the 'man with the shy smile' had left behind.

It is notable, however, that in his praise of such friends and admired individuals as Owen, Boyce, Aloys, Gwilym, he tends to stress their qualities as men, rather than as scholars or artists, although he makes the connection patently clear—especially in respect of their integrity. True to their art or scholarly discipline, and true to themselves, they were therefore true to reality. Boyce and Aloys he particularly esteemed as individualists, men who cultivated their own garden—in the case of Boyce literally, so that all imperfections

> Become themselves, thanks to his cleansing powers,
>
> While the great No-God winces. . . . .[1]

Gwilym, Evans, Owen, and Gavin he valued as men who gave themselves up to life.[2] His comprehensive 'Fanfare for the Makers' canto in *Autumn Sequel* he concludes: 'To make is such. Let us make . . .'; and the making is, by clear implication, the activity simply of men and women, as well as creative artists. He repeats this in his 'Lament for the Makers' canto, where Gwilym, as man and poet, becomes a part of all he has made.[3]

It was in the image of such men and makers that he came increasingly to view his own life and work, the two being creatively integrated in his art, and the ideal conditions for the operation of both being identical. He was well aware that significant insights cannot be contrived. They have to come directly as a result of one's individual nature and activity: 'You cannot collect them with scissors and a pot of paste. You must work for them. They must be related to your work and come to you in the course of it.'[4] In 'Prognosis' he is waiting and watching.

[1] *C.P.D.*, p. 359 (*A.S.*, VII).

[2] Graham Shepard ('Gavin') was also a writer. He had published one novel, and left behind a large number of unpublished MSS., into which I was permitted to look by his widow, Mrs. Ann Shepard. The novel, *Tea-Tray in the Sky*, was published by Arthur Barker, London, 1934.

[3] These cantos are, respectively, VII and XVIII; *C.P.D.*, pp. 357 and 402. The allusion is to Dunbar's poem. [4] *Minch*, p. 156.

Throughout the cumulative interrogatory of each verse he is restlessly alert to the thrill of some revelation at hand:

> Will he give a champion
> Answer to my question
> Or will his words be dark
> And his ways evasion?

The stranger of 'Prognosis' returns again in 'Mutations', waiting in the wings for his cue to make another annunciation that will result in new 'mutations in the mind'. Surveying contemporary man against the ages, as 'the millennia cool', MacNeice can see no hope of a spiritual change; but such surprises or annunciations both 'keep us living' and help to make the meaning plain. Throughout the poems of these two decades he rings the changes of image on this same theme, sometimes stressing the aspect of revelation, sometimes the rigours of waiting, watching, studying the signs; but always he emphasizes the active role of mind as it makes sense of the moments of illumination, edits what is given. Despite the constant menace of the unassimilated, mere Not-Self, the watchers keep their vigil on the wall, visitations come and come again, renewing the pattern of awareness, promising renewals without end, transforming walls to windows opening on the timeless, assuring, in 'Selva Oscura', 'that the world, though more, is also I'.

Elsewhere it is the search that is stressed. In 'The Dowser' the subject is explicitly searching for the underground well with his divining rod, remembering 'some old fellow/(Dead long ago) who remembered the well', when 'the hazel rod bent, dipping, contorting', and he knew he had found it. What he actually found when he dug, however, was blinding illumination, an erupting 'geyser . . . of light'. At other times the illumination is more limited, the search for the way more hazardous, the need for skill and control more acute, as in 'The Wiper', where 'the road', which runs emphatically through each of the five stanzas, is scarcely held, seen with difficulty, 'sucked in under the axle' to be immediately 'spewed behind us and lost' as we race through the darkness and the rain, trying to see a little of the way ahead, but content if we just manage to 'hold the road'.

Thus when, in 'Prayer Before Birth', he prays for protection against all those who would dissipate his entirety, his oneness with water, grass, trees, sky, and birds, it is to the white light at the back of his mind that he appeals for guidance.[1] In three of his long poems of the mid-1940s, 'Letter from India', 'Mahabalipuram', 'The Stygian Banks', the illumination is presented as an avatar. In the last-named, the 'golden avatar' is the Spring of perpetual renewal, when the high winds are swaying the tree-tops on which the cradle/coffin of beginning/end is swaying, and the subject is moving at one in the dance with the eternal, cosmic rhythm. It is not only the private way ahead that is the object of constant search, the individual illumination, the relation of the private Me to the Not Me. The road he is trying to hold in 'The Wiper' is the common highway, on which other drivers are making a similar effort; and from their effort and their passing presence he takes comfort.

This determination to face, and interpret, the facts with ruthless and disciplined integrity is perhaps even more marked in his search for the general than for the individual pattern. After his inconclusive debate with Thucydides he was only too pleased to turn from the 'bleak reading' of history to 'the private sphere/ Where waste and loss are felt as waste and loss'.[2] Nevertheless, he continually attempted the bleak reading, daring, with Eliot:

> The backward look behind the assurance
> Of recorded history, the backward half-look
> Over the shoulder, towards the primitive terror.[3]

His tragic awareness at the time of Munich that history was repeating itself in a pattern of evil and wrong becomes more profound as he studies the later evidence of the cruelty, violence and intolerance, and can see few signs of a new cycle of renewal in the general life of mankind. We are all, with King Thyestes,

---

[1] In his broadcast, *India at First Sight*, MacNeice similarly connected the white light that came into the mind of Buddha, after he had sat in meditation all day under the fig tree, with his awareness of his identity with the universe.

[2] *C.P.D.*, p. 410 (*A.S.*, XIX).

[3] *F.Q.*, p. 29. Mr. Renford Bambrough reminded us that 'Eliot's backward half-look was over the shoulder of a keen student of Bradley's *Appearance and Reality*'. (*Listener*, 27 January 1966.)

'Messmates in the eucharist of crime', and Here and We 'in perfidy are linked' to There and Them.[1]

It is in controlling the inflow of such appalling factual data, mastering it and making sense and shape of it, that mind comes to full awareness of itself, in creative association with not-mind. In the process it inevitably loses some of its innocence, as the false dichotomy of the naïve and the know-all mind is resolved. In 'The Messiah', as frequently elsewhere, he presented his two selves, 'one naïve, one know-all'.[2] The latter answered the simple questions of the former with ridiculous cocksureness, describing the new Messiah in terms applicable to himself as:

> . . . A new mutation of man
> He knows the answers to everything. . . .

As the mind grows towards maturity, the two selves come closer to the composite self, the naïve self losing some of its innocence, as the know-all mind loses some of its arrogant assurance. Even if 'the years destroy/The courage of our ignorance', it is equally true that:

> The tree of knowledge stands the test of joy
> And evil strops our wits. . . .[3]

In 'Thalassa' he can proclaim his faith in 'a high star' by which our course may be set, in spite of, though also because of, our certain knowledge that our 'wills are fickle', our 'values blurred', our 'hearts impure', our 'past life a ruined church'. There is no alternative. We must continue by the way of knowledge on which we have set out, coming eventually and painfully to understanding:

> But let your poison be your cure.[4]

---

[1] 'Thyestes'.

[2] The self-communings, the interior dialogues of these two aspects of mind, are what he esteems in the heroes of Kafka and Beckett, with their 'nagging concern with truth' (*V.P.*, p. 120).

[3] *C.P.D.*, pp. 350–1 (*A.S.*, V).

[4] The interweavings, in these poems, of the personal and historical themes, the juxtaposition and conjunction of the innocent and the knowing minds, within a metaphysical framework of Being and Becoming, all strongly recall the similar pattern in 'Little Gidding': 'History may be servitude,/History may be freedom. See, now they vanish,/The faces and places, with the self which, as it could, loved them,/To become renewed,

It does seem reasonable to claim, at the very least, that underlying this poet is 'a speculative metaphysician, of an unfashionably ambitious sort'.[1] Indeed, even if the mind behind this poetry lacked the assurance of a dogmatic faith, it might not be stretching the term too far to say that it did not lack belief—recalling especially his own assertion that 'to shun dogma does not mean to renounce belief'.[2] Poetic creation of the order of MacNeice's best poems could almost certainly not have been achieved even by a craftsman of his skill and an observer of his intelligence without the driving and binding force of belief firmly held. It gave him what as a young poet he had said admiringly it gave Hopkins: not only 'hands and an eye', but also 'a heart, a mainspring'.[3]

transfigured, in another pattern' (Part III, *F.Q.*, pp. 40–1); 'We shall not cease from exploration/And the end of our exploring/Will be to arrive where we started/And know the place for the first time' (Part V, *F.Q.*, p. 43). Eliot, like MacNeice in 'Apple Blossom', symbolizes the innocence in his image of 'the children in the apple-tree' (p. 44).

[1] See Preface.   [2] Ibid.

[3] 'A Comment' (on Hopkins) in *New Verse*, no. 14, April 1935.

Part II Maker

5 Metaphysical Image

If it is true that beliefs affect the form of the poem, this movement in MacNeice's thought towards a disciplined interpretation of his subject matter should be paralleled by a similar movement towards formal, technical discipline. His awareness of the problem, in formal terms, is again an early one. Just before he went up to Oxford he was enthusiastic about Significant Form, and 'Images and rhythm were the most important things in the world.'[1] He soon modified this enthusiasm:

> It had not occurred to me that the theory of Significant Form, which I took from Clive Bell, is a contradiction in terms. In any object, poem or picture, which shows 'significant form', according to this theory, the shape is valuable *for the shape's own sake*. But 'significant', on any analysis, ought to mean significant of something outside itself.[2]

Thus, in the summer of 1928 we find him

> full of intentions e.g. to make an exhaustive study of 17th century English prose (e.g. Donne, Jeremy Taylor, Sir T. Browne, Milton, etc) and show how its cadences and imagery are a better union with God than any English prose before or since (except possibly Malory, in quite a different way). . . .[3]

His attitude again seems to be basically a metaphysical one: the subject matter comes to full awareness of itself only through submission to the 'brute Other' that gives it form and so identity. This he expresses pointedly in *The Poetry of W. B. Yeats*:

> The paradox of poetry is like the paradox of individual freedom. An individual is not less free, but more free, if he recognises the factors which condition him and adjusts himself to his context; a poem is not less of a poem, but more of a poem, if it fulfils its condition of corresponding to life.[4]

Consequently, he was particularly hostile, as we noted, to Croce's devaluation of the creative act, and insisted that the poet does not fully realize what he has to say until he has said it.

[1] *M.P.*, p. 59.   [2] Ibid., pp. 59–60.
[3] Letter to J.R.H. from Carrickfergus. This is the kernel of the theme he elaborated more than thirty years later in *V.P.* The case of Malory he examined in his essay, 'Sir Thomas Malory': see Bibliog.
[4] Op. cit., p. 227. See below, pp. 171–3.

Many other modern poets and critics have placed equal stress on this connection, which seems to force itself strongly upon the contemporary creative and critical awareness. Thus, MacNeice, in his essay on 'Subject in Modern Poetry', defended 'Mr. Eliot's eccentricities of form' as being 'largely evoked by and appropriate to his subject';[1] but he qualified this significantly in *Modern Poetry*:

Eliot became notorious for his technique, but his technique was suited to his subject-matter:

'These fragments I have shor'd against my ruins'

was always his early cry (till he took up Anglo-Catholicism) and his verse was carefully fragmentary to match the world as he perceived it. But the contemplation of a world of fragments becomes boring and Eliot's successors are more interested in tidying it up.[2]

The essential connection between the poet's belief, and so the content of his poetry, and the formal element, indeed, MacNeice elaborated throughout *Modern Poetry*, so that it might almost be called the theme of the work. He states bluntly at the end of his chapter on Rhythm and Rhyme that 'no formal element in a poem can properly be divorced from its content',[3] and asks the reader to bear this in mind in his next chapter, on Diction. His conclusion is explicit:

Subject is automatically formalized when it is put into any sort of words. It is impossible to write either without form or without subject. But subject can to some extent swamp form or form invalidate subject. It is the ratio between the two which makes a good poem. Subject must work itself out in pattern but not be emasculated by pattern. In this book I have tried to show how modern poetry has set out to readjust the ratio, which had been upset by various conflicting extremisms.[4]

The need to 'readjust the ratio' in himself and in his work he stressed in letters to Anthony Blunt between 1926 and 1936. For instance, he complained bitterly in a letter from Birmingham

<hr/>

[1] *Essays and Studies* by members of The English Association, vol. 22, Oxford, 1937, p. 147.
[2] Op. cit., p. 13.   [3] Ibid., p. 134.   [4] Ibid., p. 199.

on 10 November 1935 that he was 'all form and no content'. As early as 1927 (9 June 1927, from Oxford) he was inveighing against the artificial division of form and content: e.g. '[Wyndham Lewis] will try to build a wall between the idea (or spirit) and the form—as in the book on Shakespeare, i.e. between Craftsman and Creator . . .'. Twenty years later he stressed emphatically the need for organic structure, specifically in the context of value and belief:

A poem must have some relation to life and maybe that life is messy, but it must also emerge as a thing in itself, an organism. And therefore it must be shaped, it must have an internal structure. And by that I do not mean merely a formal pattern; I mean also the sort of structure which will creep in willy-nilly if a poet has some positive values or, if I may risk the word, beliefs. . . .[1]

Shortly afterwards, in his Introduction to his translation of *Faust*, he was particularly firm in defence of his technical attitude:

I aimed at a line-for-line translation and also . . . at a prosody equivalent to or, if possible, identical with Goethe's. Some of my friends regretted that I did not turn the whole thing into blank verse or 'free verse' but in my opinion that would have ruined the sense of it. For the rhymes in Goethe are part of the sense and he uses them again and again to clinch his point.[2]

The same theme dominates the late *Varieties of Parable*. In reference to Dante, for example, he makes the equation in absolute form:

Anyhow, whereas I was implying before that in poetry the formal elements are part of the meaning or the content, I would add at this point that the content, which includes of course any beliefs expressed in a poem, must *ipso facto*—at least if that poem is to be valid—have a part in the shaping of that poem. Which means that in this respect the beliefs are formalizing elements.[3]

As with the metaphysical problem, however, the critical distinction may have to be made between the appearance and the reality. So that, even if form and content may be indistinguishable in reality, it may be convenient to adopt the necessary fiction that

[1] *Listener*, 2 September 1948. Article entitled 'English Poetry Today'.
[2] Op. cit., p. 9.   [3] Op. cit., p. 19.

they are separable. As a critic, too, MacNeice experienced the need for this fiction. For example, he is obliged to preface his study of parable writers with just this postulate:

As every poet knows, one cannot draw any clear line between form and content. Yet, as every critic knows, without drawing such a line criticism is impossible. So, just as with any other kind of writing, in order to discuss parable writing at all one has to use what Aristotle would call a 'bastard reasoning' and pretend that form and content can be separated.[1]

This pretence is similarly adopted in all the instances that are bound to occur throughout the following chapters where the mechanism of the poem appears to be treated in isolation from the matter of life that informs it.

In his chapter on imagery in *Modern Poetry*, MacNeice made a basic distinction between 'the properties and the images of a poem'. These terms he both defines and, significantly, qualifies, as follows:

The properties are the objects which enter a poem by their own right, as flowers enter a poem about a garden, whereas the images enter a poem by right of analogy, as flowers entered Plato's descriptions of his mystical and abstract Heaven. But, conversely, the properties themselves may be, in the ultimate analysis, only symbols. Was, for example, Wordsworth's celandine really all celandine and nothing but celandine?[2]

As he develops this theme, he expresses admiration for Baudelaire, whose 'great quality is concentration, shown often in the comparison of physical to spiritual and vice versa', and in whom 'there is a fine balance between wit and intuition, statement and suggestion'.[3] Similarly, he deplores the rejection by Baudelaire's followers, the Symbolists, of 'both rhetoric and brute reality', as they 'devoted themselves to suggestion', so that image and property merge in their poems, which 'maintains their status as dreams'.[4] This trend, as he notes with some relief, is now being reversed:

The present trend, however, is to reduce images in proportion to properties. This is because . . . poets are now more interested in subject,

---

[1] *V.P.*, p. 5.   [2] Op. cit., p. 91.   [3] Ibid., p. 100.   [4] Ibid., pp. 100, 101.

and that a subject from the concrete objective world. The few poets today who ... philosophize in their poetry, *have* to use images because bare philosophy belongs to science rather than to poetry. Witness Norman Cameron's excellent poem on the principle of Love:

> 'He bloomed in our bodies to the finger-tips
> And rose like barley-sugar round the lips'

But most of the other poets 'philosophize', if they do philosophize, more in the manner of Wordsworth. For Wordsworth the objective world of nature is an embodiment, not a concealment, of something like the Platonic Forms. He does not therefore require many images because his properties carry their own message.[1]

In his own poetry, too, he seemed to develop increasingly towards the image that is as factual as a property, and the property that is as suggestive as an image. In *Varieties of Parable* he is perfectly willing to adopt Professor C. S. Lewis's term 'sacramental', or Professor Graham Hough's term 'incarnational', for the property that has this quality.[2] He comments with some interest in the same book on Professor Hough's examination, in terms of the points on a clock-face, of the ratio between 'theme' and 'image', where the extremes of dominant 'theme' and dominant 'image' are, respectively, twelve o'clock and six o'clock. At three o'clock stands Shakespeare in whom 'theme and image seem equally balanced'.[3] This is the ideal, the balance that Mac-Neice considered modern poetry was trying to redress, whereby the poet could 'once again ... make his response as a whole ... presenting something which is (a) communication, a record, but is also (b) creation—having a new unity of its own, something in its shape which makes it poetry'.[4] In 'Experiences with Images' he is even more explicit, pointing out that, where Shakespeare was universal in his use of images, the eighteenth and nineteenth centuries tried to confine the poet, but he is once again free, for

---

[1] Ibid., pp. 112–13.   [2] Op. cit., p. 59, and *passim.*
[3] Ibid., pp. 17–18, and *passim.* Professor Hough's book, *A Preface to 'The Faerie Queene',* MacNeice reviewed enthusiastically in the *Listener,* 31 January 1962, noting with approval his detection of 'a metaphysical spectre' behind both allegory and symbolism, and supporting his contention that 'allegory in its broadest possible sense is a pervasive element in all literature'.
[4] *M.P.,* pp. 29–30.

as luck or T. S. Eliot would have it, today's fashion makes a good deal more allowance for human multiplicity. Mr. Eliot's essay on *The Metaphysical Poets* (1921), which could well be regarded as the modern poet's manifesto, is something far more than a piece of special pleading for Donne and Co. It is a challenge to poets to return, if they can and if they dare, to Shakespeare's catholic receptivity.[1]

It is obviously difficult to say with any degree of assurance how far a poet's properties may be regarded as sacramental, or even to what extent his images are present as legitimate properties. MacNeice considered that Eliot, for instance, 'indulged' his images, complaining that 'the images he uses are arrogant, they think they are there in their own right'; and recalled that Eliot 'has himself written of the almost magical compulsion exercised upon a poet by certain remembered objects or events in his own experience: their significance is something he cannot explain, but he *feels* it'. There *may* be sacramentalism present. MacNeice finds the same characteristic in Auden, whose 'poems are full of "sacred objects"; but, more often than not, this means that they are sacred to him as a private individual and for reasons which may be mainly accidental. . . .'[2]

Mr. Geoffrey Grigson insisted in the preface to his anthology, *New Verse*,[3] that

To be an imaginative poet, of the best kind, you need to see objects as themselves and as symbols, all at once. . . . You need to be able to impart ideas through objects . . . and my conception of what a poet, *at his best*, should be now is some one with a moral sense who is more than ever careful to convey the inner by the outer shape of things. I agree with Louis MacNeice: 'I would have a poet able-bodied. . . .'

And so he goes on to give MacNeice's definition, from *Modern Poetry*, of the poet as a man actively interested in current affairs. It is for this reason that Mr. Grigson asserts:

As far as it is possible to judge now, I should say that there were no better poets in England, after Yeats and Eliot, than Auden and Louis

[1] 'E.I.', p. 126.

[2] The quotations in this paragraph are from *V.P.*, pp. 105–7, upon which the paraphrases are also based.

[3] *New Verse. An anthology of poems which have appeared in the first thirty numbers of 'New Verse'*. London, 1939.

MacNeice. Both have this exact, material view. . . . Both make familiar use of objects. . . .

He does not consider, however, that 'their simple power of vision, touching, hearing, etc., is as great and as wide as would be ideal at the present moment'; and finds that, while 'MacNeice is aware of gleam and colour, and can make emotive use of a car brushing the cow-parsley in a lane', his 'vision, not in a bad sense, is generally superficial'. Without pausing to dispute the *mere* emotive use of the car image here,[1] one may readily agree that a good deal of MacNeice's imagery up to the later 1930s was of the surface. MacNeice himself was troubled by this. In 'Experiences with Images' he asserted that many of his poems up to and including *The Earth Compels* were 'tourist', content with enjoying and recording experience.[2]

On the other hand, he was extremely wary about attempting to achieve symbolic effects that might be factitious, unsubtle, or too pervasive. In the letter from Hetty to Nancy in *Letters from Iceland* he expresses himself scathingly against such a use of symbols in Hetty's comments on the symbolic sculptures in the museum at Reykjavik:

And the symbolism, darling, is the sort they used to have in the Academy. . . . You know—Time pulling off the boots of Eternity with one hand while keeping the wolf from the door with the other. The only one which didn't seem to be symbolic was Queen Victoria on an elephant; a welcome piece of naturalism as Maisie remarked.[3]

He is equally scathing in *Varieties of Parable* about 'the 1920s principle of Gather Ye Symbols where Ye May'.[4] Similarly, he expressed only modified enthusiasm for the 'metaphysico-mystical' poems of Edwin Muir, which he found 'so unadulterated either by topical or documentary elements or by primarily aesthetic ones, such as images used for their own sake' that reading many

---

[1] See p. 144. MacNeice was well aware long before this of the metaphysical significance of his car rides, even if here the sensuous effect considerably outweighs the latent metaphysical content, so that the presence of the latter, in this instance, can admittedly be only a matter of conjecture. (The reference is to 'June Thunder'.)

[2] Op. cit., p. 130.   [3] Op. cit., p. 159.

[4] Op. cit., p. 59. (On pp. 56–9 he is discussing interpretations of Blake's *The Book of Thel*.)

of his poems on end was 'like walking through a gallery of abstract paintings'.[1] The ideal is rather the adulterated symbolic imagery of George MacDonald, for whom the symbol was, in the words of his son, 'far more than an arbitrary outward and visible sign of an abstract conception: its high virtue lay in a common *substance* with the idea presented'.[2]

The concept, of course, is familiar. Almost thirty years before, MacNeice had praised modern poets, especially Auden, for their refusal to let metaphor be 'imposed *ab extra*', but to use it rather as 'the concrete instance of an immanent theme'.[3] Nietzsche, in *The Birth of Tragedy*, favourite reading of MacNeice's shortly before this, had stated bluntly: 'Metaphor, for the authentic poet, is not a figure of rhetoric but a representative image standing concretely before him in lieu of a concept.'[4] While Coleridge, in distinguishing between 'allegory' and 'symbol' in *The Statesman's Manual*, advanced the principle in a memorable formula. The symbol, says Coleridge, 'always partakes of the Reality which it renders intelligible; and while it enunciates the whole, abides itself as a living part in that Unity of which it is the representative'.[5]

In his post-war critical writing, MacNeice stressed increasingly the need for double-level writing in modern poetry, mentioning with approval, for instance, an editorial comment by John Lehmann in *Penguin New Writing*, to the effect that 'We cannot live without symbol', and advocating a 'return to the kind of art that conceals a metaphysical meaning behind and above what it states'.[6] MacNeice found this resurgence of 'metaphysical meaning' apparent in the work of the younger poets, who had discovered 'the half-forgotten axiom that poetry is not just a matter of externals or of rational content'. In 'Experiences with Images', he postulated three essential elements in a successful

---

[1] Op. cit., pp. 124–5.

[2] Ibid., p. 94. MacNeice adds that this is what Professor C. S. Lewis, a great admirer of MacDonald, meant by 'sacramentalism'.

[3] In his essay on Poetry in *The Arts Today* (see Bibliog.), p. 55.

[4] On p. 55 of the translation by Francis Golffing, New York, 1956.

[5] Op. cit., 1816, Appendix B. Quoted by Professor Hough in *A Preface to 'The Fairie Queene'*, p. 100.

[6] 'The English Literary Scene', in *N.Y.T.B.R.*, 28 September 1947.

lyric: the dramatic, the ironic, and the symbolic. By the first two he meant that a lyric should be a monodrama, with the lyric poet alone on the stage and deliberately choosing a tone of voice for his utterance; but indicating by the slightest changes of mood, diction, imagery, the presence of a latent content of which both poet and reader are aware. As for the third essential element, the symbolic, he comments:

And finally the lyric, which is thus dramatic and ironic, is also—it should go without saying—from the first, and, above all, *symbolic*. Language itself is by its nature a traffic in symbols, but these symbols are plastic—an endless annoyance to the scientist but God's own gift to the poet; for the poet, who is always trying to say something new, must take the rough and ready symbol of a general A and mould it to stand for his own particular a; that is at his least ambitious—sometimes he will mould it to stand for b or even x. Which procedure is itself both ironic and dramatic. . . .[1]

We have already noted poems in which he attempted ambitious equations with innocent looking images from the concrete world, such as the windscreen wiper, the request stop, or the taxi meter. In *Modern Poetry*, moreover, he commented on the fact that poets like Day Lewis and Spender, 'whose theme is the modern industrial world, its economics and its politics', and who take their images from this world, can still be 'very free with the stock mystical symbols—roses, crystal, snow, stars, gold'.[2] This is equally true of MacNeice himself, who was attracted to certain of these symbols, as he was to those that he grouped more vaguely as 'the great traditional evergreens'.[3] As we noticed throughout the last chapter, he makes regular and recurrent use of traditional and non-traditional, general and particular symbolic material with, true to his metaphysical outlook, little or no distinction between the kinds. Crystal or snow, or a traditional evergreen in contemporary vogue such as the desert,[4] had no more symbolic significance than, and was put to the same poetic use as, a bus, motor-cycle, or television aerial. He also made wide use of traditional Christian symbols, biblical imagery and material

[1] Op. cit., p. 125.   [2] Op. cit., p. 111.   [3] 'E.I.', p. 127.
[4] He takes note of this symbol in 'E.I.', p. 127.

from Christian hagiology, as well as sacred matter from other religions.[1] His use of the sea as a symbol might have provided much relevant illustrative matter for W. H. Auden's study of the 'romantic iconography of the sea',[2] as could his use of the associated symbols included by Auden, the shell, the desert and the stone, the questing hero. Elemental symbols widely used by MacNeice, besides the 'stock mystical' ones, include the one universal blue of the sky, the wind, the sun, fire, and water. From the world of natural creation he made wide symbolic use of trees, flowers, animals, and birds. He used, too, the traditional matter of classical mythology, especially where it blended easily with symbolic material he habitually used from other sources, as did the maze from the Theseus myth. And he used the traditional matter of folk and fairy tale, nursery rhyme, later myth and legend, especially the Arthurian, and history.[3]

Common features of life, from whatever source, having multiple associations, have therefore multiple symbolic uses—the poet may take the 'general A' and 'mould it to stand for b or even x'. MacNeice, like other poets, fully exploited this plastic quality of symbols ('God's own gift to the poet'), but he characteristically used his freedom in a disciplined way. He very rarely moulded the general A 'to stand for . . . x', for a correspondence of private, magical, esoteric significance. On the contrary, he contrived a wide range of symbolic material drawn from common experience to meet the needs of the few basic and recurrent metaphysical themes with which he was preoccupied. Thus, such characteristic items as door and window, mirror, prism, clock, cradle, coffin, cage, aquarium consistently represent much the same metaphysical principles, although some may lend themselves more readily than others to a wider range of correspondence. This is so even where they are merged, or extended to embrace

---

[1] 'My favourite reading at about the age of eight was the Book of Revelation but, long before that, biblical imagery had been engrained in me' ('E.I.', p. 129). Cf., too, his letter from Oxford (p. 87), where he regretted missing his 'daily portion' of Bible reading.

[2] The subtitle of *The Enchafèd Flood*, by W. H. Auden, New York, 1950.

[3] In his essay on Poetry in *The Arts Today*, he suggested that there was a future for historical writing of a symbolic kind, and advised the writer who wished his 'historicised symbols to be taken seriously' to 'deploy them in verse': pp. 64–5.

related items—as the cage, for example, so common in the later poems, may illustrate both limitation and reflected reality, or the clock may be varied as hour-glass, calendar, sundial, and the mirror as any object with a polished surface. They tend to be otherwise varied only to meet the structural, especially dramatic, needs of the particular context.

The symbolic items regularly used by MacNeice are often familiar properties which other writers have used, or symbolic emblems in common use. Examples include playing cards (for sequences either contrived by skill or occurring adventitiously), games (for activity permitting free exercise of skill within fixed and understood limitations), the Old Masters (for value permanently enduring), the museum or learned library (for still life, inverted values, the illusion of control), refugees (for bewildered loss of home or identity).

Other symbolic instances of the same kind are the friends of *Autumn Sequel* (and, in a less developed form, of the catalogue in 'Last Will and Testament'); the representative figures, especially his father, of 'The Kingdom'; the makers of all times—all who, in MacNeice's personal mythology, represent the creation and transmission of value. Here, too, might be included that symbolic figure of such representative importance for MacNeice, the loved woman, whose life is instinct shaped in a dynamic pattern of value; and even MacNeice himself, so often projected in different guises as a representative figure of his time. The contemporary myth of the common man seems to make its appearance in the symbolic figures of Tom, Dick, and Harry (or Jack and Jill, or Tom and Tessy). Behind his symbolic presentation of these last figures is the metaphysical concept of the individual as both particular and universal. Thus, Jack and Jill are explicitly presumed in 'Letter from India' to be 'sacred', their lives presented in Heraclitean imagery that is also congruous with the symbolic landscape of the poem as sacred rivers, whose courses run 'through land's diversity' before merging in the sea; the conceptual figure of 'Tom-Dick-and-Harry' breaks down in 'The Stygian Banks' to 'Tom and Dick and Harry/Clapping backs in the sunshine'; Tom and Tessy, in 'The Cromlech', are

> At this point in a given year
> With all this hour's accessories,
> A given glory. . . .

being 'as sure intact a fact' as the ancient pagan symbol in the clover field behind them.[1]

MacNeice found the image of the playing card particularly useful and adaptable. The trump card in 'A Toast', which the rational will keeps behind the brain 'Till instinct flicks it out again', illustrates the harmonious balance of instinct, reason, and will that successfully combats unknown fate. The 'Shuffle of cards behind the brain' in 'When We Were Children' signifies the necessary subjective readjustment to regain contact with reality. In 'The National Gallery' the image of the swift shuffle ('the quickness of the heart deceives the eye,/Reshuffling the themes') illustrates the skill of the artist in presenting the various conditions of being ('fugues and subterfuges of being') suggested to him in different moments of insight. In all these instances the individual manipulates the cards, as player or dealer, showing skill in either capacity. In others, the cards are either dealt for him, or, if he is dealing, shuffling or cutting, or simply turning up the cards, the process is mechanical. For example, in 'Aftermath' the reader/player is invited to 'Shuffle and cut', but the play is dull, for the joker has been withdrawn from the pack, which is now 'a pack of dog's-eared chances', where, even if the cards may turn up in chance sequences, each has only its face value ('the cards are what they say/And none is wild'): life has assumed its uninteresting post-war pattern.[2] The individual cards in the pack in 'The Stygian Banks', however, are significant for the very reason that they have their face value; and, even if there are cards missing in the sequence

---

[1] Respectively: *C.P.D.*, pp. 270, 260, and 224. Behind all of these, as behind his symbolic presentation of the day that keeps 'Its time, its place, its glory' (*C.P.D.*, p. 310) is probably, again, Bradley's study of the nature of particular and universal judgements, and specifically pp. 59 ff. of *The Principles of Logic*, where he examines 'a curious illusion, now widely spread, on the subject of proper names'. See also pp. 96-8, 108.

[2] In 'E.I.' (p. 132) he includes the last-quoted lines among those of which he is 'especially proud' in his last book, because of the structural economy of the central image and the verbal wit, 'the *twist* of an ordinary phrase, the apparently flat statement with a double meaning'. Mr. G. S. Fraser discusses this further on p. 184 of *Vision and Rhetoric*, explaining that a 'card in a gambling game that can become any other card is called "wild" ', and that the joker is often used in this way.

dealt, we may be confident that they do all exist somewhere in the pack, each itself alone, but also a necessary one in a meaningful sequence:

> No more fusing them than a pack of cards is fused
> Yet the Jack comes next to the Queen. Though when they are dealt
> You will often fail of the sequence; only you know
> That there were such cards in the pack. . . .[1]

The image is used in much the same way in *Autumn Sequel*, where the theme of individual value and its survival is stressed: 'Queen and Ace/Survive, whoever deals, as Ace and Queen.'[2] In 'Country Week-End', where he remembers the 'sniggering faces' that 'Froze in surprise and fear as the cards/Kept turning up and the rain kept falling', the image represents the inevitability of fate. This is further emphasized by the dismally falling rain— the fall of rain, like all movements of water, representing either the flux, in a dismal downpour, or the permanence, in dynamic movement. It is, too, congruous with the mood that prevails in many of the poems of *Solstices*.

Within such groups as birds and beasts and fish, flowers and trees, which he used so extensively, there is the same use of recurrent symbols with more or less consistent metaphysical correspondences, although here the symbols obviously lend themselves to a wider range and variety of suggestion. The untamable black panther, for example, represents consistently 'the brute Other', as MacNeice explains in *Modern Poetry*.[3] In both the early 'Coal and Fire' and the later 'Homage to Clichés' it is equated with the granite god of the menacing absolute—the sphinx in the former and Rameses in the latter; while in both 'Coal and Fire' and the late 'The Pale Panther' it is also equated with the Heraclitean symbols of fire, in the former, and sun in the latter. The differences in mood, however, are extreme. In 'Coal and Fire'[4] there is no fear, but rather delighted identity. The panther is out of her trap, as black coal blazing:

> Here no golden mean is, here no damned middle:
> All is purity of extremes. . . .

[1] *C.P.D.*, p. 259.   [2] *C.P.D.*, p. 342 (*A.S.*, III).
[3] Op. cit., p. 112.   [4] *B.F.*, pp. 45–7.

She is a 'coal-black sphinx' who 'knows everything'—and
one day he might ask: 'What answer to your riddle?' In the
two later poems there is only the dread of the absolute, with the
answer to the riddle implied in 'The Pale Panther', where
the panther, now apparently representing the pale instrument of
death to the present cycle of creation, makes the spring that it
was crouching to make in 'Homage to Clichés'.

Similarly, the seal regularly represents the principle of instinctive accommodation to a natural environment. The horse,
as a more common feature of experience, is used with more varied
metaphysical implications, especially in conjunction with water
imagery. In the early 'River in Spate', horses are merged throughout with the water as undertakers' horses jangling their bells and
harness in the waves of phenomenal experience, in which the
corpses and coffins roll and tumble. At one point the horse image
is even fused with the panther:

And helter-skelter the coffins come and the drums beat and the waters
flow
And the panther horses lift their hooves and paw and shift and draw
the bier . . .

The absolute thus draws the corpse of the relative down the
river of phenomenal experience. Throughout the later 'London
Rain' the horses are fused with the wildly falling rain, and as

. . . . . . violent
Horses black as coal—
The randy mares of fancy,
The stallions of the soul. . .

are identified with his wild wish to reject all moral sanctions. At
the end of the third movement of 'Our Sister Water', in the mood
of exaltation of a psalm of David, he prays that all the 'white and
randy horses' should become Pegasuses.[1] The rebellious mood that
he explicitly rejected in the latter part of 'London Rain' returns

[1] C.P.D., p. 303. The white and the black horses seem to represent phenomenal experience, flux, and plurality, in their creative, harmonious, and pleasurable, and in their
destructive and painful aspects.

in the later 'Dreams in Middle Age', with its despairing invocation of 'the black horses, spluttering fire' to help him revive his
'dying values'. Thus the symbol is used dramatically to express
the value theme with which he was preoccupied at the time. In
the following poem in *Visitations*, 'Sailing Orders', however, the
image of the white horses and white waves correlates with the
calmer theme of accommodation to the flux by way of the beliefs
that 'are still to make'. In the dedicatory poem to the last collection the horse is used as one of the transportation symbols, in the
mood of 'Dreams in Middle Age', as the bucking nightmare that
is to carry him along the cinder path of bleak experience to the
'green improbable fields' of another visitation; while it is again,
in the linked parallel movements of 'Birthright', the symbol,
along with the sun, of his movement through life.[1]

Flowers regularly represent evasion of the habits and routine
pattern, as in 'Hidden Ice' and 'The Suicide'. They also frequently
express the connected theme of visitation, delighted discovery,
as in 'Selva Oscura', where the delight is the keener as the bewildered subject, lost and stumbling in the dark wood, suddenly
becomes a universal once more:

> . . . finding bluebells bathe my feet,
> Know that the world, though more, is also I.

The same bluebells are also used in the poem of that title, rather
in the way of the sand or snow symbols, as giving an unreal
unity, as an abstract universal:

> . . . so here the bluebells flow
> Athwart the undergrowth, a merger of blue snow.

Boyce's well-ordered flowers in *Autumn Sequel* represent nothing
less than the Greek scholar's ideal of beauty and truth, harmonious
and patterned experience:

---

[1] In 'Birthright' there is again the fusion, for dramatic economy, of image and verbal
wit. The horse is also a 'gift horse', which looked *him* in the mouth. As the given was, for
MacNeice, the real, his despair could hardly have been more concisely evoked. The
cinder path, besides having its obvious general symbolic significance, had particular
significance for MacNeice as a place of danger and especial taboo in Carrickfergus.
It was here that drunks might be encountered at any hour. (E.N.)

KA

> . . . . . he brings
> Me out to show me his garden with its straight
> Borders and close-napped lawns and apple trees
> And specially printed blooms which he can annotate
>
> As well as his Greek texts; what the eye no longer sees,
> As the twilight catches us out, some other sense
> Divines—the huge chrysanthemums floating at their ease
>
> Regardless of their stalks, and the optative tense
> Of bulbs in beds that Boyce with his usual care and skill
> Has made for their winter sleep. . . .[1]

This pattern is to be contrasted with the different, unmeaning, non-optative pattern of the flower-beds in the 'urban enclave' townscapes of *Solstices*, or the even less optative tulip beds of 'Another Cold May', where, in vain, 'The tulips tug at their roots. . . .'[2] The bulbs that Boyce beds down with care and skill presuppose, on the other hand, the spring resurrection that MacNeice so often uses asphodel, jonquil, or daffodil to symbolize. And the absence of natural renewal in the artificial tulip beds becomes the active, deadly menace of the massed artificial blooms of 'Flower Show', without even roots to tug at; they are 'too many, too unreal', and if 'their aims are one', it is 'the controlled/Aim of a firing party'.

The wood is very frequently Dante's *selva oscura*. In this sense it is generally used in the same way as the equally recurrent maze of the minotaur. It is also equated with the deadly obelisk symbols in the third movement of 'Day of Renewal', where individual possessions seem 'small things lost in a vast/Forest of marble obelisks'. Similarly, in 'Postscript to Iceland', his library is a 'forest of dead words' in 'a land of stone', where he longs to hunt 'the living birds', 'the gulls who weave a free/Quilt of rhythm on the sea'. The wood may also represent a place of escape and re-generation, as it is explicitly for himself, though not for his father,

---

[1] *C.P.D.*, p. 382 (*A.S.*, XIII). The central image of the vase of flowers in 'The Window' represents the same principle of the creative form and pattern imposed by the artist.

[2] In his Oxford paper 'The Policeman' (see p. 88) he said: 'No one knows what the soul is like who has not seen a flower drunken, tousled, flushed and swaying, tugging and swearing at its stalk and trying to break away and failing.' See also *S.A.F.*, p. 274.

in 'Woods'; or it may represent both slinking evasion, and in-
advertent acceptance, of the task of communicating, as in the
two-way movement of the image in 'Conversation'.

The tree is very often the Tree of Knowledge, either with the
blossom still bright, as in 'Apple Blossom'; or with the noose of
guilt and shame dangling from it, as in 'The Tree of Guilt'; or
as one of the 'Bleak trees' in 'Sunday in the Park' that 'whisper
ironies', being beyond good and evil: 'The Tree/Forgets both
good and evil in irony.'[1] Most commonly in the later poems it is
presented as the Tree that has to be lived with, now that its fruit
has been eaten, so that we may let our poison be our cure;
although in 'Jungle Clearance Ceylon' the 'bleached/Skeleton
trees' and the bare branches of 'the bonewhite trees' starkly
dramatize the effects of the poison.[2] In 'The Truisms' the 'tall
tree' that 'sprouted from his father's grave' is a resurrection symbol as moving as the daffodils in 'The Kingdom'. The glades that
often open out in his woods represent the place and moment of
necessary illumination, as in the parting of the trees in 'Vistas',
when

> The creature found itself in a roadless
> Forest where nothing stretched before
> Its lack of limbs but lack of hope. . . .

The trees of the wood also represent unity in plurality, continuing
tradition, abiding value:

> And every tree is a tree of branches
> And every wood is a wood of trees growing
> And what has been contributes to what is . . .

even if the unity and the way are not clear:

> . . . the wood of our desires
> Consists of single yet entangled trees
> Which maybe form a wood the world requires

---

[1] The fusion of traditional and non-traditional symbols is remarkable in 'Idle Talk',
where the central image of the tree, developed in the manner of Keats's tree putting out
its leaves, or the tree in 'To Hedli', is superimposed on that of the radio transmitter.

[2] It is noteworthy how many of the poems of *Sol.*, in particular, contain the Tree not
only as a symbolic image, but also as the main structural feature.

> But yet a wood which none distinctly sees
> Or fully finds his way in. . . .[1]

Finally, in 'Tree Party' every tree is emblematic of one or another of MacNeice's metaphysical preoccupations.

Symbolic bird images are used, perhaps, more often than any others in this group of natural creation. The bird is regularly the emblem of free movement, weaving its own pattern, finding its way by marvellous instinct. The gull in the air, like the seal in the water, is instinct moving easily in its environment, even if there are poems of recantation, such as 'Explorations', where

> The swallows drawn collectively to their magnet,
> . . . .
> . . . . are merely patterns
> To wonder at—and forget . . .;

for, as we noted in another context,

> . . . their imputed purpose
> Is a foregone design—
> And ours is not. . . .[2]

The same ambivalence appears in the 'urban enclave' poems, where the hissing 'father and mother goose', the courting pigeons and the arrowheading ducks of 'The Lake in the Park' insult the 'small clerk/Who thinks no one will ever love him', although in 'Sunday in the Park' the 'Carolina duck and Canada goose' that 'forget/Their world across the water' are as lost as everyone and everything else.[3] The pigeon in many poems represents the survival of instinctive values in the town: 'And now the woodpigeon starts again denying/The values of the town...'.[4] In 'Time for a Smoke' it is contrasted with the world of learning, over which it contemptuously exults in 'October in Bloomsbury': 'a pigeon scores an outer/On a scholarly collar ...'.[5] The pigeon is

---

[1] Respectively: *C.P.D.*, p. 144 (*A.J.*, XXI), and *C.P.D.*, p. 439 (*A.S.*, XXVI).

[2] The connection between free flight and pattern is concisely emphasized in the dramatic juxtaposition of 'sonnets and birds' in 'The Sunlight on the Garden'. See below, p. 174.

[3] Again, it is notable how extensively the bird symbolic image is used in *Sol.* (and in *Visit.*).

[4] *C.P.D.*, p. 110 (*A.J.*, V).

[5] The contempt is more bleakly expressed by the pelican on the bleached trees of 'Jungle Clearance Ceylon'.

used, too, like dove and raven, as a communication symbol (in 'The Window', for example, all three are used), or, as in *Autumn Sequel*, as the symbol of both communication and 'blithe annunciation'.[1] In other poems it is simply the visitation of the Holy Ghost as 'The grey dove of the future still descending'.[2] Similarly, in 'The Return', the birds that 'Come back throwing shadows on our patience' are the tokens of the unseen presence, as are the swallow flitting through the woodsmoke in the first of the 'Dark Age Glosses', the 'piping birds' of 'Vistas', or the birds of 'Visitations, I' 'flying/Beyond the ridge to lands unknown'.[3] The lark song of 'Good Dream', like the dawn song of 'All Over Again', represents the calm ecstasy of unity with being.[4] The voice of the Parrot, Pretty Poll, that utters its litany of doubt, 'I told you so', throughout *Autumn Sequel*, is a more factitious version of the Petrine cock, which is normally used with much more dramatic power, as in 'Charon'. The Parrot replaces the Weathercock, with neat irony, in *Autumn Sequel*;[5] while this symbolic role of recording the movement of the winds of time was taken in earlier poems by rooks and gulls.[6] The cooped hens of 'Greyness is All', like the battery hens of 'After the Crash', belong to the late symbolic group of caged and perverted natural creation, while the twittering emblem of the caged budgerigar is one of MacNeice's most bitterly ironic and concise later commentaries on his time.[7]

MacNeice's symbolic images from elemental sources and his 'stock mystical symbols' show the same regular and repetitive pattern of connotation, with some lending themselves to a wider

---

[1] *C.P.D.*, p. 358 (*A.S.*, VII).   [2] 'Visitations, VI'.

[3] They symbolize the same manifestation in the more hieratic form of the toast to 'The here and there and nowhere birds' in 'A Toast'.

[4] The nesting birds and the dawn song are integral parts of their emblematic seascape.

[5] *C.P.D.*, p. 379. In 'Barcelona in Wartime', the first poem of 'Entered in the Minutes', the 'crazy laughter' like that of the dead that 'shivered the sunlight' obviously suggests the lunacy of the Spanish Civil War. This is even more obvious in his description of the episode in *S.A.F.*, p. 186.

[6] A striking example is the image-question of 'The Closing Album, V': 'And why should the rooks be blown upon the evening/Like burnt paper in a chimney?' The image is used, with others, to indicate his astonishment at the apparent continuation of the regular pattern of phenomenal experience in time/space despite the monstrous outbreak of war.

[7] 'Budgie'.

range of more particular significance. Again, inevitably, we noted many of these correspondences in earlier chapters. The more unvarying of these symbols are the Heraclitean fire and sun, the moon that generally signifies the remote controlling principle in the universe, the winds of dynamic, transcendent cosmic influence, the sand, desert, and snow images of arid or artificial oneness obliterating identity, the one universal and infinite blue of pure Being in sea or sky (more often the latter). It is, naturally perhaps, within the group of water images that the correspondences vary most. These, whether of sea or river, or any movement or state of water, including the frozen, static, are also probably the images of most frequent occurrence in MacNeice's poetry. There may well be particular reasons for this, over and above the general awareness of this commonest of natural phenomena. He himself stressed his earliest intimate associations with the sea,[1] and noted the fascination exerted upon him at Oxford by 'the sluices of Mesopotamia'[2] at the very time of his concentrated studies in metaphysics; while water itself, by its essential nature, physical and metaphysical, obviously accommodated itself readily to many of MacNeice's most recurrent themes. It is 'heart's, world's best' in 'Our Sister Water', the 'dear Sor Acqua' of Saint Francis, 'Useful and humble and precious and chaste', accommodating itself perfectly to the form most appropriate to its essence. In the same poem 'Thales was right', and 'Keats was right', to insist on the primacy of water.[3]

Both sea and river are obvious emblems for the main Heraclitean themes of the One and the Many and constant flux, but MacNeice's variations are considerable, some of them traditional and some more personal. In his discussion of the symbolic significance of the sea in *Varieties of Parable* he calls it 'an enormous symbol of escape and freedom', signifying 'almost a return to prelapsarian purity', and stresses the modern *dialectical* (MacNeice's italics) attitude to the sea as 'the Alpha of existence, the symbol of potentiality', while it 'also remains what the ancients

---

[1] *S.A.F.*, passim.; 'C.M.'   [2] 'Twenty-One', p. 236.
[3] *C.P.D.*, p. 300. The Keats conundrum, 'Whose name was writ in . . . Keats was right', alludes to Lord Houghton's epitaph (*Life of Keats*, II, p. 91).

thought it, the first and last symbol of primeval chaos, of the indefatigable destroyer', corresponding to the figure of Shiva in Hindu mythology.[1] Thus the sea is 'an enormous symbol of escape and freedom', or more simply, perhaps, of daring experience, in such poems as 'The North Sea', 'Sailing Orders' and 'Thalassa'; while it is further, in 'The North Sea', a symbol of the continuous, universal presence of phenomenal time/space, the unity of all experience, the permanence of all value. It is destroyer and primeval chaos in 'Mahabalipuram', and also in 'Homage to Wren', where it is fused with the fire image; in 'Vistas' it is both the primeval chaos out of which life arose and the preserver of the 'Glinting fish' that manifest the real. Its tides are controlled by the moon to make a rhythmic pattern, a pattern that contrasts in 'House on a Cliff' with the disturbed pattern imposed on the cooling blood of the

> . . . purposeful man who talks at cross
> Purposes, to himself, in a broken sleep.[2]

The same moon, like the sun, glints on individual waves to indicate the real manifest in the actual, as in the 'Shining and slicing edge that reflects the sun', in 'All Over Again', or 'a wave/ Touched to steel by the moon twists a gimlet in memory', in 'Round the Corner'. Similarly, in 'Train to Dublin', the image of the 'real' face glinting with joy in cunning is superimposed upon the image of the 'toppling wave':

> And I give you the faces, not the permanent masks,
> But the faces balanced in the toppling wave—
> His glint of joy in cunning as the farmer asks
> Twenty per cent too much. . . .

And in both 'Train to Dublin' and 'Round the Corner' the shell is evidence of the eternal presence of the unseen real, in the former fused with the bell as a menacing and monotonous absolute ('the mere/Reiteration of integers . . . the monotony of fear'), in the latter 'union in solitude' with value and purpose in the

---

[1] Op. cit., p. 84. The quotation 'the Alpha . . . potentiality' is from W. H. Auden's *The Enchafèd Flood.*

[2] In 'The Island' (*C.P.D.*, p. 305), the image of 'Tides invading the tideless' neatly indicates his theme of experience in phenomenal time/space set against absolute experience.

universe. This potentiality of the sea is more dogmatically asserted in the last emblem of 'Nature Notes', where the sea is 'capable/At any time at all of proclaiming eternity', being an element at once 'ruthless' and 'subtle'.

It is the last-mentioned qualities of water that MacNeice illustrates in many of his various water images—its Protean ability to assume any form, and, in so doing, to proclaim aspects of the eternal manifest in time/space. The basic Heraclitean river image appears, as we have noted, in many variants: waterfall; bubbles beneath, and froth upon, the surface; the flow controlled as fountain, tap, sluice, weir, or drain. The mood, which may be an expression of metaphysical outlook, or a simpler expression of pathetic fallacy, may vary considerably with the same image. Bubbles may represent individual identity precariously maintained, identity merged in the dance of bubbles and finally lost, identity without value, or even indestructible identity in the permanent flux.[1] The waters of the weir may represent wild excitement, or order arising out of confusion, or the dead residue of experience.[2] And images merge readily, the bubbles from drowning mouths in the waves becoming, in 'Radio', the 'Bubbles upon bubbles/Out of the unknown', bubbles in sound waves—in each case an image of individual identity and communication;[3] or the image from film-editing, in Canto III of *Autumn Sequel*, fusing with the weir image to indicate the impossibility of arranging and perpetuating experience:

> . . . the silences of ice
> And solitudes of height washed out in flux,
> A weir of whirling celluloid.[4]

The images of water as rain that recur so frequently, first and last, seem to indicate, in MacNeice's more individual dialectic, the flow of phenomenal experience in a less predetermined pattern —flux as an abstract rather than a concrete. Hence the rain lashing

[1] Cf. 'The sly weir/Of sunset drags them down to merge together/Their separate bubbles. . . .' (*C.P.D.*, p. 353, *A.S.*, VI); 'The bubbles in the football pools/Went flat. . . .' ('Hold-Up'); 'the bubbles rise/From someone drowned in a sack an age ago' ('Constant').

[2] Cf. 'a mad weir of tigerish waters' ('Entirely'); 'And the water combed out/Over the weir' ('Galway', part IV of 'The Closing Album').

[3] *C.P.R.H.* p. 312 ('Octets', IV).   [4] *C.P.D.*, p. 341.

the car as it tries to hold the road in 'The Wiper', the cleansing rain of 'Precursors', the obliterating wash of rain in Canto XVII of *Autumn Sequel*, the revivifying fall of rain in 'Country Week-End', the rain falling quietly over the ruins of Clonmacnois,[1] or the rain that 'comes pimpling/The paving stones with white' in Section VII of *Autumn Journal* as the 'national conscience' after Munich came 'creeping,/Seeping through the night'. (Pathetic fallacy seems to operate strongly in the last two images.) There may also be a strong underlying Heraclitean significance in certain of the rain images as the elemental link between sea and sky, and between both and earth, as in the third movement of 'Donegal Triptych':

> . . . let the rain keep sifting
> Into the earth while our minds become, like the earth, a sieve,
>
> A halfway house between sky and sea. . . .

Another way in which MacNeice used his freedom to mould the plastic material of symbols was in his transferences, fusions or juxtapositions, or in the occasional dramatic shifts in correspondence. Some of these, such as the 'panther horses' of 'River in Spate', we have already noted. The cage, for example, he readily transformed into his widely used aquarium symbol; the traditional river and mountain into particular symbolic landscapes; the staring eyes of the Gorgon into his own symbol of dread or into the wider range of petrifaction images. Many of the points of interconnection among these groups were exploited by MacNeice in imaginative fusions or cross-fades. For instance, the eyes that dominate the later part of the actual and symbolic train journey of the last canto of *Autumn Sequel* are interfused with the eyes that haunted Theseus; and the 'Long lanes of rock' by which Theseus 'twisted and descended/To find his level and untwist his fate' are superimposed on the corridors of the empty train along which MacNeice went to untwist his own fate. This fusion continues the previous one, in which the maze and Ariadne's ball of wool are identified with the communication cord of the train and the smoke from the engine:

[1] 'A huddle of tombs and ruins of anonymous men/Above the Shannon dreaming in the quiet rain' (Part V of 'The Coming of War', *P.P.*, p. 37).

> And, slow or fast, no one can ever pull
> The communication cord; this train goes on,
> Unravelling its endless strand of wool
>
> Like Ariadne's ball which led the wan
> And doubtful Theseus through the empty maze.

The symbolic cross-fades of *Autumn Sequel*, which are perhaps too facile and frequent, may well derive, in part, from the governing metaphysical search of the poem to find unity and value in apparent diversity and waste. To take another example, he generally fuses that favourite symbol, the coffinlike cradle (for the end present in the beginning—itself a fusion), with the high wind of destiny—as in the late 'Off the Peg':

> . . . when the coffinlike cradle pitched on the breaking bough
> Reveals once more some fiend or avatar. . . .

In Canto IX of *Autumn Sequel*, however, he fuses this symbol, in an excess of facility, with the symbols of London, Blake, and Bunyan (for courage, prophetic insight and value enduring), siren and high explosive (for menace and destruction), the old wives' tale of the prince transformed to a toad who found his princess in the end (miraculous visitation, the questing hero):

> . . . . . . William Blake
> And Bunyan tenant Bonehill Fields where high
> Explosive rocked them lately. Rocked them asleep? Awake?
>
> Coffins and cradles airwise. Rockabye,
> Mein Prinzchen, little toad on the spinning top
> That weaves a siren note through the breaking sky
>
> And begins to tilt and stagger. . . .

Other fusions are often more simple and natural, such as those involving his favourite fires of pentecost.[1] Sometimes the fusions are visual paradoxes: for example, the ice and fire of

> A cone of ice enclosing liquid fire,
> Utter negation in a positive form. . . .[2]

Conversely, the symbols may be brought into frontal opposition, as the rock and sea of 'Mahabalipuram' ('and the waves assault

---

[1] See below, e.g., p. 143.   [2] 'Troll's Courtship'.

the temple,/Living granite against dead water') or the third movement of 'Areopagus': 'Their living rock was the death of sea.'[1]

The symbolic figures of Tom, Dick, and Harry, in the same way as those of Jack and Jill, Tom and Tessy, are fused with traditional symbolic imagery and the symbolic figure of his father, in the description of the worst of his dreams in Canto XXII of *Autumn Sequel*. Here, Tom, Dick, and Harry represent, 'peeping, dirty, red/In the face with shouting', the mob at the eternal crucifixion, presented in terms of that other MacNeice symbolic property, the funfair.[2] His father, approaching the rim of the amphitheatre where the holiday mob is enjoying the funfair-crucifixion, represents the traditional acceptance of the meaning of the crucifixion. Later, in 'The Blasphemies', he thinks aloud about his use of these symbols:

> Ten years later, in need of myth,
> He thought: I can use my childhood symbols
> Divorced from their context, Manger and Cross
> Could do very well for Tom Dick and Harry. . . .

The image of the bell is a striking example of a shift in correspondence, its symbolic equivalence altering, in some instances with dramatic abruptness, as his attitude to religious belief changed, or as the bell itself acquired a wider range of personal associations. Thus, in the very early 'Jack and the Beanstalk', there is no joy in the frozen kingdom of the ogre, where 'The cold wind rang the bells of ice', until the heroic Jack released the blackbirds who, at liberty once more, 'peal upon the rusted bells of joy'.[3] It is the chill bells of ice that peal most often in the early poems, where they connote the deadening Christian absolute. In the Oxford poem 'Laburnum' (May 1929), the 'cold bell' murders the 'little mockery bells at ankles/Jingling under the motley sun';[4] and in 'The Sunset Conceived as a Peal of Bells', the bells 'ring . . . up conqueringly' the death of the day and the

---

[1] The 'living rock' is the Areopagus of the title, the ancient judgement rock of Athens beneath which dwell the Furies.

[2] *C.P.D.*, p. 422. Cf. *S.A.F.*, p. 101, where he describes this nightmare.

[3] *Marlburian*, 29 March 1926.   [4] *O.P.* (*1929*), p. 26.

sun, the advance of night, while the 'blind belfry' is a place of gloom and evil, and the bell ropes are 'shadow boxers' who 'twist and sway,/Plunge and lunge on the tomb of day. . . .'[1] In 'Sunday Morning' the bells are 'skulls' mouths' emphasizing that there is no 'Escape from the weekday time'; in 'Homage to Clichés' the bell is the terrifying 'two-ton bell', the tenor bell that cannot be rung, the absolute; in 'Train to Dublin' it is equated with the shell, reiterating in his ear as it 'tolls and tolls, the monotony of fear'; and in 'The Sunlight on the Garden' the birds that defied

> . . . the church bells
> And every evil iron
> Siren and what it tells

were still compelled back to earth. In 'The Heated Minutes' the 'tiny hammers' of the cash register 'chime/The bells of good and ill'; while in the later 'Schizophrene' the church bells of the fourth stanza are described, in an extended frozen image, as 'disembodied', without belfry, ropes or ringers, expressing 'The claims of frozen Chaos . . .'. The tolling bell in the much later 'Half Truth from Cape Town' evokes early memories of religious violence in Belfast. In 'Entirely', the bell, again linked with the siren, represents the monotonous pattern of experience that defeats all attempts at evasion as it 'almost hourly . . . banishes the blue/Eyes of Love entirely'; and it has the same correspondence in 'Meeting Point', where, however, it is explicitly 'silent in the air/Holding its inverted poise', becoming instead

> Between the clang and clang a flower,
> A brazen calyx of no noise.[2]

Its 'under-sea ding-donging' in 'Nostalgia' is the voice that calls the lonely and homesick spirit to an unreal home.[3]

In 'Carol', however, the church bells ring pure joy throughout, blending their notes with other sacred symbols from the Bible

---

[1] B.F., pp. 52, 53.

[2] MacNeice's flowers, as we saw, frequently symbolize evasions of routine, moments out of weekday time, as here, and as MacNeice himself elucidated in connection with 'Hidden Ice' (M.P., p. 176).

[3] Cf. 'I wish one could either *live* in Ireland or *feel oneself* in England. It must be one of them ould antinomies' (Letter to E.R.D., 31 July 1945).

and church architecture, illustrating the explicit belief of the poem that 'man is a spirit/And symbols are his meat...'. Similarly, Owen's pure spirit of delight in Canto XXII of *Autumn Sequel* made him 'a walking belfry' as 'the sun/Strode through his lips and boomed in his steps'; and the bells ring joy in Canto XXV, their 'eight great bronze muzzles baying//The blurred moon', their 'bouncing ropes', equated with the hazards of the symbolic mountain, 'belaying/Our lives'. Finally, in the ecstatic expression of oneness with Being, in 'All Over Again', the 'outward rippling bell' unites him with all the other natural, sacred, elemental symbols manifesting the unity and joy of experience—the birds and their dawn song, the one universal blue of sea and sky, the pentecostal 'fires of the tongue', the 'Shining and slicing edge that reflects the sun . . .'.

Much of MacNeice's imagery is deeply affected by the mental climate of his times, which 'inevitably conditions our poems and the images within them'.[1] He had, from the first, a deep and characteristic love-hate attitude towards contemporary imagery. The 'tall gasworks' at Oxford were sharply resented in his villanelle 'Paradise Lost', as symbolic of the world that seemed to vitiate his destiny as an Apollonian poet. And the actual paddling by the gasworks, pleasurably anticipated in his letter in the early spring of 1927,[2] resulted in different feelings in the summer, when Graham Shepard and he 'used to paddle along the evil-smelling canal through the slums or up the Isis past the gas-drums'. Suddenly 'one May morning' they realized the symbolic significance of their surroundings. As they were 'watching a dragonfly among the cow-parsley and shards on the bank' a goods train crossed the bridge. They chanted the names on the waggons, and

This incantation of names at once became vastly symbolic—symbolic of an idle world of oily sunlit water and willows and willows' reflections and, mingled with the idleness, a sense of things worn out, scrap iron and refuse, the shadow of the gas-drum, this England. . . . The placid dotage of a great industrial country.[3]

As his eye was compelled to move from the 'dragonfly among the cow-parsley' he must have had a deep sense of a poetic destiny

[1] 'E.I.', p. 127.   [2] See above, p. 53.   [3] *S.A.F.*, p. 108.

vitiated; the moment may well have been the occasion of the villanelle.[1]

Yet his eye had already looked with holy, if ironic, pleasure on petrol pump and telegraph wires, and he had described both in sacramental terms in very early poems. In the strongly meta-physical 'Jack and the Beanstalk',[2] the beanstalk up which Jack climbs to kill the frost ogre is described, with only faint irony, in terms of a telegraph pole:

> The beanstalk burst the clouds and the white insulator doves
> Sat cooing softly. . . .

Before him and his generation lay 'an eternity of Auto-car . . . a heaven where all the petrol-pumps wear halos'.[3] And so, for 'B' in the 'Eclogue between the Motherless', the memory of the wife he has divorced is intimately fused with the image most appro-priate to her excitingly remote nature—lighted petrol pumps:

> I remember her mostly in the car, stopping by the white
> Moons of the petrol pumps, in a camelhair rug
> Comfortable, scented and alien.

The petrol pumps are there by right of property, a legitimate part of a remembered physical landscape, but they have also acquired the power of an image, an integral part of an emotional, and even a metaphysical, landscape.

Much of the contemporary imagery that MacNeice began to use increasingly shows this same movement of property towards image and incarnational instance. The same eye begins to look with equally critical and observant interest on both new and traditional sense-data, the same mind and emotions to respond to both kinds in the same creative manner. Thus, in 'June Thunder', the car and the cow-parsley are fused in one image of sensuous delight as he moves freely in time with time:

> The Junes were free and full, driving through tiny
> Roads, the mudguards brushing the cowparsley. . . .

---

[1] See p. 52. The poem appeared on 21 February 1929, in the first number of *Sir Galahad*.

[2] *Marlburian*, 29 March 1926.   [3] *Marlburian*, 23 June 1926.

The cars 'crashing the amber' in the 'Letter to Graham and Anna' are observed and used in the same way as the seals in the 'Last Will and Testament', written at the same time: 'the seal-swim crashes the island-narrows'.[1] In each case the image, as well as being a legitimate property of the landscape, is a neatly condensed metaphysical instance.

Again, in 'Breaking Webs' the motoring image, swift, dramatic and sensuous, is fused with a cerebral content to become a metaphysical instance:

> Over asphalt, tar, and gravel
> My racing model happily purrs,
> Each charted road I yet unravel
> Out of my mind's six cylinders.
>
> Shutters of light, green and red,
> Slide up and down. Like mingled cries,
> Wind and sunlight clip and wed
> Behind the canopy of my eyes.

The theme of the poem, more clearly indicated in the earlier title,[2] is the self-contained sensuous and cerebral universe isolating the individual from the ultimate realities, which MacNeice emphasizes in terms of the traditional imagery of the 'Shadow fingers of the trees' that

> Wistfully grope and grope again
> After the indoor mysteries.

The expression 'Each charted road', fusing the sensuous and the cerebral, has the same metaphysical and mystical undertones as the 'each charter'd street' of Blake's 'London', of which it is possibly an echo.

The same image recurs, but with very different autobiographical and metaphysical implications, almost ten years later, in 'Now that the Shapes of Mist':

> Or when wet roads at night reflect the clutching
> Importunate fingers of trees and windy shadows
> Lunge and flounce on the windscreen as I drive
> I am glad of the accident of being alive.

[1] *L.I.*, p. 237.   [2] 'Impermanent Creativeness' in *O.P.* (1928) and *B.F.*

The 'fingers of trees and windy shadows' may be 'clutching/ Importunate', but they are now an integral part of the dramatic entity, not wistfully groping 'After the indoor mysteries'. This is further emphasized in the sacramental image that follows:

> So many visitors whose Buddha-like palms are pressed
> Against the windowpanes where people take their rest.

In both poems, however, what matters is that MacNeice is using the motoring image in the same way, and for the same purpose, as the traditional images of reflection of, separation from, reality—shadow and window, the traditional window easily and naturally merging with the contemporary windscreen. He may still be tempted to indulge this imagery, in a mood of exhilaration, as mere décor, or, in a mood of depression, to indulge it morbidly as a poet whose poetic destiny has been vitiated. But his development towards poetic maturity may well be measured in terms of the extent to which the same eye and mind creatively record busy traffic crashing the amber; the seal-swim crashing the island-narrows; the cow-parsley and the goods-train—using both kinds of image with firm structural control, properly proportioned to the shape of the poem, corresponding to his theme.

As MacNeice begins to move more freely between property and image, he experiments with a widening range of contemporary sense-data to match the range and complexity of his themes. He finds it more and more natural to use motor-car, train, bus, taxi, ocean liner, radio transmitter, public telephone; and to juxtapose, without structural or thematic disproportion, images sacred and profane, traditional and non-traditional: as in the passing train and the holy stigmata of 'A Contact'; the miracle of the fish at Rimini and the humming telegraph wires, the effulgent headlights, of 'The Dowser'; the callbox and the tutelary spirits of 'October in Bloomsbury'; the London bus, the crowing cock and the ferryman of 'Charon'. If the metaphysical correspondence sometimes comes too pat or too repeatedly, he much more often startles with the freshness or aptness of a well-observed instance or a simple variation upon a much-used one: for example, 'the quick lock of a taxi' at the end of *Autumn Journal* as a symbol for the well-integrated individual who is 'more than a crowd', negotiating the crowd and crush with swift efficiency;[1] the clock that 'showed sixpence extra', in 'The Taxis', for the more complex themes of value, judgement, and the 'illusion of Persons'; the very simple image variations in 'Restaurant Car' on the train symbol, fusing the themes of communication and value, appearance and reality in time/space.

[1] *C.P.D.*, p. 152 (*A.J.*, XXIV).

6 Image and Structure

When MacNeice described many of his poems up to and including *The Earth Compels* as 'tourist', he went on to say that in his later poems he had been attempting a stricter kind of drama that largely depended upon structure. On analysis, he found that this structure was based on four things:

1) the selection of—or perhaps the being selected by—a single theme which itself is a strong symbol, 2) a rhythmical pattern which holds that theme together, 3) syntax (a more careful ordering of sentences, especially in relation to the verse pattern), and 4) a more structural use of imagery.[1]

Disregarding the second and third items for the moment, we might look more closely at the first and last.

An essential preliminary towards the achievement of this structural and symbolic unity was the development of the tendency we have already noted for property to merge in image and both to merge in symbol, the observant eye retaining its sharpness while the metaphysical mind perceives the correspondence. This movement was well described by Dr. T. R. Henn in his study of Yeats's symbolism, where, in distinguishing between the 'so-called archetypal symbols' and the more 'personal mythology' and its 'related symbolism', he considered that, in the latter, 'success will depend on a gradual building up of determinant points of meaning through the use of the symbols in varying contexts'.[2] The 'dominant' symbols begin to 'develop and fuse with the minor symbols', and 'As the work grows more mature, the symbols, without losing their processional character, become more closely associated in time. It is a natural step in the perception of unity. . . .'[3]

We have seen many instances of this developing fusion and unity, as more and more of MacNeice's minor symbols were fused with his older dominants in a unified pattern. This movement had developed such momentum by the time he was writing *Ten*

[1] 'E.I.', p. 130.
[2] *The Lonely Tower: Studies in the Poetry of W. B. Yeats*. London, 2nd, rev., ed. 1965, pp. 127, 128.
[3] Ibid., pp. 131, 139.

Burnt Offerings and *Autumn Sequel* that it seems to have been virtually impossible for him to observe an object without making a mental note on its correspondence, and the reader often longs, like Hetty, for 'a welcome piece of naturalism'. Thus, at the end of Canto X of *Autumn Sequel*, with its theme of 'Summer time ends and good riddance', he observes that

> . . . . The smoke
> Flies from the power house chimneys at half mast.

> Pepys would note this in his diary, perhaps with a joke,
> If he still kept a diary . . .[1]

MacNeice, too, is clearly taking note of a metaphysical correspondence. Again, at the beginning of Canto VIII, he has an acutely observed Thames vignette:

> . . . . . . her skies as yet not overblown,
> Her river, though brown and crumpled, with a bright
> Polish; the one small tug that plods upstream alone

> Trails a long strand of smoke which, black as night,
> Seems softer than fine wool. . . .

Immediately, however, the wool becomes part of his dominant Theseus and maze image, as he gathers the soft wool in his hand and begins to unravel it, moving on to the theme of value surviving. The forward movement of the poem as a poetic whole, in which the past is recalled, recorded and evaluated, depends very largely on this careful articulation of images. The patterned movement, however, from the very nature of the poem, tends to be relaxed and diffuse, however skilled the individual articulations may be.

In the second emblem of the late 'As in Their Time', on the other hand, the symbol of the cretinous god is used with perfect structural concision, centrally, fusing wit, image and symbolic suggestion:

[1] MacNeice who was (I have been frequently and reliably informed) an inveterate scribbler of such details on scraps of paper, has clearly made a similar note. Cf. his admiration in *M.P.* for Tennyson, 'the most concrete of the Victorians', who 'had an excellent eye and like Keats uses images to convey the look of objects—a distant waterfall is "like a downward smoke". Sometimes he goes further and approaches wit: "thousand wreaths of dangling water smoke/That like a broken purpose waste in air . . .".' (p. 99).

> Polyglot, albeit illiterate,
> He stood on a crumbling tower of Babel
> Cured of heredity, and though
> His idol had a brain of clay
> He could not read the cuneiform.

This is the direction followed by the structural movement in all the best lyrics of the collections after *Autumn Sequel*, but MacNeice was consciously aware before this of the kind of structure he was after. In *Experiences with Images* (1949), although it is rather the metaphysical correspondences of many of the images that he stresses, some of the poems he instances also illustrate a high level of structural integration: for example, 'Circus', with its image of the child whose face 'pops/Like ginger beer', and the rhetorical and cerebral images of 'Convoy'. These are obvious and pertinent examples, which illustrate basic metaphysical preoccupations of his that we have been examining. The properties of the scene in 'Circus', 'The child's face' and 'the air/Alive with bowlers', are articulated with the image, the popping bottle of ginger beer, into a neatly joined unity. The transference of images, upon which he placed such stress in *Modern Poetry*, is smoothly effected.

In 'Convoy' the images are, as MacNeice says, more rhetorical and cerebral.[1] In the first stanza, the proportions appear equal, with property, cerebral image, and rhetoric in equipoise. Property has a very square deal in the second verse. The balance, however, is basically upset in the last verse, where rhetoric predominates. This in itself need not have spoiled the poem, but here it does, largely because of the tone of the rhetoric. The jarring note of casual, homespun philosophizing in the opening phrase, 'This is a bit like us', is maintained in the prosy didacticism that follows, and the correspondence is needlessly explicit in the final words to the reader. Where the rhetoric is subdued, and blended in due proportion with property and image, the correspondence is suggested with deftness and tact, as in the second sentence of the first stanza:

[1] 'E.I.', p. 130.

> . . . No Euclid could have devised
> Neater means to a more essential end—
> Unless the chalk breaks off, the convoy is surprised.

The rhetorical reference to Euclid follows easily and naturally from the property/image fusion of the ships keeping their orderly lines 'Across the blackboard sea in sombre echelon', and is neatly and pointedly concluded in the rhetorical after-image: 'Unless the chalk breaks off, the convoy is surprised.' The image of the ships in terms of a blackboard diagram of Euclid is a variant of a recurring and generally metaphysical image of MacNeice's that suggests the dull monotony of a regular pattern imposed on the waves of flux.[1]

Property receives its fair due in the second stanza, with an unobtrusive suggestion of the metaphysical principle. The cranks going up and down and the signals clacking are properties he used frequently to suggest mechanistic ordering of the universe, and communication both with other individuals and with an unseen ordering mind. Image is appropriately blended with property in 'the smoke-trails tendril out' and 'The little whippet warships romp and scurry about'; while rhetoric enters with quiet effectiveness in the guise of property as

> All is under control and nobody need shout,
> We are steady as we go . . .

Thus he has, in the first two stanzas, presented, in dramatic and appropriately rhetorical form, one of his metaphysical preoccupations: life as a rationally devised, ordered system, precarious, but offering some hope of reaching a destination. Yet he wishes to emphasize one aspect of this principle with which he was particularly concerned at this time—the need for 'pragmatic/And ruthless attitudes'; and, in so doing, he upset the structural balance of his poem by using direct unassimilated rhetoric.

In the same context[2] MacNeice instances other poems, such as 'Snow', 'The Springboard', 'The Dowser' and 'Order to View',

---

[1] Cf. 'The ducks drew lines of white on the dull slate of the pool', in 'Eclogue between the Motherless'. It reappears, e.g., in *A.S.*, III (*C.P.D.*, p. 343), and 'The Lake in the Park'.
[2] 'E.I.', p. 131.

where the images 'attached to details, were usually details themselves', and 'could therefore be judged by their correspondence
to particular objects or events'. Here, however, he considers they
'carry the weight of dream or of too direct an experience' and so
'will require from the reader something more—or less—than
reason'. Thus, in 'Snow', where the experience is overwhelmingly
direct, the images 'are not voices off, they are bang centre stage'.
Here, the intricate fusion of rhetoric, property and image, which
was flawed in the final stage of 'Convoy', comes off in the rhetorical conclusion, which incorporates the three main property/
images of the poem: 'There is more than glass between the snow
and the huge roses.' The line is weighted with the quiet menace of
the implication that the reader must body out for himself—the
uniqueness, finality, and mystery of particulars that are both
'collateral and incompatible'. In 'Order to View', the experience
is equally direct, especially in the dramatic suddenness of the
last stanza. The structural integration is more loose than in 'Snow',
and, rather as in 'Circus', image is perhaps indulged excessively
as the poem grows:

> The shrubbery dripped, a crypt
> Of leafmould dreams. . . .
>
> .   .   .   .   .
>
> And beyond the sombre line
> Of limes a cavalcade
> Of clouds rose like a shout of
> Defiance. . . .

MacNeice does, however, deftly bring the soaring image of the
'cavalcade/Of clouds' back to earth and property by way of the
neighing horse:

> . . . Near at hand
> Somewhere in a loose-box
> A horse neighed
> And all the curtains flew out of
> The windows; the world was open.

As in 'Convoy', the simple properties of the windows, the upper
and lower winds, the 'tarnished/Arrow over an empty stable',

are favourite ones of MacNeice's, loaded with metaphysical suggestions. Unlike that of 'Convoy', and like that of 'Snow' (though perhaps less skilfully), the explicit rhetoric in the close of each of the last two stanzas, 'The world was closed . . . the world was open', rounds off a dramatic/descriptive unity with calm inevitability.

'Order to View' does call for a limited exercise of dream logic from the reader; but the other two poems, 'The Dowser' and 'The Springboard', call for considerably more. The very nature of a poem structured on dream logic enabled MacNeice to indulge his recurrent hope that he might eat his cake and have it.[1] It is obviously very difficult to make any valid property/image distinction in the first part of 'The Dowser', for example, where the inklings and adumbrations, all equally congruous within the dream logic terms of the visitation theme, prepare the way both structurally and thematically for the central dramatic image of the dowser himself. This, in its turn, wavers, merges with, and leaps with dramatic congruity into, the final blinding experience of revelation, the well now 'More of a tomb', a sudden 'geyser . . . of light' that 'erupted, sprayed/Rocketing over the sky azaleas and gladioli'.[2] The preparatory images of 'The Dowser' are not only related in terms of thematic congruity, their suggestions of a revelation at hand; they also 'cross-fade' (a favourite technical expression of MacNeice's) in terms of visual or allusive landscape. The unseen headlights 'beyond the rise in the road' form part of a landscape that easily includes the 'Humming wires', and even, with a stronger exercise of dream logic, the 'shadow of a passing bird'. Similarly, the 'whisper in the bones/Of strange weather on the way' moves naturally, not only into 'feel of a lost limb/ Cut off in another life', but also into the central image of the dowser, his 'rod bent double', assured of the vital unseen presence. The 'Trance on the tripod', and Saint Francis united with the unknown glory that drew the waves and fish to his feet, share

---

[1] Cf. 'To eat one's cake and have it? Perhaps/In the end we can . . .' (*C.P.D.*, p. 313).

[2] Cf. his presentation of the same theme, using a different but related set of images, in 'The Return', with its similar climax: 'The acclamation of earth's returning daughter,/ Jonquils out of hell, and after/Hell the imperative of joy, the dancing/Fusillade of sunlight on the water.'

the same sacramental mood, which is assumed again as the down-to-earth image of the dowser and the well becomes the biblical one of the tomb and the blinding light of resurrection, whether of Lazarus or Christ. Again, the 'shadow of a passing bird', with its traditional undertones of divination, fades easily, through similar undertones, into the 'Trance on the tripod'. The 'more of a tomb' suggests Lazarus or Christ and the Easter resurrection and 'imperative of joy', as the erupting geyser of light and flowers suggests both the Easter resurrection and Persephone. The 'Trance on the tripod' suggests in brief the mystery and sanctity of the Delphic communication with the godhead, as the episode from the life of Saint Francis may well contain for the reader an allusion to the wider background of miracle and sanctity from the *Fioretti*.[1]

'The Springboard', as increasingly in MacNeice's later poems, is constructed around one central image, abruptly and dramatically presented, taking the reader *in medias res* without preparatory 'build' (another favourite technical expression from the structure of the radio play). An equally strong exercise of dream logic is, however, called for. The theme of the poem seems to be the one that was beginning to preoccupy MacNeice at the time—value realized in activity based upon belief. The central image of the man 'crucified among the budding stars' does, however, as it is imaginatively developed, demand considerable agility in the reader in the disentangling of its associated details. The subject fuses in himself the daring trapezist or high-diver and the crucified Christ; the highly dramatized ritual sacrifice of the saviour of mankind, and the simple gesture of the ordinary man who commits himself to the way of faith:

> His friends would find in his death neither ransom nor reprieve
> But only a grain of faith—for what it was worth.
>
> . . . .
>
> One man wiping out his own original sin
> And, like ten million others, dying for the people.[2]

[1] The reference here is apparently to the episode at Rimini, in Chap. XL of the *Fioretti*. Cf. the 'Sharp and straight on the ear like stigmata' of 'A Contact'.

[2] This is a direct allusion to John 11:50: '. . . it is expedient for us, that one man should die for the people . . .'.

The fear of the 'I' of the poem, first identified with the fear of the 'he', is then identified with the unbelief of the 'he'; so that the personal remains strongly present in the impersonal, and Mac-Neice once again appears to be speaking of himself through the *dramatis persona*. In the 'we' of the last stanza, the identification is further widened, so that the impersonal 'he' includes the reader and his and MacNeice's generation, their original sin localized as the inhumanity of the air-raids against the wider historical background of a broken faith and the grinning face of denial—all of which is fused with the momentary act of faith and commitment in the last integrated and condensed image, so neatly balanced and made quietly explicit with rhetoric:

> And yet we know he knows what he must do.
> There above London where the gargoyles grin
> He will dive like a bomber past the broken steeple. . . .[1]

In the poems we have just been examining, both the property/images and the themes to which they correspond, while often familiar and repeated, or even obsessive, in the poetry and thinking of MacNeice, cannot be said to be private, although some may be 'sacred to him as a private individual'.[2] An image[3] such as the 'jonquils out of hell' of 'The Return', or the classical myth of Persephone, or the cockcrow much used by MacNeice, are part of our active mythological and religious symbolic awareness, all associated with resurrection, the jonquils and cockcrow more specifically with Easter. Easter was also, for MacNeice, as it probably is for many of his readers, a time of deeply mingled feelings of tragic gloom and joy. He had especially poignant associations with Good Friday and Easter Sunday: deep distress at his mother's illness, recollections of nightmare and dread at the crowing of the cock, reflected joy in his father's joy on Easter morning. Easter Day was a day of particular gladness in the Rectory. MacNeice recalled how his father 'would come into

---

[1] Cf. 'your past life a ruined church' in 'Thalassa'.   [2] See p. 122.

[3] Having drawn attention to MacNeice's distinction between 'image' and 'property', I feel it would be both pedantic and confusing to maintain the distinction hereafter. I have therefore reverted to the common term, 'image', with no distinction implied, except in a few contexts where it is again explicitly employed in contradistinction to 'property'.

breakfast on Easter Day beaming as though he had just received a legacy'.[1] On the other hand, it was on Good Friday that his mother had her operation, and, although he was only five, the association lingered strongly—connected in his memory, perhaps, with his last memory of her weeping in the garden. He also had deep feelings of guilt towards his mother, mainly because he felt he had been ungracious and disloyal in refusing a box of chocolates from her.[2] The cockcrow of guilt and betrayal is also the cockcrow of the resurrection, intimately connected in his memory with the nightmare hauntings of his childhood.[3]

The daffodils of the resurrection dominate two of his most moving poems, the seventh part of 'The Kingdom', on the death of his father, and 'Death of an Old Lady', on the death of his stepmother. To take another example from the same area of association, 'The Strand' deals, like 'The Dowser' and 'The Springboard', with the themes of value subsisting in one man's faith, and communication with the world of unseen values. The seascape of the poem is obviously not only an actual one, precisely localized with the mountainscape behind ('these contours of Slievemore/ Menaun and Croaghaun and the bogs between'), but also a symbolic one, whose correspondences do not fundamentally depend upon an awareness by the reader of the full meaning, for the poet, of the personal associations. The simple image of the wet sand, for instance, a central one in the poem, is used, in the manner of so many of his other very common reflection images, to mirror both an illusion and a reality. The illusion it mirrors is made quite clear in the first stanza: it 'imputes a lasting mood/To island truancies', the familiar illusion, which tantalized MacNeice, of the permanence of what passes.

The reality that is mirrored is much more complicated, being

---

[1] *S.A.F.*, p. 233.

[2] Ibid., p. 43, especially footnote by E.N. This memory was obsessive, and features dramatically in *O.G.*, pp. 44–5.

[3] He placed the blame for much of this (unfairly, in the opinion of E.N.) on Miss Craig, with her grim: 'Aye, you're here now but you don't know where you'll be when you wake up' (*S.A.F.*, p. 42). In *A.S.*, XVII, he quotes this again, and adds '. . . I lay/Fearing the night through till the cock should crow//To tell me that my fears were swept away/ And tomorrow had come again . . .' (*C.P.D.*, p. 399). Cf., too, the 'every cockcrow a miracle after the ogre's night' of 'The Stygian Banks' (*C.P.D.*, p. 258). (The henhouse was on the other side of the nursery wall at the Rectory.)

inextricably involved in the illusion, for the permanence of what passes may be no illusion. Even if the One, the sea, obliterates the Many, the 'bright reflections', these reflections will recur end-lessly, linked in the permanency that is bestowed upon them by the eternal principle whose brightness they reflect. The 'bright reflections' are, like 'the flange of steel in the turning belt of brine', in the category of the jigging or glinting manifestations of the real. The difficulty for MacNeice, as it was for F. H. Bradley, or, presumably, for anyone who looks for certainty in manifestations of the 'evasive universal',[1] is that we have ultimately to take the manifestation on trust. In this reflection image, how-ever, there is, for MacNeice, one added element of the deepest significance—the earlier 'bright reflection' was of his father; and, despite what we are told about his father in the poem, we are not told enough to know that behind the image lies twenty years of spiritual conflict, or to know that MacNeice is openly and honestly conceding that his father's reflected image may have been valid evidence of reflected reality, communication with the guid-ing principle in the universe.

The only hint we are given of this is in the line that immediately precedes his abrupt and moving introduction of his father:

> A square black figure whom the horizon understood—
> My father. . . . .

His father, through his faith in the Christian absolute, which his life and his permanent/impermanent reflection manifested, was at one with the obliterating One: the horizon understood him. This hint is enlarged in the 'responsibly compiled/Account books of a devout, precise routine'. His father could confidently present his account on judgement day, and so was not haunted by the same fears as MacNeice and so many of his generation. Moreover, he achieved what was, for MacNeice, perhaps the most elusive ideal of all: integration within his individual self of the particular and the universal, for he 'Kept something in him solitary and wild'.

MacNeice is thus working in this poem within a highly

---

[1] 'Departure Platform', *L.D.*, p. 20. See above, p. 102.

complex area of spiritual autobiography and metaphysical speculation, but he so clarifies this with his structure of simple image and comment that the reader is not baffled by awareness of these complexities. At the same time, the reader must be in little doubt that the images in the poem are sacred ones.

It is the same in his late poem 'The Truisms', where he again deals with the theme of belief. Here, the imagery is again of the very simplest, although its integration into a dramatic and symbolic unity demands the exercise of dream logic: the coffin-shaped play-box of truisms on the mantelpiece, the coffin 'his father skulked inside', the truisms become birds that 'flew and perched on his shoulders', the 'tall tree' that 'sprouted from his father's grave'. The correspondence between imagery and theme is clear, and even if the element of spiritual autobiography and personal association appears to be densely present the reader has no cause to feel confused or antagonized by his awareness of these deeper layers. MacNeice, although a highly allusive poet, does not normally use personal (or general) allusion to complicate the poem, but rather to add layers of significance that give structural depth and richness, even where they are only partly visible, or wholly taken on trust.[1]

It is easy for the reader, in the excitement and novelty of the episodes in a long poem, to lose sight of the 'single theme'; and even easier for him to forget that the poet may be treating this theme in such a way that it 'itself is a strong symbol'.[2] In *Autumn Journal* and *Autumn Sequel*, for instance, where the theme is the recollection of the poet's personal past and the search for pattern and value in that past, much of the power and interest of the theme lies in the fact that it is viewed and interpreted in the symbolic terms of its reference to the general past, present, and future, their evolving pattern and residual value. The microcosm becomes a symbol for the macrocosm, and *vice versa*. The events recollected, the visual properties of the poem, regularly have a deeper and wider significance as universals; property easily

---

[1] Cf. his remark in *M.P.* (p. 90) that 'the famous obscurity of modern poets is largely due to their use of imagery'.

[2] 'E.I.', p. 130. See above, p. 148.

attracts to itself image, symbol, sacramental instance. Moreover, as the theme is the metaphysical search for the real principle made manifest as the recurrent strands in a patterned condition of being, it is obviously desirable thematically, as well as structurally, to pattern the visual properties in a coherent system of reappearances and cross-references. The interdependence of form and content is absolute, an essential condition of the poem.

This is obviously less true of *Autumn Journal* than of *Autumn Sequel*, the sections of the former corresponding rather to the separate entries in a journal, whereas the cantos of the latter are concatenated in a much more self-conscious search for unity in diversity. Although there is a highly organized structure of image reappearances and cross-references *within individual sections* of *Autumn Journal*, there is very little attempt to extend this structural device to connect sections with one another. This does, however, illustrate clearly the congruity of structure and theme, for the main effect is to isolate days and episodes. This patterned use of images in *Autumn Journal* is easily exemplified in an interesting instance, 'the cock crowing in Barcelona', which, with its visual and verbal repetition, effectively rounds off Section XXIII, recalling him sharply from his moral and metaphysical speculations to the more precise contours of his earlier air-raid description:

> And the sirens cry in the dark morning
>
> .   .   .   .   .
>
> The cocks crow in Barcelona
> Where clocks are few to strike the hour. . . .

(It is possible that the 'spotlight roving round the scene', at the beginning of the next section, is a visual carry-over from this air-raid vignette.)

We have already seen instances of the same kind of structural movement within individual cantos of *Autumn Sequel*—for example, the vignette at the beginning of Canto VIII containing, by right of property, the 'one small tug', with its 'long strand of wool' that instantaneously becomes the ball of wool unwinding through his days and ways. It then reappears in various places until it makes a climactic appearance in Canto XXVI, merged both in the smoke from the funnel of the actual and emblematic train, which also becomes an 'endless strand of wool', and in the mythical

> ... Ariadne's ball which led the wan
> And doubtful Theseus through the empty maze.[1]

This linking is part of a wider system of developing inter-connections from canto to canto, which reaches its climax in the concluding cantos, XXV and XXVI. These are structurally analogous to the last section of the final movement of a symphony, where the thematic and episodic variations re-emerge to join in an integrated pattern, the Many as the symphonic One. Thus, the telegraph poles and the radio hook-up are a diversification of the smoke and wool image; the barbicans of the earlier cantos crumble once more; and once again the earlier 'Jack/Of Wrecks' has 'trumped and burst the dykes'.[2]

The articulation of the symbolic imagery in the last two cantos is a great deal more elaborate than this, but the structural principle is obvious. MacNeice's inspiration here seems as much Dionysian as Apollonian, and the extreme technical elaboration is the formal equivalent of the poet's mood and inspiration. He is ecstatically convinced that the nightmare of chaos, horror, and meaningless repetition are subordinate elements in a pattern characterized by order, delight, and meaning*ful* repetition. It is in fact, as Nietzsche keeps insisting in *The Birth of Tragedy* it should be, as if Dionysus had helped him to a vision he is deter-mined to express in terms of an ordered Apollonian dream-vision.

The structural interplay of images in *Ten Burnt Offerings* (as differing from the mere repetition of images within the same area of symbolic correspondence—water, flower, or sea images, for example) is contrived more in the manner of *Autumn Journal*. That is, there is considerable interplay within each of the ten individual poems, and a more limited interplay between poem and poem. There is, however, a resemblance to the structure of *Autumn Sequel* in that an analogy with musical composition

---

[1] C.P.D., p. 437. And so MacNeice obtains full value for his property/image, letting his contemporary property carry its double load.

[2] Respectively: C.P.D., pp. 351 and 433 (*A.S.*, V and XXV).

readily suggests itself—the quartet form of the poems in *Ten Burnt Offerings*.[1] In the birthday poem, 'Day of Renewal', for example, the image of either the birthday cake or the candles is deftly threaded into the pattern of all four movements, a thin thread, but vividly there and used in imaginative variations. It makes its first appearance with dramatic brevity: 'Candles increased, then vanished'; but the brief phrase is a kind of *leit-motiv* for the rest of the movement. It makes another unobtrusive entry early in the second movement, concealed rather than revealed in the swinging rhythms of nursery rhymes and Bow Bells: 'Eat your cake, have your cake, last time lucky. . .'. The candles then re-enter briefly as 'Five farthings for what? For turtles? Candles?' and then make their main entrance to dominate the last half of the movement in the sad intricacies of the 'dark cupboard' image, where 'Memories/ Flitter and champ'. The cake is eaten and the candles that gave a brief and illusory light are now mere

> .   .   .   stubs of candles
> Twisted, snuffed out, still in their holders,
> Relics of Christmas, birthday butts.

Almost inevitably the 'butt' leads to the rather flat metaphysical pun: 'Who put us here? The daily Why,/The Birthday But.' And the theme of the illusory candlelight is continued in the interplay with other guiding lights, the 'light at the top of the well' and 'The light up above us' that 'is one big candle./To light us to what?'[2] In the third movement, the cake image immediately follows the brutally ugly image of the sunlight that 'catches the spikes/On the boot that is raised to blind', on which it makes its own bitter commentary:

> .   .   .   So what is own?
> One's birthday is a day that people die on—
> Shorthand of wavering shadow on white icing
> Scribbled by tiny candles. . . .

The interplay of the light and darkness themes, woven around the image of the cake and unseen candles, is resumed again in the second stanza of the final movement:

[1] This may be indicated in the ambiguous title, 'Suite for Recorders'. (See p. 106.) He also called the poems 'experiments in dialectical structure'. (See p. 167.)

[2] The image of the 'light at the top of the well' is probably a recollection from his Oxford poem, 'From Down Here', *Sir Galahad*, no. 2, 4 May 1929. ('Lying in the bottom of a well I cannot make/Contact with you. . . .')

> A child inside me lights the beacons
> Which spell both victory and defeat,
> Candles that he cannot see
> Around a cake he dare not eat.

And the image makes its final quiet entry in the last stanza, in the rhetorical question-and-answer ('To eat one's cake and have it? Perhaps/In the end we can . . .') that both takes up again the phrase from the second movement and leads, by way of a ghost image of the candles, to the concluding sacramental image:

> .   .   .   when no one flame
> Shines less than all and through blown smoke
> There drifts a god who needs no name.

This last image is also, though with a vital transformation, a variation on the image earlier in the movement of all his years

> Blurred with blue smoke, charred by flame,
> Thrusting burnt offerings on a god
> Who cannot answer to his name.

(And both are probably recollections of the biblical image of the altar to the Unknown God, repeated in the second and third movements of 'Areopagus'.) Other quietly contrived image-links unite the movement and carry it forward, such as the 'pocket full of plumstones' of the second movement, ironically duplicating Whittington's 'pocket full of milestones', implying all the eaten birthday cakes, and re-entering as a gay phrase in the fourth movement: 'The plumstones blossom in my mind.'[1]

The same interplay occurs throughout this collection, the framework of the imagery forming a whole structure that carries the related themes of value subsisting in an ordered sequence of constant renewals; the apparently dead and done finding new life in surprising new manifestations; the eye of the anxious searcher occasionally seeing the pattern. The structure of the poems in *Ten Burnt Offerings*, at least in terms of the integration of images, seems to illustrate the work of a more tactful and less ostentatious craftsman than the one who shaped the theme of *Autumn Sequel*

---

[1] The last line of the first stanza.

into an organized whole. Nevertheless, whether the final impression is of tact or ostentation, it may well be that the exercise of skill in integrating such masses of material helped him a long way towards the firm and confident architectonics of the best of the late poems.

The same kind of skill was marked in the long poems of the late 1940s, such as 'The Stygian Banks', 'The North Sea' and 'The Window'; a skill, that is, concerned to shape a coherent whole in terms of the ideal expressed in 'Experiences with Images', where there is a close equivalence between a central theme that is itself a strong symbol and the images that embody this symbolic theme. 'The Stygian Banks' especially shows an elaborate structural integration of images. The title, and the title-image in Chaucer's lines, however, illustrate and round off, rather than dominate, the unfolding theme. The theme itself is the complex one that is central in MacNeice's thinking: reality as the tension uniting the longing, separate Me and the existent, separate Not Me beyond. This is symbolized, certainly, in the figure of Troilus (for whose entry we have to wait until the seventh movement), who

> Patrols the Stygian banks, eager to cross,
> But the value is not on the further side of the river,
> The value lies in his eagerness. . . .

It is, however, the 'perpetual Spring' aspect of the theme that provides the dominant symbolic imagery, especially the symbolic figure of Alison, 'for ever aged fifteen'.[1] Thus, spring images dominate the poem, both the traditional natural images and the more literary, but perpetually fresh, ones of Chaucer's England, which characterize the first movement—the mediaeval ring-dance, the wandering clerk, the monk-and-lover in the abbey, the jongleur taking his stance beneath the high, grilled window, the 'drums of the Judgement' (that roll throughout the poem); with, to stress quietly the theme of the linked 'rondel of the years',

---

[1] The anonymous 14th-century lyric, *Alysoun*, was one of MacNeice's enthusiasms in his last year at Marlborough (*S.A.F.*, p. 99). It is presumably the love song he connects with the monk-and-lover in the abbey. (His reference to 'Chaucer's England' may also have called to mind the description of the slender Alison in *The Milleres Tale*, despite her 'eightetene yeer . . . of age'.)

the child of today, 'your/Child', either bowling his hoop or taking part in the dance. These images re-enter continually throughout the remaining movements, as the *leit-motiv*, 'Now it is Spring', sounds and re-sounds. Other images that enter in the second movement, for later variation, are the coffin (to be identified with the cradle on the breaking bough),[1] the wine glasses that ring when the right note is struck, the moss-roses that link separate individuals in a common memory, Tom, Dick, and Harry, who are not Tom-Dick-and-Harry, but 'Remain respectively Tom and Dick and Harry/Clapping backs in the sunshine . . .';[2] the green corn rippling with wind, and the labourer's arm rippling with muscle, neatly repeated in the third movement in its identification with our later

> .   .   .   doing and making
> Not to display our muscles but to elicit
> A rhythm, a value, implicit in something beyond us.

The glasses that symbolized sympathetic pitch re-enter to round off this movement, by way of Tom, Dick, and Harry, to represent good fellowship in 'Fill your glasses'—with an immediate reversion to the earlier equivalence in the reminder that

> When they are emptied again, the note may be higher yet
> And your own glass may break.

✓   The wind, thus quietly introduced, becomes much more prominent in the third movement, where it is introduced along with the breaking bough and the (implied) rocking cradle, and consistently welcomed to blow its wildest and give release from the bondage of 'mere existence':

> .   .   .   Let the wind
> Lunge like a trombone, draw back his hand to his mouth,
> Then lunge again and further; he is welcome . . .

And it becomes an integral part of the dominant garden image of the fourth movement, although it is now distinguished under two aspects: the limited wind that stirs to life within the high
✓ garden walls, and the unlimited wind that blows from the un-

---

[1] This image tightens the *H.S.* text, which, for 'from the coffin the retired life', has 'the figure who has retired'.   [2] A rejection, of course, of the 'illusion of Persons'.

confined spaces beyond. Again, the images from previous movements are repeated (for example, Alison, the hoop, the song-dance and its unchanging burden), and new symbols introduced for later development: the factory hooter and the eight-o'clock news, those reminders of 'mere existence'. At the end of the fifth movement there is an imaginative symbolic variation to meet the needs of a variation in theme. As everything is in constant flux, we are reminded of the illusion of moments out of time—and so Tom and Dick and Harry are not everlastingly drinking and clapping backs in the sunshine,

> .   .   .   but in fact
> They too are for the road, they too have heard
> The roll of recruiting drums beyond the horizon. . . .

And the ambiguity of the 'recruiting drums', their essential connection with 'the drums of the Judgement' (like that between coffin and cradle), is deftly stressed in the immediate juxtaposition of the fresco of 'The bearded Judge and the horned figures with prongs', which, to conclude the movement, is contrasted with that 'mere existence' symbol 'the blonde in the poster', repeated from earlier in the movement.[1]

The flux is further emphasized in the opening of the sixth movement: the watchman who, in the original vignette in the first movement, was about to cry, has now cried, and the lover 'must kiss his hand/Up to the grille and go.' So we, too, must go; but there are two ways of going—one in tune with the infinite, unafraid of the sound of 'the drums of the Judgement' that is borne on the infinite winds, the other in dread of the absolute, turning to all that is relative, confined, phenomenal for solace. And so the symbolic image of 'Alison's poise in the orchard' recurs, for

> .   .   .   the wind
> Which they dread, the wind which passes Alison by
> Without even ruffling her dress, yet once in a way
> Passes not by but into her. . . .

[1] The image of 'the blonde in the poster' may very well be connected with one of MacNeice's earliest uses of a strikingly contemporary image with symbolic undertones —the 'princess in the poster' in the school poem, 'Spring'. See below, pp. 167-8. She contrasts sharply with Alison.

Like all who are thus accommodated to the absolute, she under-
stands the meaning of the silence—the 'cone of silence' that was
the guiding daemon of Socrates, that links the martyrs in the
arena with one another and with the absolute. (He thus re-uses,
for a variation in the theme, a variation of the arena image that
he had used at the end of the third movement for the theme of
the defiance of what must be, the bondage of time, place and
causality.) Thus the symbols of the hooter, the queue, the grinding
gears, 'the end of the news', end the movement, as MacNeice
prays that we may break from these phenomenal bonds and attain
the wisdom that 'being silence/Is love of the chanting world'.

It is this love that dominates the last movement, where he
naturally brings together in a triumphant symphonic finale all the
earlier dominant images, either separately or in excited blend.
Bee and blossom merge in friar and jongleur: 'friar and wandering tumbler/Smuggle a pollen of culture into the villages . . .'.
And 'the fertilizing paradox' is emphasized in a juxtaposition that
makes the metaphysical sense clear:

> .   .   .   The closed window,
> The river of Styx, the wall of limitation
> Beyond which the world beyond loses its meaning,
> Are the fertilizing paradox, the grille
> That, severing, joins, the end to make us begin
> Again and again, the infinite dark ·that sanctions
> Our growing flowers in the light, our having children;
> The silence behind our music. . . .

A similar analysis of the interplay of symbolic images in 'The
North Sea' or 'The Window' would reveal the same level of
integration. 'The North Sea' is a particularly good example of
the identification of theme and symbol, the theme being, again,
the relationship between the absolute and the relative, the flux
and the permanence, with the sea itself the symbol both of the
annihilating absolute and the phenomenal present in time and
space in which value is made absolute. It is interesting to note the
use of the window image in 'The Window' for a theme different
from (though, of course, related to) that illustrated by the *closed*
window and the grille in 'The Stygian Banks'. Here the window

appears to be open,[1] though it is, to begin with, rather like the window in 'The Stygian Banks', a window in terms of art—the theme of the poem being the difference between the equipoise achievable in art and that achievable in life; the difficulty of achieving in life the same balance of inflow and outflow.

The 'froth of otherness'[2] in life, exemplified in 'The Window' as the potentially disintegrating images, continued to trouble MacNeice during the final period of his most assured craftsmanship, although he allowed himself to hope he was gaining the mastery. On the publication of *Visitations*, he commented:

This is the first book of short poems I have published since 1948. In between I have published *Ten Burnt Offerings* (ten long poems which were experiments in dialectical structure) and one very long poem, *Autumn Sequel*. . . . It is hard to put labels on one's own work but I like to think that my latest short poems are on the whole more concentrated and better organised than my earlier ones, relying more on syntax and bony feature than on bloom or frill or the floating image. . . .[3]

This new concentration and better organization in the later poems frequently takes the form (to disregard once more, for the moment, the matter of 'syntax and bony feature') of a noticeably tighter structural organization of images, with the dominance of a theme-symbol even more marked. This could be illustrated almost at random from the last three collections, where, in poem after poem, the theme is absolutely identified with a central symbolic image that entirely dominates a short lyric, or binds a longer one in the manner of the longer poems just discussed.

MacNeice stressed the structural importance of irony,[4] which is the element that supports many of his later structures when the force of their violent contemporaneity threatens a flaw. It had served the same role from the beginning, perhaps even before he became consciously aware of its use by Eliot. Thus, as we have just seen in one of his earliest poems, his much-used image of the Sleeping Princess is fused with that of a bill-hoarding to express his horror of *stasis* in the image of 'the princess in the poster', who 'combs her tresses/Prisoned for ever in a crypt

---

[1] At least, I take the window to be open. If it were not open, there seems no point in stressing the fact that the flanking curtains cannot be discomposed, or the window opened a hair's breadth *more*. If the condition were that of life they could, but as it is the condition of art they cannot.

[2] *C.P.D.*, p. 277.   [3] *P.B.S.B.*, no. 14, May 1957.   [4] See above, p. 125.

of paper'.[1] The irony here may be incipient and tentative; but it is soon conscious and controlled, strictly subordinated to theme and structure—for example, in his Oxford poem 'Utopia', where Mr. Jimp sings to the world that 'We got a lil gay-boy sparking plug' to replace the old sun that is setting, 'a neat lil sun' in 'patent leather shoes'.[2] The irony here serves the imagery and overall structure of the poem in much the same way as it does in, say, 'The Pale Panther', with more than a hint, too, of the savagery in the later irony.

The real power of irony as a formative element obviously lies in the contrasts it states or implies. The world may be one where MacNeice is skating easily 'on the lovely wafers of appearance'; where the trains are running smoothly, announcing their presence with a whistle that falls 'Sharp and straight on the ear like stigmata'; where

... Pentecost-like the cars' headlights bud
Out from sideroads and the traffic signals, crême-de-menthe or bull's
   blood,
Tell one to stop, the engine gently breathing, or to go on

to where the factory chimneys are 'like black pipes of organs'.[3] The images cohere, the traditional co-exist with the non-traditional, the sacred with the profane, largely because of the poet's delighted sense of the oneness of his universe. Where this sense is weak or absent, its place may well have to be taken by irony, the sense that perceives contrast, but, by the very strength of its perception, gives form and substance.

Both these unifying forces are well exemplified in the contrasting images of 'An Eclogue for Christmas', where the loving sense of the metaphysical unity, and the ironic sense of the disunity, of appearance and reality both operate strongly. In his description of the contemporary urban scene, the irony that points the lesson by historical parallel also provides the structural unity:

The street is up again, gas, electricity or drains,
Ever-changing conveniences, nothing comfortable remains

[1] 'Spring', *Marlburian*, 29 March 1926.   [2] *O.P.* (1930), pp. 20, 21.
[3] The references are to 'Thank You' (*E.C.*, p. 51), 'A Contact', 'Birmingham'.

Un-improved, as flagging Rome improved villa and sewer
(A sound-proof library and a stable temperature).
Our street is up, red lights sullenly mark
The long trench of pipes, iron guts in the dark,
And not till the Goths again come swarming down the hill
Will cease the clangour of the pneumatic drill.

In the vignette that follows, the loving sense of unity makes the image purely incarnational:

On all the traffic-islands stand white globes like moons,
The city's haze is clouded amber that purrs and croons,
And tilting by the noble curve bus after tall bus comes
With an osculation of yellow light, with a glory like chrysanthemums.

The ironic sense alone, however, organizes the images in 'New Jerusalem'. Here, too, the street is up, and irony points the lesson even more savagely: the foundations being laid for the 'new city, vertical, impersonal' not only involve the bulldozing of 'all memories and sanctuaries', but also open up 'forgotten and long-dry water-pipes', which are champed up by these earlier bull-dozers, 'dinosaur, pinheaded diplodocus'. The ironic sense also expands the central bulldozing image into a coherent symbolic townscape that includes such 'ever-changing conveniences' as stimulant, sleeping pill, transistors, television screens, wide win-dows, a traffic jam, and, without incongruity, Lazarus with 'a steel corset/And two glass eyes' and a police dog to help him 'to navigate the rush hour', Ezekiel among the 'Wheels upon wheels never moving', Daniel feeling his way through the packed streets 'in search of a carnivore', a new Babel arising on the bulldozed foundations. In poem after poem in the late collections MacNeice's sense of irony, combined with metaphysical wit or deep tragic awareness, enables him to make creative structural use of the sense-data that assailed him in a world of mass production and lost spiritual value. And so, in such poems as 'The Habits', 'As in their Time', 'In Lieu', 'Spring Cleaning', 'Memoranda to Horace', 'Jericho', 'Yours Next', often with an obvious effort to control the force of his irony, he adapts to the structure of his theme such contemporary properties as hypodermic needle, adgirl, tranquillizer, computer, smokeless fuel, plastic gear, skinfood, frozen sperm, cosmic radiation, blurb for a detergent, dentures, hearing aids, contraceptives, funerary urns from the supermarket, pennies for spastics, jet trails, vacuum cleaners, deep freeze, spacemen, fish farms, radio telescope, space ship, weightless cage, television monitor, cosh, flick-knife, fruit machines, pin tables, gas chamber.

7 Prosody

In book reviews, broadcasts, and critical articles of all kinds, as well as in *Modern Poetry*, MacNeice elaborated his views on prosody, displaying a notable consistency of view throughout. He summarized them in a broadcast discussion with Mr. L. A. G. Strong in 1941.[1] Here he affirmed, without ado, his acquaintance with traditional prosody: 'Well, I have read a good deal about the theory of metre and I do know how to analyse the various traditional metrical forms, and actually I do know how to practise them if I want to.' Yet he made it quite clear that 'the laws of versification aren't laws: they're just conveniences'. He went on to qualify this, however, by asserting his belief in the benefit to the poet of submission to even highly artificial verse forms:

For poets like Petrarch or Shakespeare, or Horace or Villon for that matter, it was in a way an advantage to start writing within these . . . very artificial limits which these intricate forms like the sonnet impose—forms like . . . the Horatian Ode or the Ballade that Villon used.[2]

This led him to a pointed attack on his old bugbear 'inspiration', which he nevertheless modified to agree with a distinction made by Strong between 'the poet's singing', which is based on 'an intuitive perception of rhythm', and his 'academic knowledge of metre'. He not only agreed with the distinction, but accorded the primacy to rhythm: 'I would agree that rhythm is a far more important thing than metre, strictly.' The burden of the remainder of MacNeice's contribution is the paradox of the freedom given to the poet by his submission to metrical discipline, the accommodation of the intuited rhythm to the enforced metrical pattern: 'The point of having rules is that you can break them. The artist needs a limit within which to work and he needs a norm from which he can deviate. . .' Invited to give an example from his own poetry of this interplay of intuited rhythm and regular

[1] Entitled *Are There Any Rules?*. Broadcast in the Home Service, on 13 June 1941.
[2] He instanced his own writing, the previous year, of 'five very regular ballades straight off just for the interest of it'. These are the ballades dated August 1940, and included in *C.P.R.H.*

metrical pattern, MacNeice quoted the poem 'Didymus', instancing specifically the last line:

Now it's just the last line I want to mention. I could have written there—'Into the wrong, the reflected sky'—that would have been a smoother rhythm, but the order of epithets wouldn't have been so good, and quite apart from that . . . [there is] the sheer sound. I prefer in this poem to mass the two stresses 'wrong' and 'sky' together. 'Wrong' and 'sky': that I feel makes you dwell on the wrongness of it.[1]

The early poems leave the reader in little doubt about Mac-Neice's faith in rhythm as 'a far more important thing than metre'. He seems determined to stress this in his Foreword to *Blind Fireworks*:

As for my versification, there are lines which may, by the incautious, be (wrongly) read in a merry slap-on-the-back fashion; thus—'The Mán in the Móon is long yéars dead and góne' (= 'O young Lochinvar is come out of the west'); which should be read 'The Mán in the Móon is lóng yéars déad and gone', 'long' and 'dead' being heavily stressed. And in general I stress the important words.

In what was probably his last written comment on poetic theory, he remarked of the poems in *The Burning Perch*: 'I notice that many of the poems here have been trying to get out of the "iambic" groove. . . .'[2] In between lie over thirty years of effort to play intuited rhythm against traditional metre in the musical counterpoint that was the ideal of disciplined freedom.

We find MacNeice throughout *Modern Poetry* insisting in various contexts that 'the normal business of poetry is the conveying of information through certain kinds of word-patterns',[3] and, in his 'Alphabet of Literary Prejudices', deprecating 'Chunks of Life', insisting on the need to formalize:

All pattern is artificial and most patterns need smashing up on occasions; we cannot, for all that, get away from artificiality. The writer who despises form must still formalise, even in selecting his material. To despise 'form' will not bring him nearer reality but may very easily take him further from it. . . .[4]

---

[1] MacNeice's line is: 'Into the reflected, the wrong, sky.'
[2] Article on *B.P.* in *P.B.S.B.* no. 38, September 1963.
[3] Op. cit., p. 40.   [4] Op. cit., p. 38.

Although he admitted no essential distinction between poetry and prose, he did nevertheless admit an important technical distinction by contrasting the movements of verse and prose in terms of rugby and netball:

The contrast between verse and prose is like the contrast between rugby football and games like netball. The mere arranging of verse in lines serves the same purpose as the offside rule in rugger and the rule against forward passes; instead of the meaning being passed vertically down the field, as it is in prose, each line in verse when it comes to an end passes back to the beginning of the next (and I am not only thinking of typography). This method, as in rugger, gives a sweeping movement, an impression of controlled speed and power—an impression which is enhanced when the verse is on a recognizable rhythmical pattern.[1]

In a late review of a book on Robert Frost,[2] he made the same point in terms of golf and squash:

A sentence in prose is struck forward like a golf ball; a sentence in verse can be treated like a ball in a squash court. Frost, as Brower brings out, is a master of angles: he quotes Edwin Muir on his poetic 'method': 'starting from a perfectly simple position we reach one we could never have foreseen'.

In each case, he goes on to disparage, or give limited approval to, free verse: 'It is refreshing to find Professor Brower quoting Frost himself as saying: "I had as soon write free verse as play tennis with the net down".' In *Modern Poetry* he admits 'the legitimacy of even the baldest free verse', where the phrases 'can be more poised and therefore more effective and memorable than if merged in the hurry-scurry of prose', but expresses a preference for 'the more regular kinds of verse because . . . if you are going to poise your phrases at all they will usually need more poise than can be given by the mere arranging of them in lines . . .'.[3]

In the Introduction to *Varieties of Parable* MacNeice refers to Martin Esslin's contention that 'the Theatre of the Absurd strives to express its sense of the senselessness of the human condition

[1] *M.P.*, p. 116.
[2] Review of *The Poetry of Robert Frost* by Reuben Brower, in the *N.S.*, 12 July 1963.
[3] Op. cit., pp. 116, 117.

and the inadequacy of the rational approach by the open abandon-
ment of rational devices and discursive thought', but affirms that
it 'can at least be disputed: Mr. Eliot's theory, put forward in
1921, that in a dislocated world poetry must be dislocated too,
has been disputed now for several decades'.[1] Again, the connection between form and content is seen not only as a technical,
but also as a metaphysical, issue. He further suggested, in his
essay on Poetry in *The Arts Today*, that where the subject matter
is particularly complex the poet ought to help his readers by
using a deliberately simple form: 'When we are esoteric (mystical
or metaphysical) we shall prop them up with a palpable outward
form (like Yeats or Valéry) till they have time to collect our
tenuous implications.'[2]

This shaping of words that is the poem is in effect a challenge
to the disorder of the Many, an attempt to stabilize the Many as the
One, however fragile the stability. In a review of Edward Lear's
Teapots and Quails,[3] he commented: 'As Auden wrote of Tennyson and Baudelaire: "It may well be . . . that the more he (the
poet) is conscious of an inner disorder and dread, the more value
he will place on tidiness in the work as a *defence* . . .".' Thus, in
'Sunday Morning', the futile attempt to shape a self-contained
unity out of the flux is described as the attempt to

> . . . abstract this day and make it to the week of time
> A small eternity, a sonnet self-contained in rhyme.

In 'The Sunlight on the Garden' the attempt to soar in disciplined
freedom is again equated symbolically with the sonnet:

> The earth compels, upon it
> Sonnets and birds descend. . . .

And in 'The Stygian Banks' the sonnet again represents an artificially imposed unity:

> . . . The slab in the floor of the nave
> Makes one family a sonnet, each name with a line to itself,
> But the lines, however the bones may be jumbled beneath,
> Merge no more than the lives did. . . .

---

[1] Op. cit., p. 15. He discussed this at some length in the chapter entitled 'A Change of
Attitude' in *M.P.*, referring in particular on pp. 14–15 to Eliot's essay on the Metaphysical
Poets.   [2] Op. cit., p. 66.   [3] The *N.S.N.*, 5 December 1953.

The sonnet is seen in the same metaphysical terms as life itself—
the embodiment of the same formal unity that allows the members
of the family to be both concrete particulars and concrete universals.

'Sunday Morning' is nominally a sonnet. It is a patterned
arrangement of words in fourteen lines, with end-rhymes, but
the pattern is so arranged that many reading it possibly feel
themselves in the presence of something at once familiar and
new. The division into a ten-line section and a quatrain is an
uncommon structure; the system of end-rhymes is actually a
sleight-of-hand arrangement of couplets; the number of feet in the
metrical register varies from five to seven; and the number of
stresses in the stress register appears to vary between five and six.
Yet MacNeice, as we saw, believed that the poet ought to be able
to practise the traditional formal skills. Thus, his early poem entitled
simply 'Sonnet'[1] is in the traditional Petrarchan or Miltonic form.
He showed that he could compose skilfully in such French forms
as the villanelle and ballade, and he wrote a perfectly regular
sequence of octets. Of the commoner traditional forms, he used,
for example, octosyllabic couplets in the early 'Child's Unhappi-
ness'[2] and in the late 'Birthright', while in 'Autobiography' they
are set in moving isolation, as couplet stanzas, by the refrain.
Heroic couplets and blank verse are used in, respectively, the
'Letter to Graham and Anna' and 'The Hebrides'. The *terza
rima* that is used throughout *Autumn Sequel* in near-regular form
is also used with skill in 'The Strand'. The rhyming pattern of the
tercets in *Autumn Sequel* is regular, and the pentameter line is the
metrical base, although it is occasionally varied by a hexameter.
It is the same in the heroic couplets of the 'Letter to Graham and
Anna', where the couplets rhyme regularly (with, of course, as
in *Autumn Sequel*, much half-rhyme and assonance), and an
occasional hexameter is substituted, not necessarily in each line
of the couplet: 'And lóok alóng the gróund, one cánnot sée the
gróund/For the féet of the crówd, and the lóst is néver fóund.'[3]

---

[1] *P.R.H.*, p. 90. [2] *B.F.*, p. 12.
[3] *C.P.D.*, p. 62. The three anapaests, however, seem to swell the strictly metrical count
of the pentameter.

Hexameters are also occasionally substituted for the blank verse pentameters of 'The Hebrides', where there is a further variation technique in the repeated short opening line, 'On those islands'. The heroic quatrain is used in 'Place of a Skull', in a *very* nearly regular form that equates with the theme—the basic inadequacy of the Christian ultimate to meet the needs of the whole of his experience.

For the rest, MacNeice tirelessly creates sleight-of-hand patterns where the reader is wooed into acceptance of an original, or at least a fresh, verse form through his sense of familiarity with the residual elements of the old one. This applies to almost every verse or stanza unit, from the line of blank verse, to couplets, tercets, and quatrains, quintets, sestets, and the longer stanzas. Thus, in the late 'Dark Age Glosses', the reader feels himself familiarly in the presence of blank verse, although there is, in fact, very considerable, and studied, variation in the form of tetrameters and hexameters; and hexameters are used throughout the dramatic and rhetorical 'Rites of War'. Blank verse, in fact, of all the traditional forms, he was most determined to resolve:

... some forms in English have been overworked. . . . This is especially so with blank verse. . . . The poet to-day, I suggest, should use blank verse with freedom, varying the length of the lines and the groupings of the stresses; and he must avoid (what he is still more liable to suffer in the sonnet) falling into obsolete turns of phrase which blank verse will automatically suggest to him. . . .[1]

Although he was fond of couplets, he preferred, like some other poets,[2] to use them in different stanza units, especially quatrains— for example, the early 'Postscript to Iceland' and the late 'The Grey Ones'. In such poems as 'Solitary Travel', 'Icebergs' and 'October in Bloomsbury', he alternates rhymed and unrhymed couplets. This pattern is varied with considerable ingenuity in

[1] *M.P.*, pp. 126–7.

[2] Notably Blake in his *Songs of Innocence* and *Songs of Experience*. MacNeice used the octosyllabic couplet and quatrain for a similar mood of deep, tender, or fierce pathos. He remarked in *M.P.* (p. 38) that 'at the age of about 7' he 'had an anthology of verse which included some of Blake's *Songs of Innocence*', and that he was most struck by 'The Chimney-Sweeper', whose metre he liked and whose story he saw in 'a succession of very vivid pictures'. This poem seems directly to underlie 'Autobiography', in which its opening line might easily have been incorporated.

'Icebergs', where the couplet in the third stanza is enriched with an assonance ('alone') in the second line, and the rhymed couplet precedes the unrhymed in the last stanza, thus musically following the previous rhymed couplet and permitting the poet to end both with a near-repetition of the opening line and with the word 'water', which has already ended the foregoing first lines of stanzas. In 'Half Truth from Cape Town' he arranges his regular heroic couplets in sestets; while in 'Windowscape' his regularly rhyming couplets have an irregular pattern of metrical feet, the basic hexameter being varied with pentameters and heptameters. MacNeice, indeed, had a particular liking for the hexameter, or alexandrine, couplet, which he used in such early poems as 'Evening Indoors', 'Valediction', 'Spring Voices', 'Museums', 'Nature Morte', 'The Glacier', 'Chess'. It is again notable how the modulations of the general pattern in these poems suit the theme. In 'Nature Morte', 'The Glacier' and 'Chess', the couplets are regular, for a thematic reason that might be summed up in the concluding couplet of 'Chess':

> Choose your gambit, vary the tactics of your game,
> You move in a closed ambit that always ends the same.

In 'Evening Indoors' the calm is not absolute ('And so come other noises through the noise of the clock'), and it is appropriate that there should be slight ripples on the surface of the pattern (pentameter lines); while the vainglorious, self-indulgent mood of 'Museums' seems to be reflected in the many swelling fourteeners. In 'Spring Voices', a break in the mood of flowing joy is abruptly indicated in a couplet where a near-regular alexandrine is followed by a long and menacing twelve-stress line:

Bréathing on his néck and múttering that áll thís has háppened befóre,
Kéep the wínd óut, cást nó clóut, trý nó unwárranted jáunts úntríed
    befóre. . . .

An alexandrine couplet follows, but the mood has been broken, and the final couplet is wildly irregular, packed with onomatopoeic devices. And in 'Valediction' the couplets vary even more wildly to match his mood.

There can be few possible variations that MacNeice did not attempt on the quatrain, which is perhaps his favourite stanza. Many of them have the surface simplicity of Blake's, or the 'hymn tune' quality of Housman's;[1] and many illustrate an almost obsessive determination to ring all the changes. He has a marked preference for the tetrameter quatrain, or for a pattern of longs and shorts, and a marked disinclination to use the pentameter quatrain, especially the heroic version. Thus, in 'August' he uses only one regular stanza of heroic quatrain—for the thematic climax. In the first two stanzas he rhymes the first and last lines—an attempt, as it were, to confine 'The living curve that is breathlessly the same'. As the individual's tentative efforts continue in the next two stanzas, the rhyme shifts about, until in the last stanza it falls into the finality of the heroic quatrain, expressing, by its form, dead awareness of the finality of the eternal rhythm of time: an endless Form of fixed alternations.

The same equivalence to theme is marked in the quatrains of 'The Individualist Speaks', where the lines, as one might almost expect, vary (from tetrameter to heptameter, on a pentameter basis), and there is a highly individual system of rhyme, half-rhyme and assonance in the first three lines of each stanza. For the same reason, the quatrains of 'Snow', and the near-full rhyme in the last stanza, convey the unity, while the varying lines and the absence of rhyme, apart from the weak and unstressed repetition in the first line, convey the variety. In other quatrains the variations have the regular opening and closing precision of a concertina, as, for example, those of 'Departure Platform', 'Babel', 'Slow Movement'. This gives, in 'Departure Platform', a pattern in which the first pentameter line makes a positive assertion, which is punched home in the following trimeter (or tetrameter), and then elaborated in the swinging pentameter (or hexameter) of the third and fourth lines:

> Love, my love, it is high time to travel,
> The brass bell clangs escape
> And summer in a porter's cap will punch our tickets
> And launch us where the shining lines unravel.[2]

---

[1] See below, p. 191. [2] *P.P.*, p. 17.

In 'Slow Movement', the highly musical interweaving of the first three lines of each quatrain, varying from tetrameter to heptameter, is rounded off with a regular trimeter that stands out in sharp relief.

MacNeice contrived similar emphatic juxtapositions of long and short lines in his other stanza forms, as well as in his blank verse or free verse. In 'Perseus', for example, in the first three stanzas the short lines swell to the descriptive, narrative, or rhetorical finalities of the long, and very long, concluding lines. The open-shut theme of 'The National Gallery' is suggested in the pattern of the tercets, with their glad repeated rhymes, and their regular opening pentameter or hexameter swelling to the very long second and third lines. The nightmare panting of 'Bad Dream' is sharply suggested in the controlled concertina of its sestets, with the concerted jabs of their very short lines.

The very simple trimeter or tetrameter quatrain he employed either to match a mood of gentle pathos or to simplify the reader's task where the theme is especially complex.[1] The trimeter quatrains in 'Leaving Barra' serve both purposes, even if the theme is not particularly difficult. His unusual rhyming and linking device here, where a repeated end-rhyme links the stanzas, also suggests the linked points of glitter on the waves; but again he eschews absolute regularity in the unobtrusive 'buddha/Buddha' variation. The tetrameter quatrains of 'The Revenant' have a calm inevitability and controlled passion that strangely recall Herbert:

> To die in a moment is a small thing
> Like a sea-shell in a quiet room,
> Yet from that shell the sea will fling
> The thunder of uncharted doom.

In the two notably simple quatrains of the octet 'Corner Seat', he deals with a complex metaphysical theme. The trimeter quatrains of 'Carol' are representative of the most pellucid and simple of his hymn-like structures, which he used intermittently up to the late poems—such as 'Apple Blossom', the opening poem of *Solstices*.

The variations just noted in his rhyme patterns in the quatrain

[1] See above, p. 174.

are exploited to the full in his other stanza lengths, from the
tercet upwards. Nor is it only, as one critic aptly observed, that
'he needs rhyme, chime, clink of some sort, to keep his verse going
properly'; he also clearly, as he said Goethe did, considered
rhyme to be a 'part of the sense'.[1] The flow of repeated rhymes
and assonances in the tercets of 'The National Gallery' is as
suited to the glad theme of the unity of experience as is the
clever clinking of the repetitions in the tercets of 'Coda', with
which he rounds off *The Burning Perch* (and, perhaps, a whole
continuous process of metaphysical thinking). The placing of
'better' at the end of a different line in each *unrhymed* tercet of
'Coda', together with the quiet tense-variations in the repeated
phrase, 'knew', 'know', 'shall know', stresses the theme of a
pattern of illuminations unfolding from the darkness.

An intricately woven rhyme pattern frequently, and obviously,
indicates a mood or theme of unified experience—either of the
excited, dynamic kind, or the paralysing, static (the rhythms
showing which is which). The intricate rhymes in the sestets of
'The Sunlight on the Garden', with their rich and regular system
of alternating masculine and feminine endings, and head-and-tail
rhymes added for full measure, in an extraordinary manner
suggest both the fullness and delight of experience, and the sad
acceptance of inevitable destiny—the inevitability being stressed
in the inverted repeated half-rhymes of the first and last stanzas:
'garden/pardon', 'pardon/garden'. The same intricate, though
less obvious, precision marks 'The Brandy Glass', with its similar
theme, where the simple and regular end-rhymes (A B C C D A
C D A), together with the slightly varied repetition in the first
and last lines, suggest both the inexorable pattern of fate and the
hopeless pathos of the plea for a precise repetition. Again, in
'Entirely', the delighted awareness of both plurality and unity is
ironically suggested in the counterpoint of excited image and
rhythm and the strict rhyming pattern of the octets. Similarly,
the agitated rhythms within the sestets of 'London Rain', with
their even tighter system of rhyme and repeated rhyme, suggest
both the wild resistance to 'the fences/That fence about my soul'

[1] Respectively: G. S. Fraser in *Purpose*, no. 2, Autumn 1938, and *G.F.*, p. 9. (See p. 119.)

of the first part, and the glad acceptance of the world as 'what was given' and the world as 'what we make' of the last part. This kind of rhyming virtuosity perhaps reaches its climax in the 'Visitations' sequence at the end of that collection, with its theme of destiny and free will, patterned experience and the visitations that testify to a meaningful pattern. The stanzas and lines are of all lengths with a plethora of repeated rhymes and phrases. In Part V of 'Notes for a Biography', where he rounds off his theme of the renewals and repetitions of experience, the rhyme scheme of the sestets, with their repetitions and regular pattern of long and short lines, and much play of repeated rhyme, is meticulously precise: A B C A B C / D B E D B E / F B G F B G. And in 'Sunday in the Park' the rhythmic anaphora of the repeated end-rhymes ('ironies' and 'forget') crushes the reader under the weight of the inevitability and the acceptance of oblivion. His comment in *Modern Poetry* on Edward Lear's use of the repeated end-rhyme seems relevant here:

I now think that though the new end rhyme is obviously a great asset to the kind of limerick which is essentially witty . . . Lear's scheme is more suited to the limerick *as lyric*. It gives a better balanced and more assured statement; we do not anxiously wait for the virtuoso ending.[1]

Often, too, a very regular rhyme pattern seems to be a device to contain, and so challenge, doubt and confusion. This is conspicuous in the dedicatory sestina 'To Hedli', which prefaced the 1949 collection and in which his theme is overt dismay and anxiety. He also used at times a disciplined irregularity of end-rhyme for much the same purpose, placing his rhymes with deliberate casualness where they best concentrate the expression and point the theme. As he said in *Modern Poetry*:

The case against rhyme is that, being obviously artificial, it suggests insincerity and that it lulls the reader into a pleasant coma. There are many ways in which one may compromise. . . . One can use rhyme in a poem, but not continuously or not in the expected places (compare 'Lycidas').[2]

This technique is marked in the last collection, in such poems as

'The Suicide', 'Constant' and 'Star-Gazer'. In the first, the near-regular placing of the single 'act' rhymes (fact, stacked, packed, cracked, tract, lacked, act, intact) weighs heavily in forming the mood, for the sound is, in a curious way, both sad and ugly, and yet crackling with a kind of electric vitality. The rich, but very irregular, rhymes of 'Constant' accord well with the ironical title and theme, while the simple, irregular cluster of 'night/ sight/bright/light' in the first stanza of 'Star-Gazer' suggests the child's wonder and excitement. (The starkly isolated 'Anyone left alive' in 'Star-Gazer' is also a good example of the effect of a varied line pattern.) The regular pattern of *remote* end-rhymes in otherwise unrhymed stanzas he also used to much the same effect. In the grim 'After the Crash', this remote regularity (second and last lines of the sestet) equates unobtrusively with the theme, which is given further emphasis in the last stanza by the repeated rhyme and phrase:

> The pan on the left dead empty
> And the pan on the right dead empty,
> And knew in the dead, dead calm
> It was too late to die.

It is small wonder that MacNeice exclaimed with some exasperation in a late review: 'Some idiot recently stated that rhyme in English poetry was now a thing of the past.'[1]

Some of the other devices listed by MacNeice in *Modern Poetry* by which the poet could combat artificiality or insincerity were 'internal rhymes, off-rhymes, bad rhymes, "para-rhymes"', and the rhyming of stressed against unstressed syllables.[2] He also mentioned with approval the 'ghost rhymes' of Spender, where 'the balance of the end words is still perceptible and therefore pleasurable'.[3] All of these devices, as we have in part noted, he himself exploited to the full. Indeed, as he remarked in a late review,[4] the risk had become that many poets should regard such devices as the norm:

---

[1] The *N.S.*, 12 July 1963, in a review, already referred to, of Professor Brower's study of the poetry of Robert Frost.   [2] Op. cit., p. 131.   [3] Ibid., p. 133.

[4] Of *Wilfred Owen*, by D. S. R. Welland, in the *N.S.*, 22 October 1960. (Mrs. Anne Ridler illustrates this point, with interesting examples, on pp. 38–9 of her introduction to the 1951 re-issue of *The Faber Book of Modern Verse*.)

Technically, however, Owen's innovations have long been assimilated; half-rhymes and such no longer draw any more comment than does a 'cubistic' touch in a poster in the Underground. In fact at one time they were taking the place of full rhymes as the regular thing to use; some even came—absurdly—to consider the full rhyme a vulgarism. Here, as always, we must avoid a canonisation of technique. . . .

Closely connected technically with the binding and emphasizing effects of rhyme is his use of refrain and repetition, which we have noted, and which is so marked a structural feature of MacNeice's poetry. An equally marked, and perhaps even more basic (though less obvious), structural feature is his use of enjambment. In terms of his own analogies from rugby football and squash, this represents the flick of the wrist passing the ball back that the movement may continue, or the thwack of the ball as it angles off to be returned once more. It is a feature so intimately bound up with the technique of rhyming that it is very often not to be distinguished separately from it, as in several of the rhyming or assonating links we have just been noting, such as the 'lost/Wisps' of Section XXII of *Autumn Journal*. It is used almost obsessively, and most obviously, as an emphasis device—for example, in this same section to emphasize the dominant theme of value: 'So here where tourist values are the only/Values . . .'.[1] And it plays a vital part in the composition of the verse syntax—although a part about which it could be misleading to dogmatize, if only for the reason that the effect is as closely associated with rhythm and music as it is with logic. Nor is analysis simplified by the fact that behind MacNeice's own obvious disinclination to use the end-stopped line (or the end-stopped thought process) is, presumably, the strong technical influence of both Spenser and Horace, in whose verse patterns enjambment is also such a basic feature:

> And forth he cald out of the deepe darknes dredd
> Legions of Sprights, the which, like litle flyes
> Fluttring about his ever-damned hedd,
> Awaite whereto their service he applyes . . .[2]

The almost thud-like effect of the 'Legions', 'Fluttring', 'Awaite' illustrates precisely what MacNeice meant by his analogy, as the

[1] *C.P.D.*, p. 147. [2] *The Fairie Queene*, I. i. 333–6.

ball is neatly taken by hand to be carried forward, and passed back once more. This kind of verse movement seems to be behind much of MacNeice, with appropriate changes made for different mood and idiom, as do lines such as the following illustrative Sapphics from Horace:

Iliae dum se nimium querenti

iactat ultorem, vagus et sinistra

labitur ripa, Iove non probante, u-

-xorius amnis.[1]

This seems to be very like the kind of verse syntax to which MacNeice said he was approximating his own in the 'Memoranda to Horace' and other poems in the last collection,[2] but it is surely marked from the earliest poems. It is obvious, naturally, in the traditional Sapphics of 'June Thunder' or 'Christmas Shopping', where he even, in the latter, has a split-word enjambment as in Horace's stanza above:

Hands from above them as of gods but really

These their parents, always seen from below, them-

Selves are always anxious looking across the

Fence to the future. . . .[3]

The cumulative, descriptive-reflective movement of the verse here is unthinkable without these hinges on which the syntax swings.

---

[1] Horace, *Carm.*, I. ii. 17–20. [2] See below, p. 192. [3] *C.P.D.*, p. 96.

MacNeice's overriding technical problem, then, was how to work his rhythms into the patterns of the traditional prosody. He is very self-consciously aware of trying for virtuoso rhythmic effects in all his poems up to the time he left Oxford, feeling obliged, for instance, to point this out in a letter to Anthony Blunt in the summer of 1928: 'Most of my poems need reading several times over; also the prosody may be a little difficult—try reading them aloud.' There is much over-obvious verbal music, with elaborate counterpointing and showy onomatopoeic effects of all kinds. This was the period when 'images and rhythm were the most important things in the world'.[1] He knows his metres intimately in his head, but he is carried away by the excitement of the rhythms he feels intuitively. Many of these are heavily and demonstratively lugubrious ('The déep wáys of mán are dóped now and déad and góne') or weary-eerie ('Wéep, fóuntain, créepily, só créepily').[2] His characteristic lilting nursery-rhyme rhythms are also very marked. Indeed, rhythmic variations to suit the mood might be illustrated almost at random from *Blind Fireworks*: for instance, the Hopkinsesque movement of hissing and dying flames in 'Evening Indoors' ('The flámes blénd and páss, incénd and énd and páss'). MacNeice was excited by Hopkins just then, however much he may have warned against him in a few years' time.[3] Another marked feature is the compressed stress cluster for rhetorical/dramatic effect. This is notable from the first—for instance, in the very early descriptive lyric, 'Nocturne', where the stressing is ingeniously used in the conclusion, the reader being suddenly dropped from the dreamy rhythms of a fulgent Sitwellian night sky to the unexpected bump of: 'I will láy me betwéen twó clóuds/But I wíll nót sléep.'[4]

---

[1] *M.P.*, p. 59. See above, p. 117.

[2] Respectively: 'Sailor's Farewell', *B.F.*, p. 23, and 'Gardener Melancholy', *B.F.*, p. 22.

[3] In a letter to A.F.B., tentatively ascribed to March 1928, he said: 'I am reading Gerard Manley Hopkins' poems—exciting.' See below, pp. 188 ff.

[4] *Marlburian*, 22 October 1925. MacNeice remarked in *M.P.* (pp. 51–2): 'Someone having told me that my poems were just like those of the Sitwells, I began reading the Sitwells.' He 'liked their surprise effects', their transposition tricks involving 'ordinary speech'.

The later Oxford poems show the same exuberant skill of the young poet <u>for whom rhythm is everything</u>. One example might be noted from this period, the last stanza of the self-questioning, wryly self-conscious, 'Epitaph for Louis':

> Péddling his vocábulary,
> Múttering, véxed
> With thís wórld, gúttering
> Ínto the néxt.
> In a whíte flúx he dípped
> His dúnce-cáp únder
> And slípped in a fít
> To the crýpt of it,
> It was nó wónder
> Óbiit.

The guttering, muttering decline in the rhythm matches the mood of waning identity that is the theme of the poem:

> Loúis was a cándle ónce.[1]

The idiom that he has been peddling is clearly as vague and unsatisfactory to him as the pedlar himself. Playing with rhythms, however skilled the play, is not enough. The *obiit* of man and maker is one. He was, as we saw, 'tired of University life', for he 'knew all the moves in advance'; when he did leave, he felt 'it was high time', and did not consider it surprising that 'for about three years after leaving Oxford' he 'almost gave up reading or writing modern poetry'.[2] He found at first that he had exchanged 'a public hothouse for a private one', but 'the panes of glass fell gradually out of their frames' and he 'began to smell the life that went on outside'.[3] He himself put it shrewdly from a technical point of view in a letter home half-way through his Oxford years:

In a few years I imagine I shall have gradually stopped writing verse. This is because my verse and prose are becoming more and more like

---

[1] *Sir Galahad*, vol. I, no. I, 21 February 1929.
[2] *S.A.F.*, p. 120; *M.P.*, p. 74.   [3] 'Twenty-One', p. 239.

each other and they promise a most remarkable compound. You see, some time ago my prose was intellectual and crisp and my verse sensuous and florid (all according to established regulations) but now my prose is becoming more sensuous and my verse more intellectual. These combined will form a sponge to soak in quantities of experience.[1]

The connection between his programme to absorb new experiences (which we have noted: 'lots of lovely particulars'),[2] and the new idiom in which to absorb and express it, is absolutely basic. It is no exaggeration to describe it as his joint programme for the 1930s—and, in altered form, following yet another re-appraisal of himself, his writing, and his world, for the later 1940s and the 1950s. His letter certainly describes accurately in advance the idiom of the poems in the 1935 collection, on the assurance and the individuality of which so many critics commented. It is the idiom of the new man and poet, absorbing the particulars of the actual world, and expressing them in what is partly the collo-quial forms of that world, and partly the particular idiom of the poet himself. The attitude it voices is close to Wordsworth's, especially as MacNeice summed it up later in *Modern Poetry*—the poet as a man like other men, using the speech of other men and making no essential distinction between the language of prose and the language of poetry ('. . . I do not recognize any great gulf between poetry and prose').[3]

He still emphasized, however, the need for rhythmical varia-tions to correspond to changes in theme, and admitted his delight in variety for its own sake:

. . . I think that many poems (especially those which come from more subtle or sophisticated subjects or moods) are the better for rhythmical variations, (a) because rhythmical variations can often be significant of variations in content, (b) because variety is delightful for its own sake.[4]

Yet he made it quite clear, with analytical examples, that the whole point of variations or counterpoint effects is that we accept them

---

[1] From Oxford, 30 June 1927.
[2] Letter to J.R.H. from Birmingham in the autumn of 1930. See p. 95.
[3] Op. cit., p. 114.　　[4] Ibid., p. 117.

'because we are aware of the basic rhythm on which they are variations'.[1] The variations, moreover, enhance the value of the pattern:

Metre, verse-pattern, and rhyme are therefore conveniences for the poet, but they are not laws of nature. If he can do without them he is entitled to. I . . . hold that, once there is a pattern, the pattern is often more effective the more it is varied. . . .[2]

One of his illustrations showed perfectly the kind of syncopation he was aiming at (thereby repeating, in effect, what he had said in the Foreword to *Blind Fireworks*):

In my own practice I find that a poem of the blank-verse kind, unless short, usually requires pedestrian lines as foils to the others; every line should not be equally heightened. And blank verse should be strong rather than pretty. For this reason syllables naturally weighted should be given their weight instead of the weight being shared out over the line.

'The polar bear prowled on the ice'

is a better line than

'The polar bear was prowling on the ice.'

What classical metrical theorists would call the 'syncopation' of the former line throws a proper stress onto all the important words, which is dissipated in the latter line.[3]

Although he thus admittedly writes poetry for the ear, he is not prepared to sacrifice 'system' or 'significance' to music:

. . . my own preference is for poetry which is musical, but . . . the characteristics of this music are not superficial prettiness or smoothness, but (a) system and (b) significance. When I write poetry myself, I always consider the sound of each line conjointly with its adequacy as meaning. . . . Sometimes I am conscious that a line is roughly onomatopoeic, but I do not think it is possible *deliberately* to suit the sound continuously to the sense. I suspect that here again a poet has to compromise between poetry as representation and poetry as creation, between something recorded and something invented.[4]

MacNeice supported the poet's desire to reproduce in his verses the richness and fullness of natural speech rhythms, but he

[1] *M.P.*, p. 118. [2] Ibid., p. 115.
[3] Ibid., p. 128. [4] Ibid., pp. 134–5.

was wary of any attempt to fake the paradigm to accommodate these rhythms. He was notably cool about sprung verse:

Hopkins wanted to introduce the licence of conversation into verse. His eye was on the Old English models and he thought that by limiting the *number* of stresses but apportioning them where he liked in the line, he would be able to achieve (a) the naturalistic richness of conversation, but not dissipated, as it is in conversation, by the lack of a formal basis, and (b) variety of rhythm for variety's sake.

Such a licence, besides being practised in popular ballads and nursery rhymes, had already been claimed as the poet's right by Coleridge in his preface to 'Christabel'. . . . Hopkins and Coleridge were both entitled to demand this licence, but were both mistaken in thinking they could sanction it merely by the counting of stressed syllables, as is shown in Hopkins's own practice where the counting is often a fraud. Witness (with Hopkins's own stress-marks):

'Christ minds; Christ's interest, what to avow or mend
   There, éyes them, heart wánts, care háunts, fóot follows kínd,
  Their ránsom, théir rescue, ánd first, fást, last fríend.'

These are strong and effective lines, but Hopkins's notation makes them vicious. Merely through sticking to his fetish of five stresses per line, he (a) goes miles away from his admired rhythms of ordinary speech, and (b) (which matters much more) slurs over, as unstressed, words— 'heart', 'care', 'rescue', 'first', 'last'—which, both for their sound-value and their meaning, *ought not* to be slurred over.[1]

MacNeice seemed perfectly happy to accept Hopkins's 'counterpointing' explanation of the metrical irregularities of English verse ('In much English verse the irregularities can be explained, in Hopkins's term, as counterpointing'), but he could not accept Hopkins's view of sprung verse as something 'different in kind from counterpointing', for, to MacNeice's ear, 'this difference is only a difference in degree'.[2] There was to be no factitious theoretical justification for the natural speech rhythms, which were to be disciplined to suit the paradigms of traditional English prosody.

In a review of Professor Tuve's book on Herbert, MacNeice

---

[1] *M.P.*, pp. 123–4.   [2] Ibid., p. 122.

suggested that Herbert and Yeats would provide better models for young poets than Donne and Hopkins:

On purely technical grounds it is a pity that young poets looking for models to the early seventeenth century should have so ignored Herbert and pondered so much on Donne; Donne is, I think, the greater poet but he is certainly a worse model, just as Gerard Manley Hopkins is a worse model than Yeats. To write like either Donne or Hopkins you have to *start* peculiar, whereas, while both Herbert and Yeats are also peculiar in their very different ways . . . their peculiarities are not so violent or deep as to subordinate their work to their psychology. To put it differently, Herbert and Yeats are more *classical*.[1]

(MacNeice, too, as a young poet, had turned to the seventeenth century, finding, as we saw, in the cadences and imagery of its prose 'a better union with God than any English prose before or since . . .'.)[2] He subscribes to Professor Tuve's praise of 'the cadences and rhythm of his [Herbert's] language', and italicizes her assertion that '*Tone of voice is a component of meaning*'. In another review two years later, he asserted the relevance of Herbert's example to contemporary poetry:

Mr. Eliot himself has long since stopped shoring fragments against his ruins, while most of the poets younger than himself, both here and in America, have returned to their traditional business of 'making', of imposing order. . . . This being so, it is time that Herbert, who (even though Cowper called him 'gothic and uncouth'!) was as classic a designer as Horace, should no longer be subordinated to Donne who, for all his brilliant gifts, was too often a ribbon-developer. . . .

He further praised Herbert thus:

A master of colloquial rhythms, he achieved, as both those critics demonstrate, a most surprising but convincing combination of these with 'elegant stanza forms and rhyme schemes', a combination attempted, to their credit, by certain modern poets such as Auden. . . .[3]

The most obvious example of Herbert's direct influence is probably in MacNeice's 'Prayer Before Birth', which echoes

[1] The *N.S.N.*, 13 September 1952: a review of *A Reading of George Herbert*, by Rosemond Tuve.

[2] Letter to J.R.H. in the summer of 1928. See above, p. 117.

[3] Review in the *London Magazine*, vol. 1, no. 7, August 1954, pp. 74–5, of two studies of George Herbert—by Margaret Bottrall and by Joseph H. Summers.

both the mood and, in part, the structure of repeated rhetorical invocation of Herbert's prayer, 'Sighes and Groans'. The section of *Springboard* which is begun with 'Prayer Before Birth' is headed by the epigraph from Herbert: 'Even poisons praise thee'.

The example of Dryden, too, he considered to be a salutary one for his time, and there are many Drydenian undertones in his idiom, apart from the almost parody antitheses of *Autumn Sequel*.[1] MacNeice admired Horace first and last, as he did Housman, and for the same reason: both seemed, in their different ways, to have achieved the admired marriage of individual tone of voice and traditional metrical paradigm. Housman's 'hymn-tune metres', however, he found restricting:

Augustan *of Auden*

> A. E. Housman, whom I join you in admiring, was a virtuoso who could get away with cliché images and hymn-tune metres, but, as you would, I think, admit his methods are not suitable to anyone who has a creed which is either profound or elaborate.[2]

And Housman's idiom was too affected:

> It is a mistake to think of him as a 'simple' poet; the simplicity is often bluff; his very directness, like his regular music, is ironic. There were already many examples in English of the poignancy of a statement so simple as to sound almost naïve. . . . Housman varied this naïveté with a grand manner—a more pompous metric and a diction involving archaisms and poeticisms. . . .[3]

It was Housman, above all, he loved to recite, as Mr. Robert Pocock recalled in the *Radio Portrait*:

> And he would always read poetry aloud; he'd recite Housman above all, lying down at full length in the devotional attitude. . . . And then invariably he'd end up with *Queen of Air and Darkness*. He returned to that almost obsessionally. . . .[4]

In the same programme, Mr. Auden stressed his belief that

[1] E.g., 'Let Demos rule the streets, they own the sky' (*A.S.*, XIX, *C.P.D.*, p. 407).

[2] Letter to W. H. Auden, in *New Verse*, nos. 26 and 27 (Double Number), November 1937, p. 12, regarding Auden's 'return to a versification in more regular stanzas and rhymes', which MacNeice considers 'a very good thing'.

[3] Review of *The Collected Poems of A. E. Housman*, in the *New Republic*, vol. 102, no. 18, 29 April 1940.

[4] Op. cit., p. 20 of script in B.B.C. archives.

'Horace, although or rather because a very different temperament, was a very valuable influence.'[1] MacNeice in 'Memoranda to Horace' certainly identifies himself closely enough with Horace, as man and as poet, sharing a similar predicament, and he asserted explicitly that in this poem

there is a conscious attempt to suggest Horatian rhythms (in English of course one cannot do more than suggest them) combined with the merest reminiscence of Horatian syntax. This technical Horatianizing appears in some other poems too where, I suppose, it goes with something of a Horatian resignation. . . .[2]

Without attempting a more exact technical identification at this point, it may perhaps be suggested that MacNeice comes closer to Horace than to any other poet in this vital matter of expressing his whole personality in a tone of voice—wry, civilized, ironic, warmly involved and coolly detached, slangy and sophisticated, laconic and garrulous—which has to accommodate itself to a strict metrical paradigm. In recalling in *Modern Poetry* his earliest admiration for Horace at school,[3] it is this aspect that he stresses: 'What should be remembered is that the *attitude* in Horace . . . is something consciously applied—one more convention within which the poet has to work.' He seems to anticipate, too, his later Horatianizing in the comment: 'I liked the glitter of Horace . . . and admired his tidiness, realizing that English with its articles and lack of inflexions could hardly ever equal Horace either in concentration or in subtlety of word-order.'

It was the technique of Eliot, however, that was paramount in showing MacNeice the way to the tone of voice that was heard so unmistakably in the poems of the 1930s. It was not Eliot's tone of voice that MacNeice was out to catch, but Eliot's order of technical achievement: the tone of voice itself was a particular, dependent upon knowledge and integration of self. MacNeice has pointed out his technical debt to Eliot in many places. In *Modern Poetry*, he followed up his deprecation of Hopkins's influence on younger poets by commenting:

[1] The difference, presumably, lies in the two main defects traditionally ascribed to Horace: that he was a time-server and a snob. Yet in Part III of the 'Memoranda' MacNeice seems to tolerate these as accidentals.

[2] *P.B.S.B.*, no. 38, September 1963.   [3] *Op. cit.*, pp. 48–9.

Poets like Eliot made a more genuine compromise with ordinary speech rhythms, writing verse portions of which, like some verse in drama, was itself on the conversational plane. . . . Eliot's verse, like a film, relies in every respect very much on its 'cutting'.[1]

In an essay on 'Eliot and the Adolescent' he gave a detailed and convincing description of the impact made upon an adolescent whose 'favourite long poem had been *Prometheus Unbound*' a year before he read Eliot.[2] The volume available to him 'began with *Prufrock* and ended with *The Hollow Men*'. Some of it was not strange:

The images, the rhythms and the hypnotic, incantatory repetitions of *The Hollow Men* were not too alien to anyone brought up on the Bible and on Shakespeare's tragedies and even on the autumnal Victorians. In the same way the pock-marked moon of *Rhapsody on a Windy Night* fell naturally into place beside Shelley's 'dying lady'. But *The Love Song of J. Alfred Prufrock*?[3]

Some of the images were 'little more daring than some images in A. E. Housman', but 'freed from Housman's ti-tum-ti-tum framework' the imagery

seemed to pull much more weight. At the time this release from limitations seemed to me mere release . . . and it was only unconsciously and insidiously that Eliot's extraordinary rhythmical skill rang its bell in my nerves. After a few readings I knew this poem by heart.

It was the modulations of the voice proclaiming its *Weltschmerz*, however, the voice of 'self-pity' and 'masochism', that struck the adolescent, for whom 'Eliot's delicate balance of satire and sympathy was shattered'. Similarly, the 'Portrait of a Lady' could not be fully appreciated,

yet this too was rendered memorable, if not intelligible, by its sheer technical brilliance. Eliot's supple line which could so exactly and

[1] Op. cit., p. 125. He analyses his reaction to Eliot more fully on pp. 56–9, summing up the technique as 'the blend of conversation and incantation, the deliberate flatnesses, the quick cutting, the so-called free association' (p. 58).

[2] In *T. S. Eliot: A Symposium Compiled by Richard Marsh and Tambimuttu*, London, 1948, p. 147.   [3] Ibid. At a Marlborough Lit. Soc. meeting (June 1926), MacNeice introduced 'a difficult new poet', T. S. Eliot.

without fuss convey the slightest *nuance*, change of mood or variation on his theme, seemed admirable even to someone on whom the main theme was largely lost.

In 'Preludes' he felt more at home. The adolescent who 'wanted to play Hamlet in the shadow of the gas-works', and who knew instinctively that the fact of great cities 'mysterious, compelling, frightening' was one of the 'great inescapables' that 'a poet . . . must recognise', appreciated that what Eliot 'expressed so succinctly and vividly' was what he and his generation 'were up against'. As for *The Waste Land*, he found it almost impossible to describe its impact. It was 'the poem in this book which most altered our conception of poetry and, I think one can add, of life'. The literary allusions, the cosmopolitan world, the anthropological symbolism were all unfamiliar.

Yet it had such an enormous impact on us that I am forced to explain it by some such hypothesis as Jung's archetypal myths. . . . The cinema technique of quick cutting, of surprise juxtapositions, of spotting the everyday detail and making it significant, this would naturally intrigue the novelty-mad adolescent and should, like even the most experimental films, soon become easy to grasp; but that the total complex of mood-and-meaning remains for me now, for all its enrichment by experience and study, qualitatively the same as it was then, strikes me as astonishing.

In the ten years between first reading Eliot and bringing out his second collection in 1935, he had enjoyed the 'enrichment by experience and study' and he had, apparently, found the novel techniques 'easy to grasp'. He had also had the benefit of Eliot's rigorous critical rejection of many of the poems he wished to include in the collection, a rejection he accepted willingly:

I am sending my book of poems back to Eliot soon—having ruthlessly struck out all the half baked ones. . . . Should be quite a good book for once, I think, which shows that old Eliot is not such a fool, as two years ago no one would have read the good poems for the bad ones.[1]

---

[1] Letter to J.R.H. from Birmingham, in the summer of 1934. Eliot had returned the original list of poems suggesting the deletions. Professor Dodds also emphasized to me the willingness with which MacNeice accepted Eliot's critical judgement on this occasion —a willingness that he rarely, if ever, showed to anyone else. Cf. the comment in *R.P.* by his sculptor friend, the late George McCann: 'You didn't talk poetry shop with him unless he invited it. He didn't invite criticism from anyone.' (McCann is 'McGuire' of *A.S.*)

Three of the longer poems in the 1935 collection, 'Ode', 'An Eclogue for Christmas', and 'Eclogue by a Five-barred Gate', seem to be particularly stamped with the MacNeice colloquial rhythms. The influence of Eliot, too, is marked in much of the idiom of the Eclogues. The self-conscious stylization, the merged colloquial and incantatory rhythms of 'Prufrock', come through in a passage such as *A*'s third speech in 'An Eclogue for Christmas':

> Í who was Hárlequin in the chíldhood of the céntury,
> Pósed by Picásso besíde an éndless opáque séa,
> Have séen myself sífted and splíntered in bróken fácets,
> Téntative péncillings, éndless liabílities, nó ássets,
>
> ·   ·   ·   ·   ·   ·
>
> They have máde of me púre fórm, a sýmbol or a pástíche,
> Stýlised prófile, ánything but sóul and flésh:
> And thát is whý I túrn this jáded músic ón
> To fóreswéar thóught and becóme an autómatón.

The colloquial rhythms are firmly imposed upon a wavering accentual-syllabic basis, where the underlying trisyllables seem to be attempting in vain the pattern of a dance, until they finally break into the jerky motion of the automaton. There is a strong infusion of the Eliotean *Weltschmerz* that impressed the adolescent, but also a precision, clarity, and ironical dryness in the self-analysis that firm up the rhythms, and illustrate the assimilation of some of Eliot's 'extraordinary rhythmical skill'.

The rhythms also show the shrewdness of his earlier remark about the merging of his prose and verse rhythms into a composite that would enable him to absorb quantities of new experience. Other examples might be selected almost at random:

> B: Whát will háppen to ús when the Státe takes dówn the mánor
> wáll,
> When there is nó móre prívate shóoting or físhing, when the trées
> are áll cút dówn,
> When fáces are áll díals and cánnot smíle or frówn. . . .

Compare these rhetorical/conversational periods with the very

similar cumulative rhythms in a passage of prose reviewing some
fifteen years later, tentatively arranged as verse

And thóse who líke a wríter to have gúts and lóyalties,/thóse who
prefér a ríver, howéver múddy,/to a póol, howéver órnaméntal,
thóse/who are ínteréšted in líving wórds or líving/wórkers, or the
stíll líving Íreland, should cértainly/táke him. [1]

The idiom, too, contains within itself, as an endemic feature, a wide
and well selected range of the contemporary sense-data it has
assimilated:

A: Whát will háppen to ús, plánked and pánelled with jázz?
    Who gó to the théatre where a bláck mán dánces like an éel,
    Where pínk thíghs flásh like the spókes of a whéel, where we féel
    That we knów in advánce áll the jógtrót and the cáke-wálk jókes,
    Áll the búmfún and the gágs of the comédians in bóaters and tóques,
    Áll the trícks of the vírtuósos who invért the úsual. . . .

This coarser, slangy colloquial strain, where he seems to be
trying to assimilate a cocktail lounge or taproom style, in a more
down-to-earth idiom, might similarly be compared with the
style of the breezy film reviews he was doing for the *Spectator*
in the early war years. He described, for example, the 'wonderful
line-up of faces' in the film *Angels over Broadway* as 'béstial,
blótto, gága and Máchiavéllian', a line that might have appeared
as a catalogue, without any incongruity, in the Eclogue, say in the
context of, 'Óld fáces frósted with pówder and chóked in fúrs'. [2]
One feature of this colloquial idiom should be noted: MacNeice
did not attempt any exclusive use of 'the common language of
men'. He referred frequently in his critical writing to the fallacy
of attempting this. [3] The problem is intricate. There are many

---

[1] Review of *Inishfallen, Fare Thee Well*, by Sean O'Casey, in the *N.S.N.*, 19 February
1949. Note the characteristic enjambments.

[2] 21 March 1941.

[3] e.g. his item 'Kersey Noes' in 'A.L.P.': '*Kersey Noes*—and honest russet yeas—are still
recommended by those who take Wordsworth at his word and preach "the common
language of men". I needn't go into this fallacy as Coleridge exposed it at the time.'
(The reference is to Shakespeare's 'russet yeas and honest kersey noes' in *Love's Labour's
Lost*.)

different contemporary idioms. We have, therefore, a basic problem of rhythm and speech that might well be expressed, in metaphysical terms, as the problem of the individual considered as both a particular and a universal.[1] Idiom, like the individual, may be a particular, or it may be a universal, depending upon which aspect the user wishes, or has the catholicity, to stress. To assimilate sufficient elements from the range of contemporary particulars to make his idiom a contemporary universal, linking the speaker with a wide variety of other speakers, and harmonizing his particular selves so that they form a concrete universal: this is a large, but not an unrealizable, ideal.

MacNeice's almost exact contemporary, William Empson, remarked in his *Seven Types of Ambiguity*:

The demands of metre allow the poet to say something which is not normal colloquial English, so that the reader thinks of the various colloquial forms which are near to it. . . . It is for such reasons as this that poetry can be more compact, while seeming to be less precise, than prose.

It is for these reasons, too, among others, that an insensitivity in a poet to the contemporary style of speaking, into which he has been trained to concentrate his powers of apprehension, is so disastrous, can be noticed so quickly. . . .[2]

There is much truth in this claim, even if Mr. Empson's own poetic idiom is so far from an illustration of it. However much the later MacNeice may have admired it, and even worked it into his own idiom in parody imitation, the highly punning and allusive idiom of William Empson the University Wit did not impress the earlier MacNeice. He began a review in *New Verse*[3] of William Empson's *Poems* by saying: 'I should not perhaps be reviewing these poems as this is definitely the kind of poetry I don't like.' He admitted his admiration for the wit and the 'tricks', but concluded: 'All the same I would not say that Mr. Empson is either a good poet or the kind of poet that is required at the moment. . . .

[1] See pp. 96–7 above.
[2] Op. cit., p. 28. First published 1930; 2nd (rev.) ed. 1947, from which this passage is quoted.
[3] No. 16, August, September 1935.

In poetry we want a spareness and clarity (whether Wordsworthian, Drydenic, or Freudian). The clever fellows must wait to show off some other day.' Yet there is much of the contemporary University Wit in the MacNeice idiom of the 1930s, which MacNeice obviously had some trouble in accommodating to the plainer idiom of the Ordinary Man. The important thing is that he was aware of the need to accommodate the two, and continually attempted to find a tone of voice that would avoid the extremes of over-sophistication and dull plainness.

Indeed, this whole problem is treated analytically and descriptively by MacNeice in his 'Eclogue by a Five-barred Gate', which is as much a discussion of the contemporary poet's problem of speech and rhythm as of the spirit of the times. The 'honest, kersey noes' of the shepherds:

> 1. There seems no nater in 'em, they look half dead.
> 2. They be no South Downs, they look so thin and bare. . . .

quickly move, urged by the menacing insistence of Death, to the ironic mock pastoral tones of the University Wit:

> D. Your sheep are gone, they can't speak for you,
>   I must have your credentials, sing me who you are.
> 1. I am a shepherd of the Theocritean breed,
>   Been pasturing my songs, man and boy, this thirty year—
> 2. And for me too my pedigree acceptances
>   Have multiplied beside the approved streams.
> D. This won't do, shepherds, life is not like that,
>   And when it comes to death I may say he is not like that.

As Death questions them more closely, their idiom veers away even more grotesquely from any language of ordinary men:

> D. Have you never thought of Death?
> 1.   Only off and on,
>   Thanatos in Greek, the accent proparoxytone. . . .

Death then loses all patience with the rustic figures of fun ('Cut out for once the dialect and the pedantry'), and tries to tell them unambiguously something about the poet as one dealing in realities, able to 'quote the prices/Of significant living and decent dying', to 'lay the rails level on the sleepers/To carry the powerful train of abstruse thought', and not only

>   .   .   .   the surface vanity,
> The painted nails, the hips narrowed by fashion,
> The hooks and eyes of words. . . .

Here Death explicitly connects the idiom with the attitude and the thing expressed, as MacNeice has been using the varying colloquial rhythms to suggest the varying attitudes of reality and unreality they embody. In the quiet, relentlessly regular flow of Death's rhythms, the firmness and clarity of his idiom, we have the equation with reality, as the wavering, grotesque amalgam of the shepherds' idiom equates with unreality. Death's idiom becomes more pointed and stern as he warms to his theme, his periods developing almost imperceptibly from the rhetorical and incantatory to the more natural and colloquial:

> D. All you do is burke the other and terrible beauty, all you do is
> hedge
>
> And shirk the inevitable issue, all you do
> Is shear your sheep to stop your ears.
> .   .   .   .
> There you go again, your self-congratulation
> Blunts all edges, insulates with wool,
> No spark of reality possible.
> Can't you peel off for even a moment that conscious face?

As the shepherds recite their dreams at Death's insistence, they move from the postured diction of the stage rustic, recalling, perhaps deliberately, Bully Bottom ('2. I'm going to sing first, I had a rare dream'), to the natural rhythms and diction of the ordinary man:

> Well, I dreamt it was a hot day, the territorials
> Were out on melting asphalt under the howitzers,
> The brass music bounced on the houses. . . .

This idiom is more acceptable to Death:

> Thank you, gentlemen, these two dreams are good,
> Better than your daytime madrigals.

The shepherds are now fit to enter the new pastures, the pastures of Death, going, perhaps, from one unreality to another, but now at least properly equipped as poets to enter, with credentials of the right kind. Thus a parable of MacNeice's own time has been told largely as a parable of idiom and speech rhythm. (It is notable that many of the MS. emendations are in the direction of a more natural colloquial flow: for example, Death's comment on the first shepherd's dream, 'Your dream, shepherd,/Is good enough of its kind . . .', is emended from '. . ./Is weak but valid . . .'.)[1]

MacNeice almost certainly has his own dilemma in mind here, as the Apollonian dream poet entering Death's kingdom with something like genuine credentials, now aware, at least, of the kind of idiom to avoid if he is going to deal in realities. In the two Eclogues of *The Earth Compels*, 'Eclogue from Iceland' and 'Eclogue between the Motherless', in the 'Letter to Graham and Anna', and in 'Homage to Clichés', he experiments further with colloquial rhythms, juxtapositions, rapid cuts. The colloquial rhythms and idiom vary as his conception of self varies, or as one aspect of self is pushed to the fore by his theme or the nature of his interlocutors—both the University Wit and the friendly agreeable rattle in the letter to his close friends Graham and Ann Shepard; the neurotic intellectual in the 'Eclogue between the Motherless'; the cocktail lounge wit in 'Homage to Clichés'; very much the shepherd in Death's kingdom in the 'Eclogue from Iceland', trying to make his poet's colloquial speech express not only the realities of that kingdom ('the other and terrible beauty'), but also 'abstract thought':

> You cannot argue with the eyes or voice;
> Argument will frustrate you till you die,
> But go your own way, give the voice the lie,
> Outstare the inhuman eyes. That is the way.

The influence of Auden seems to be marked in some of the more astringent colloquial rhythms of this Eclogue, especially in the speeches of Craven (Auden), where one would expect them:

[1] H.N.

> . . . but this dyspeptic age of ingrown cynics
> Wakes in the morning with a coated tongue. . . .

but also, sometimes not too happily, in those of Ryan (MacNeice):

> And so today at Grimsby men whose lives
> Are warped in Arctic trawlers load and unload
> The shining tons of fish to keep the lords
> Of the market happy with cigars and cars.

This assured accommodation of tone of voice to rhythm and metre is marked in the shorter poems, with the same occasional tendency to resolve the rhythms very far towards colloquialism, the same incantatory effects as the major stresses fall more regularly on the accented syllables, the same counterpointing and juxtaposing for particular effects, the same virtuoso word music, and, in the best of the lyrics, a marked correspondence between rhythmic and speech pattern and theme. Thus, in 'To a Communist' there is a rounded fullness in the broad vowel and diphthong sounds of the first three lines suggesting not only the soft smoothing over of all irregularity, but also the over-simplifying thoughts of the Marxist. This is contrasted, in the thin sounds and jerky rhythm of the first half, and the broad bumps of the second half, of the fourth line with the angularities and particulars that are smoothed over: 'Particular pettiness of stones and grasses.' The menacing conversational silkiness (rather reminiscent of Death's tones in the Eclogue) of the three following lines leads to the anti-climactic bump of the conclusion, 'For óne dáy ónly'

(which takes up in ironic repetition, as so often in other poems, the 'óne níght ónly' of the first line).

The same metrical precision might be illustrated almost at random from the best lyrics of the collections up to *Springboard*. (It seems superfluous to do more than instance a very few such felicities, which are a commonplace of MacNeice criticism.) These include such lyrics, generally acknowledged to be among his very best, as 'The Sunlight on the Garden', and 'Snow'. The theme of the latter being, as he said in his own comment upon it in a broadcast reading, quite simply (despite all the critical exegesis)[1] 'the drunkenness of things being various'. He indicates his awe and excitement in the intimacy and directness of his conversational rhythms, where we *overhear* his innermost astonishment and delight.[2] There is a more elaborate display of onomatopoeic skill, too, of the same kind as in 'To a Communist', in the broad vowels and slow music for the snow and the principle of unity, contrasted with the jerky rhythms and thinner vowel sounds in the music of the tangerine and pips and variety theme, and the flames and gaiety and spite theme. What is perhaps most ingenious of all is this attuning of the *abstract* thought of the poem to the same pitch as that of the *concrete* sense-data. Thus the rounded fullness of the vowel music and the liquid consonants of 'Soundlessly collateral' suggest the theme of unity, the One—the music being at exactly the same pitch as 'the great bay-window was/ Spawning snow and pink roses against it'. Then 'incompatible', with only one broad stressed vowel in its five syllables, provides a hinge for the swing to the jerky music of the lines from 'World is suddener . . .' to the end of the second stanza, the music of variety and the Many, which hits the pitch of variety most precisely in the thin vowels, and the plosives and fricatives, of 'I peel and portion/A tangerine and spit the pips . . .'. Similarly, the onomatopoeic fire music ('And the fire flames with a bubbling sound'), and the music of the abstract statement '. . . for world/Is more spiteful and gay than one supposes . . .', both suggest the spite and gaiety. Finally, the jerky onomatopoeic music of the stress rhythm over the trisyllabic metrical base gives a movement both mesmeric and exciting, which passes naturally to the affirmation of the metaphysical awareness in the last line, an emphatic repetition of the physical awareness of the first two lines:

[1] See Bibliog.

[2] In his radio commentary (broadcast on 18 July 1949) he remarked that the thought struck him as he was sitting by a fire in his room, peeling a tangerine, and became simultaneously aware of the snow outside his window and a vase of huge roses at the window. Professor Dodds told me that he had invited MacNeice and other friends to a party in December. Snow was lying outside and he had roses from his hothouse at his 'great bay-window'. MacNeice was immediately struck, on entering the room, by the contrast. No doubt both occasions are fused in the poem.

On the tóngue on the éyes on the éars in the pálms of one's hánds—
There is móre than gláss betwéen the snów and the húge róses.[1]

'Bagpipe Music' well illustrates both MacNeice's technical
skill and his attempt to make a composite out of the Wit and the
Ordinary Man. The technical skill has received its fair share of
critical comment. The girning and droning of the pipes tuning up
is reproduced in the 'It's no go . . . it's no go' repetitions, which
move swiftly into the skirling rhythms of the reel (predominant
iambs and trochees) interwoven with the slower trisyllabic
rhythms of the strathspey:

The Láird o' Phélps spent Hógmanáy decláring hé was sóber,
Cóunted his féet to próve the fáct and fóund he had óne fóot óver.
Místress Carmíchael hád her fífth, lóoked at the jób with repúlsion,
Sáid to the mídwife, 'Táke it awáy; I'm thróugh with óver-
                                                    prodúction.

Here the cruder and simpler 'peasant's sense of humour', for
which he was grateful in the 'Last Will and Testament', is unobtrusively pointed by the more sophisticated wit into a harmonious blend acceptable to both the University Wit and the Ordinary
Man. Commenting on the verse technique, MacNeice said:
'One of the points about it was to try to suggest by the sound of the
lines the noise of the bagpipes.'[2] (It should be quite clear that
MacNeice is not attempting any precise and virtuosic *mimesis*.
It is perfectly possible to reproduce precisely the rhythms of a
bagpipe composition in meaningful word-music, which is,
indeed, an ancient Gaelic tradition, but MacNeice is simply adapt-
ing the musical pattern to the needs of his theme and poem.[3])

---

[1] The rhythms of the second-last line recall those of the Chorus in *Murder in the Cathedral*: e.g. 'In the mews in the barn in the byre in the market place/In our veins . . .', etc.
(pp. 67–8). Eliot, of course, was working on exactly the same metrical problem as Mac-
Neice, but, as he had been studying MacNeice's poems carefully at this time for the 1935
collection, it is possible that MacNeice's rhythms influenced him directly, however
unconsciously.

[2] In a programme, *The World of Books*, produced by Jocelyn Ferguson and broadcast
on the Home Service on 24 January 1967, introduced by a recorded comment and reading
by MacNeice.

[3] *Cantaireachd* is the name of this traditional syllabic notation, in which melody notes
are represented mainly by vowels, and grace-notes by consonants. It is not improbable

In the dedicatory poem 'To Hedli', which prefaced *Spring-board*, he announced his intention to eschew 'the lilting measure', and it is in the longer poems of the 1940s that one can perhaps see most clearly MacNeice striving for a different tone of voice and a different kind of harmony. The rhetorical tones are still dominant, in a flat and prosaic take-it-or-leave-it manner, in 'Plurality', and there is much false rhetoric in 'The Kingdom'. In 'The North Sea', 'The Window' and 'The Stygian Banks', however, he is dealing with abstract thought as Death had told the shepherd the poet must, and only in 'The North Sea' do the conversational rhythms sag to anything like the rhetorical dullness of 'Plurality'. In 'The Stygian Banks' above all, perhaps, he achieves the colloquial tone of voice he is searching for at this time, with an easy and natural accommodation to the 'lilting measure' about which he was feeling guilty—perhaps because he is dominated throughout by a hopeful metaphysical outlook and the happiest early personal associations.[1] Even the baldest rhetorical periods are very quickly caught up in the rhythmic warmth and dance, to sing in a memorable phrase:

> . . . Nó cáptions and nó járgon,
> Nó dímínútion, distórtion or stérilizátion of éntity,
> But cálling a trée a trée. For thís wísdom
> Is nót an abstráction, a wórdiness, but béing sílence
> Is lóve of the chánting wórld.[2]

In *Ten Burnt Offerings* and *Autumn Sequel*, and even in many of the poems of *Visitations*, the colloquial rhythms appear to express a personality that is wavering and uncertain, seeking a new, or a re-, integration. The voice is questioning, often querulous, perhaps happier when it may shelve the question, escape from self and indulge in verbal elaboration of all kinds. MacNeice remarked admiringly of Sir Thomas Browne in *Autumn Sequel* that he

that MacNeice heard *cantaireachd* in the Isles, or heard of it from the late Hector MacIver or Norman MacCaig. Mr. Allan Rawsthorne, the composer, who knew MacNeice well, commented in *R.P.*: 'I don't think that one would call Louis a particularly musical man in the conventional sense of the word, but on the other hand he had a very great sense of what he wanted music to be doing.'

[1] See above, p. 163.   [2] End of Part VI, *C.P.D.*, p. 266.

'managed by the way/To make our language dance a saraband'.[1]
This is what MacNeice, too, seems to be trying to do. It is not
Herbert who is dominant, but Browne. The wit of Empson,
cerebrally enjoyed, but in the 1930s written off as a fit idiom for
poetry, is indulged. There is a marked increase in the figurative
element in his idiom, the tropes sometimes functional, but often
indulged for their own sakes. This verbal elaboration is, structurally, the same phenomenon as we noted in the elaborate interplay
of images in these poems. The poet, being unsure of himself as
man, seems to be at least assuring himself, in Aristotelian terms,
of the reality of his functional self, the craftsman in words.
Moreover, he had been subjected, as craftsman, to a most rigorous discipline in his translation of *Faust*, and the skills exercised
had to find a large release. Some of the over-elaboration is tire-
some, and in places the wit undoubtedly flags (although the best
poetry of this 'middle stretch/Of life'[2] is arguably better than
might be suggested by the critical coolness with which it was
generally received).

Perhaps the cause of the general critical dissatisfaction is that
MacNeice has expanded the idiomatic and syntactic range of
his periods so far to accommodate the extravagances that the
speaker himself recedes to the dimensions of a small voice at the
mouth of a microphone. Test samples might be taken almost at
random—a characteristic sentence from *Autumn Sequel*, for
instance:

> . . .   *The small, dark hours advance*
> Anonymous tentacles *to drag us down*
> *But, given a house is home, we can seize the chance*
>
> *Of riding out the night till the waking town*
> *Rechristen itself* and the larger hours explode
> In burning trees and barking dogs *while brown*
>
> *And grey turn gold and silver*, and the slow toad
> Of London flashes the jewel in its head
> *And all the gears change up. . . .*[3]

---

[1] *C.P.D.*, p. 397 (*A.S.*, XVI).   [2] *C.P.D.*, p. 309 (*T.B.O.*, VII).
[3] *C.P.D.*, p. 368 (*A.S.*, IX).

Reading such long-winded periods, the reader is almost bound, in self-defence, to register little more than the crisper conversational expressions.[1] Compare the periods of a similar passage in *Autumn Journal*:

> And now the woodpigeon starts again denying
> > The values of the town
> And a car having crossed the hill accelerates, changes
> > Up, having just changed down.[2]

If the passages are representative, and the comparison therefore fair, it seems reasonable to assume that the rotund periods are not caused simply by the nature of the long poem itself, and the *terza rima*. They represent that much deeper effect whose cause is a continuing struggle to find a new tone of voice that can still accommodate itself to the demands of the paradigm.

In many of the poems of *Visitations*, however, the new accommodation has been achieved. Where the poet is thinking aloud, or addressing the reader directly in a dramatic projection, one is aware of a new firmness in the conception of self, especially in the tone of quiet, but assured, wonderment in such poems as 'The Here-and-Never' (in 'A Hand of Snapshots'), 'Time for a Smoke', 'Easter Returns'. In others there is an added (possibly, in part, factitious) note of nightmare, or gloom, toughness, ecstasy, or jigging high spirits, as, for example, in 'April Fool', 'Dreams in Middle Age', 'Jigsaws, II', 'Visitations, I, II'. The varying tones of voice within the patchwork sequences ('A Hand of Snapshots', 'Jigsaws', 'Visitations'), however, indicate a still wavering concept of self, with a marked preference for a Vaughan or Herbert-like simplicity, as in 'Jigsaws, I':

> What ghosts of cuckoo-spit and dew
> Veil those fields that once I knew?

crossed with a more Donne-like colloquial vigour and naturalness:

> Fresh from the knife and coming to,
> I asked myself could this be I
> They had just cut up. . . .

---

[1] Which I have very tentatively italicized.   [2] *C.P.D.*, p. 110 (*A.J.*, V).

One good reason for this colloquial simplicity is probably his old principle of a simple and natural form for a complicated theme. This, however, presents him with the difficulty of avoiding the factitious simplicity that sits uneasily on its theme, as in parts of 'Visitations, V', especially the last stanza:

> So when he slipped off into the night
> Thanking us for his supper
> And then, by the moon's light and his own light,
> Added that he was an angel,
> We were a little, but not so much surprised;
> For we had known him always, we realized.

Yet where the note is both unaffectedly natural, and dense with urgency and anxiety, as in 'Beni Hasan', he seems to have found the self he is trying to express.

Many of the older idiomatic and rhythmic features are still present. Something of the stilted rhetoric, for example, lingers, though it is generally subordinated to the tones of simple question or affirmation, as in the rhetorical periods of 'Visitations, VI'. The word-music, the variations of pace, rapid cutting and juxta-position, are all there, with, in the best, a close equivalence to theme. Thus, in 'Return to Lahore' the to–fro rhythms of the dance fit his Heraclitean theme of then-and-now, the pattern repeated, as well as suggesting the variations in the pattern. The only alteration between the original version, in the *London Magazine*, and the later, is in this direction, the casual, colloquial opening of the second verse, 'Só, nót lóng báck hére, éight yéars áfter, / I fínd . . .', being tightened to the smoother dance rhythm, ' "So lóng! Come báck!" So báck I cóme/To fínd . . .'.[1] The clump-clump of the feet of the 'illiterate seasons' in 'Wessex Guidebook' corresponds to very much the same metaphysical theme. In 'The Other Wing', the rattling onomatopoeic music of the birth of Zeus, and then the clacking, shuttling music of Pallas and the work of her craftsmen, merge via the silky accents of the

---

[1] A critic commenting on the technical virtuosity of his bagpipe imitation, remarked that 'Miss Edith Sitwell once wrote a poem which caught accurately the beat of a slow foxtrot'. ('A Bookman's Diary', in *John o'London's Weekly*, 8 April 1938.)

lecturer-guide ('This ne plus ultra. Ultra? But yes,/Gentlemen, first on the left . . .'), to the tone of voice that is colloquial Mac-Neice in the last two stanzas of the poem, which are also the characteristic tones of the last two collections.

In these collections MacNeice seems to express himself much more freely and regularly in the tone of voice that intermittently dominated *Visitations*, with a stronger infusion of the denseness, the wiry toughness, that firmed the lucid simplicity of, say, 'Beni Hasan'. What is particularly notable is the extent to which the rhetorical style has been resolved into natural thought rhythms that remain dramatic and arresting:

> But what is a practical joke in a world
> Of nonsense, what is a rational attitude
> Towards politics in a world of ciphers,
> Towards sex if you lack all lust, towards art
> If you do not believe in communication?
> And what is a joke about God if you do not
> Accept His existence? Where is the blasphemy?
> No Hell at seventeen feels empty.[1]

In the 'urban enclave' poems, 'The Park', 'The Lake in the Park', 'Dogs in the Park', 'Sunday in the Park', he seems to be almost back to the idiom of the earliest Eliotean *Weltschmerz*; but the idiom is *sui generis*, a sad and ironical music of loss, isolation and forgetfulness.

We have already noted MacNeice's comment on his attempt in 'many of the poems' in *The Burning Perch* 'to get out of the "iambic" groove which we were all born into'; and his 'conscious attempt' in 'Memoranda to Horace' 'to suggest Horatian rhythms', his 'technical Horatianizing' that 'appears in some other poems too where . . . it goes with something of a Horatian resignation'.[2] This 'technical Horatianizing' has, however, been apparent almost from the start, if by the expression we understand the attempt to fit natural colloquial rhythms to a traditional paradigm. All that has altered is the poet's concept of himself, of the tone of voice most appropriate to that self and the themes of the poetry. The strain of nightmare and savagery continues to be marked in the

---

[1] 'The Blasphemies'.   [2] *P.B.S.B.*, no. 38, September 1963.

tones, to equate with the dominant themes, along with a simplicity and wonder that seem truly unaffected in such poems as 'Round the Corner' and 'Star-Gazer'. Perhaps the prevailing tone is that of the poet determined not to be one of the 'elderly poets' who 'profess to be inveterate/Dionysians, despising Apollonians . . .'.[1] If the dream vision of the god has largely turned to nightmare, the poet must still master it, utter it in the controlled voice of the civilized man who may be disillusioned, but who refuses to lose his hope, his articulacy, his wit, or the integrity of his response to experience. It is particularly marked in the colloquial calm of 'The Suicide', which carries him to the proud and dignified assertion at the end of the poem that W. H. Auden quoted as his epitaph in his Memorial Address:

> This man with the shy smile has left behind
> Something that was intact.

And it is perhaps what makes a poem such as 'Goodbye to London' as valuable a piece of making as that other poem on London by the maker William Dunbar, whose refrain MacNeice adapts to suit his mood of rhetorical, but controlled, despair:

> Having left the great mean city, I make
> Shift to pretend I am finally quit of her
> Though that cannot be so long as I work.
> Nevertheless let the petals fall
> Fast from the flower of cities all.

Where the nightmare vision is too powerful, the poet's voice finds an escape from the scream (of 'Bad Dream', for example, in *Visitations*) in an irony that may be silky, as it is throughout 'This is the Life' ('Gracious in granite—this is the life—with their minds made up for ever . . .'), or savage, as in 'New Jerusalem':

> So come up Lazarus: just a spot of make-up
> Is all you need and a steel corset
> And two glass eyes, we will teach you to touch-type
> And give you a police dog to navigate the rush hour.

It often reflects a tired resignation, as in the cumulative refrain

---

[1] 'Memoranda to Horace'.

variations of 'The Habits', which reach their climax in 'The Lord God said it was all for the best'; and it is very often dense with subdued menace, as it seems to come coldly through the clenched teeth of Charon: 'If you want to die you will have to pay for it.'

The greater denseness seems to be especially marked where the Horatian resignation is stronger, as in 'Charon', 'In Lieu', 'After the Crash', 'Another Cold May', 'The Pale Panther'. The rhythms in these poems have been resolved far in the direction of collo-quial naturalness, and yet, as in the later poems of Yeats, they seem to have achieved an even firmer prosodic discipline, making a different kind of rhetorical affirmation, one that is characterized by sombre depth and strength. When the mood of resignation (which, as he 'was not brought up a pagan, is more of a fraud than Horace's')[1] is lightened with hope and faith, we have the tone of the last-published 'Thalassa', which may well have dominated the poems of all this last, uncompleted phase:

> You know the worst: your wills are fickle,
> Your values blurred, your hearts impure
> And your past life a ruined church—
> But let your poison be your cure.

[1] *P.B.S.B.*, no. 38, September 1963.

Epilogue: a Very Rare Everyman

In this study MacNeice has been dismembered as Metaphysician and Maker—whereas, of course, he is Metaphysician-and-Maker. And his poetry has been dismembered as image, prosody, and tone of voice—whereas it is image-prosody-and-tone of voice. The good poet, like the good poem, is a concrete universal. Such dismemberment may be defended by the critic as unavoidable in the act of critical dissection, however hard he may try to bear in mind that the parts are members one of another, that a body of poetry, like a poem, is a concrete. As MacNeice himself put it: 'A poem is a concrete, not an aggregate. It is not thoughts *plus* emotions *plus* diction *plus* rhythm.'[1] What the critic perhaps hopes ultimately to achieve by his dissection is some kind of critical synthesis, however partial.

We began this study of MacNeice with a consideration of two basic points raised by Mr. Julian Symons in connection with the value of the poetry. The first was the extent to which MacNeice might genuinely be said to speak for, and appeal to, the ordinary man, to be the spokesman for his times. The second was his lack of belief, the need for the commitment to a belief in some external guiding force that would alter the very nature of his poetry and make him 'a very fine poet indeed'. Throughout this study it has been our contention, which we have attempted to illustrate at length, that MacNeice did, in fact, increasingly become the spokesman for his times, and that his belief in an external guiding force so strengthened that he could legitimately be termed a believing poet. The time has therefore come to attempt our partial synthesis.

There can be no question that MacNeice cast himself in the part of Everyman in his 'modern morality' play, *One for the Grave*, so loaded is it with autobiographical items, with attitudes and props that appear repeatedly in the poems.[2] There is a prevailing tone of tragic despair, uncertainty and resentment in Everyman's attitude. As the Floor Manager explains of the action and Everyman's part: 'This is an actuality show and our leading actor is an

[1] 'A Comment', in *New Verse*, no. 14, April 1935. See also above, p. 120.
[2] The theme of his uncollected poem, printed in the first number of *New Verse*, January 1933, summed up in its title, 'Everyman his own Pygmalion' (*Moriturus me Saluto*), foreshadows in a striking way that of O.G.

PA

amateur. . . .'[1] Everyman resents the injustice of this arrangement, but he does his best to interpret the enigmatic instructions that come from those directing the rehearsal/performance. He fears the worst as the scene continues to darken and he becomes more and more lost. As he lies on his deathbed, his delinquent son and daughter gabble menacingly in debased Cockney, and in the room are such familiar symbolic props as the cracked mirror and the heavily ticking clock, as well as such a typical later one as the flick-knife.[2] Yet Everyman fights on, with dogged, questioning persistence. He turns his back pointedly on the Floor Manager of the show (Morty: Death) and on his 'three stooges', the Analyst, the Marxist, and the Scientist, and appeals directly to his fellow men:

> *Everyman:* I turn my back on the three of you—(*He looks at Floor Manager*) and on you also. I will talk to my fellows who *don't* know all the answers. . . . *Moriturus te saluto*. I did not choose to be put in this ring to fight, I did not ask to be born, but a babe in arms is in arms in more senses than one and since my birth I've been fighting. Conscript or volunteer—I just don't know which I am— and it may have been a losing battle but at least I've been in it, I've been in it. . . . Everyman must vindicate himself. Oh I know they say one has no choice in the matter, but I don't believe them. . . .[3]

He does not explicitly turn his back on the remote Director, with whom he is not in contact,[4] but this figure is rather unsympathetically presented, distant and unfeeling, as in the poems; and the Doctors of Medicine and Divinity are figures of grim farce. The last worthwhile word[5] is given to the Gravedigger (who sounds like Everyman's father, only 'kinder'):

> *Gravedigger:* Who am I? Most people think I'm the end but I am also the beginning. I was present when your mother bore you. . . .[6]

[1] O.G., p. 17.   [2] O.G., pp. 33–7.   [3] O.G., pp. 73–4.

[4] Nor is he seen directly by the audience. He is simply *Director's Voice*, in which designation there may perhaps be an implication of the *Dei Voluntas* that is so clearly represented.

[5] In the actual ending, MacNeice lapses, in my estimation, into one of his worst bits of maudlin and bathetic sentimentality. As occasionally elsewhere, he does not seem to know when to stop. The play, and its message, would surely have been much more powerfully impressive had it ended with the last words of the Gravedigger to Everyman—or at least with the Director's instructions to him to cue the Finale, on p. 88.

[6] O.G., p. 86.

He comforts Everyman, telling him to disregard the Floor Manager, and salutes him in the name of Life, with which he identifies himself:

Gravedigger: Stop it, Morty. You needn't listen to *him* any more. Every hour of your life he's been standing at your elbow and whispering, or breathing down your neck—and his breath has always been cold. But now at this hour of your death—that's right, hold your head up—it's I who call the tune. Everyman, here and now, I salute you in the name of Life.

Everyman: And *your* name?

Gravedigger: I've just said it. . . .

It cannot be often that a poet has given, intentionally or otherwise, such a clear indication of his attitude to his role and his relationship to his audience. And it is difficult to imagine a wide section of the audience, however critical, not identifying themselves very largely with this Everyman as their spokesman. This Everyman is also the poet who wrote some of MacNeice's best poems.

The Everyman of the modern morality, however, as MacNeice presents him, is a powerful, but dramatically simplified spokesman. He is characterized largely by an avoidance of extremes, a vigorous, clear-sighted, common-sense intelligence, which qualities MacNeice admired, and, surely beyond question, possessed. In this praise of Herbert, he may fairly be said to describe his own achievement, as well as his ideal:

Modern snobbery, like modern neurosis, prefers extremes and it is assumed that to choose a middle way implies a lack of passion, of imagination and of courage. Yet, in fact, a genuine middle way requires both a very steady head and a heart. Perhaps it is only possible for the truly educated in certain places and at certain times. . . .[1]

MacNeice's friend Mr. Goronwy Rees, in describing him in these terms in *A Radio Portrait* as one who 'shunned extremes, finding them dangerous', was nevertheless careful to point out that 'what was most refreshing and delightful about Louis' was his 'highly individual and idiosyncratic outlook'.[2] The mildly

[1] Review of two studies of Herbert in the *London Magazine*, vol. 1, no. 7, August 1954, p. 75.   [2] Op. cit., p. 11.

paradoxical situation therefore arises that MacNeice becomes even more inevitably Everyman by virtue of being so markedly an individual. Both W. H. Auden and Goronwy Rees isolated the distinguishing mark of this individuality as that of the Dandy. As Mr. Auden said: 'Whenever I think of my friend, I think first of the aesthetic Dandy. . . .'[1] And he stressed his opinion that this, together with 'the Scholar in him', saved him from going to extremes:

> The temptation during the Thirties to overestimate the social importance of poetry, and the threat of the poet to become a prima donna, was strong, but Louis MacNeice, to his eternal credit, resisted it much better than most of us. The Dandy in him, I think, was a help, and also the Scholar. . . .

However the individuality may be described, the need to be an individual, and to speak in the voice of that individual, was absolutely basic for MacNeice. This truth to self in the poet involved above all, perhaps, as Mr. Auden suggested, resisting the temptation to fake his feelings to accommodate his audience. MacNeice himself said in 'An Alphabet of Literary Prejudices':

> *Writing Down* to the presumed masses and writing up to a factitious élite are both pusillanimous activities, for in either case the writer is false to his views and to himself. Yet one and the same man can often write honestly and valuably for a small public at one time and for a large one at another; most people after all have lots of different things to say—some esoteric, some 'popular'. What we should never do is write for any public, real or presumed, which is so alien to ourselves that to meet it we have to lie.

MacNeice was well aware of the twin dangers of sentimentality and morbidity that he ran in refusing to fake his feelings. In reviewing a book on Wilfred Owen, he referred to the writer's opinion that in 'Owen's kind of poetry', the poet 'has somehow to avoid . . . the double pitfall of telling the reader about the pity, for that would become sentimentality, and of over-emphasising the suffering, for that would become painful morbidity'. His comment was:

> Yes indeed, there *is* such a double pitfall but there is a narrow way

[1] *R.P.*, p. 5.

through and it is still worth trying to walk it. For that is the human way. If you take any wide detour you may indeed produce works of art, but they will not be so germane to the life of our time.[1]

Yet he knew that finding the way through involved taking risks, and that the writer must be prepared to run them. As he said of 'Vulgarity, Fear of' in 'An Alphabet of Literary Prejudices': '. . . creative literature, which by its nature involves personal feelings, must run the risk of sentimentality. But it's better to be sometimes sentimental, overcoloured, hyperbolical or merely obvious than to play for safety always and get nowhere.'[2]

We have grown so familiar with Wilfred Owen's remark in the proposed Preface to his *Poems* about the poetry being in the pity that we tend, perhaps, to forget that he also said, with no less truth:

All a poet can do today is warn. That is why the true Poets must be truthful.

Warn. Is this not what the best poets of today, and notably Louis MacNeice, have done supremely well? Be truthful. If MacNeice was not true to himself, and to experience, who was?[3] Although they may not be his best, the poems in the 'Visitations' sequence, especially the last, give us what is possibly the best idea of the mature MacNeice. In 'Visitations, VII' ('And the Lord was not in the whirlwind')[4] we see the poet as the prophet Elijah in his cave on Mount Horeb, the holy mount ('He sat in the cave looking out and the cave was the world'), the cave of prophetic warning and hope, which is also the silent cave of making, listening for the 'still small voice in the silence', as he scans the signs in order to do God's will:

> Yet after all that or before it
> As he sat in the cave of his mind (and the cave was the world)

[1] Review of *Wilfred Owen*, by D. S. R. Welland, in the *N.S.*, 22 October 1960.
[2] Op. cit., p. 41.
[3] I began this study with an admiring reference to Mr. G. S. Fraser's remark about MacNeice as a 'speculative metaphysician', but I must admit my failure to sympathize with, even if I think I understand, his now familiar remark from the same essay about MacNeice's 'evasive honesty'. (*Vision and Rhetoric*, etc., p. 180.)
[4] The poem reads like a sermon on 1 Kings 19:11, 12.

Among old worked flints between insight and hindsight,
Suddenly Something, or Someone, darkened the entrance
But shed a new light on the cave and a still small voice in the
    silence
In spite of ill winds and ill atoms blossomed in pure affirmation
Of what lay behind and before it.

Perhaps the gravest risk that MacNeice ran, in the wider perspective, was that he refused to order his reactions to experience
in advance, that he approached experience believing only (though
with absolute conviction) that there was a meaning within the
experience, and that it would, and frequently did, reveal itself.
Such an attitude inevitably invites contrast with the believing
poet in the more orthodox sense. It might therefore be illuminating to hear just such a poet, MacNeice's friend W. R. Rodgers,
commenting on just this empirical attitude of MacNeice's:

Critics sometimes say . . . that MacNeice perhaps lacks an over-all
view, a deep intention, an inherent and linking philosophy. Quite
untrue. . . . If MacNeice's poetry—or his life—at first sight appears
fragmentary or lacking in cohesion, it is not because he failed to edit
or order it; it is simply because he positively refrained from editing or
ordering his sensations in advance. He preferred to leave himself open
to experience, to the infinitely possible and the suddenly surprising,
to the *given*. . . . This, I would suggest, is the very basis of poetry.[1]

This refusal to edit or order his sensations in advance involved
MacNeice in one of the most intractable of creative problems:
that of poetry as creation and poetry as criticism. MacNeice
voices his problem in a conversation in *Roundabout Way*, between
the (autobiographical) Devlin and his friend Hogley, where he
emphasizes the need for a dark glass to shut out too keen an
appreciation of reality:

'Well,' said Devlin, 'why not? It's a bore always seeing through things.
I'd rather have a dark glass any day? [*sic*] One can see the sun through
that.' 'What you really like,' said Hogley, 'is a mirror.' 'Yes, I do.'[2]

---

[1] From a broadcast, *Book Talk*, on the European Service, 18 November 1965.
[2] *R.W.*, p. 76. Cf. his remark in a letter to A.F.B. that 'if one keeps seeing through things
one never sees into them'. (From Carrickfergus, 31 December 1927.)

(Thus he is, essentially, faced with the old problem of the Apollonian poet.) Elaborating on this theme, he goes on to denounce the vitiating effect of a keen critical spirit: 'A born critic is a dead critic. I mean, any critic as such is essentially dead. He must have good taste and so he can't be vulgar. And if you can't be vulgar, you can't create. . . .'[1] This returns us squarely to a familiar problem—the problem, in effect, that he treats as an aspect of the theme of 'The Window', of salving 'from the froth of otherness/ These felt and delectable Others . . .', of achieving the condition of art as the equipoise of the critical and the creative spirit, achieving a creation that is also a communication, hanging a 'bridge in timelessness' and so claiming 'his own authority/To span, to ban, to bless'. Here he expresses the necessary 'surrender' to what is given, but in its positive as well as its negative aspects: the surrender to the surface of experience, but as a controller, a maker, hoping to connect surface and core.

Even if we dislike, as MacNeice himself did, the terms 'major' and 'minor' in assessing the stature of a poet, we might perhaps tentatively use them for a reason MacNeice gave in reviewing *The Letters of W. B. Yeats*:

These letters demand our attention because Yeats was a 'major' poet. It is a term I dislike but it is useful to indicate the gulf between him and such a poet as Æ (just as George Herbert can be called 'major' where Christina Rossetti is 'minor'). The word 'major', however, does carry certain implications of bulk, depth and width, and when we start trying to find these qualities in Yeats, we shall find they have changed in his hands. He *is* wide in a sense—but not the usual sense. He *is* deep in a sense—but not the usual sense. Conclusion: this is a major poet —but a very, very odd one. It will probably be years yet before critics can get this oddity in focus.[2]

Does the best poetry of MacNeice carry any 'implications of bulk, depth and width'? In the terms of our present study, we might venture the explicit claim that his poetry *has* depth, and that the depth derives from his belief in the existence of ultimates that will reveal their real presence in the face of disciplined and persistent questioning—which belief underlies his best poems. As

[1] *R.W.*, p. 78. [2] In the *N.S.N.*, 2 October 1954.

for the width of his poetry, it surely derives from the degree to which he succeeded in resolving his personal paradoxes (while the paradoxes themselves remain stubbornly present) and, in so doing, achieved the status of Everyman—a very rare and particular Everyman.

Bibliography

I. PUBLISHED WORKS OF LOUIS MACNEICE

(Place of publication London, unless stated otherwise)

Blind Fireworks, Gollancz, 1929.

Roundabout Way, Putnam, London and New York, 1932, under the pseudonym 'Louis Malone'.

Poems, Faber, 1935, and Random House, N.Y., 1937.

The Agamemnon of Aeschylus, Faber, 1936, and Harcourt, Brace, N.Y., 1937.

Out of the Picture: A play in two acts, Faber, 1937, and Harcourt, Brace, N.Y., 1938.

Letters from Iceland, with W. H. Auden, Faber and Random House, N.Y., 1937.

I Crossed the Minch, Longmans, London and N.Y., 1938.

Zoo, Michael Joseph, 1938.

Modern Poetry: A Personal Essay, O.U.P., London and N.Y., 1938; re-issue 1968, with an Introduction by Walter Allen.

The Earth Compels, Poems, Faber, 1938.

Autumn Journal, Faber and Random House, N.Y., 1939.

The Last Ditch, Cuala Press, Dublin, 1940.

Selected Poems, Faber, 1940.

Poems 1925–1940, Random House, N.Y., 1940.

Plant and Phantom, Poems, Faber, 1941.

The Poetry of W. B. Yeats, O.U.P., London and N.Y., 1941 (paperback edition, Faber, 1967, with a Foreword by Richard Ellmann).

Meet the U.S. Army, prepared for the Board of Education by the Ministry of Information, 1943.

Springboard, Poems 1941–1944, Faber, 1944, and Random House, N.Y., 1945.

Christopher Columbus: A Radio Play, Faber, 1944 (in Faber Schools Edition, 1963, with new Introduction).

The Dark Tower and Other Radio Scripts, Faber, 1947 (in paperback edition, 1964, without the other radio scripts).

Holes in the Sky, Poems 1944–1947, Faber and Random House, N.Y., 1948.

Collected Poems, 1925–1948, Faber and O.U.P., N.Y., 1949.

Goethe's Faust, Parts I & II, an abridged version translated by Louis MacNeice and E. L. Stahl, Faber, 1951 (paperback ed., 1965), and O.U.P., N.Y., 1952.

Ten Burnt Offerings, Faber, 1952, and O.U.P., N.Y., 1953.

Autumn Sequel, A Rhetorical Poem in XXVI Cantos, Faber, 1954.

The Other Wing, Faber (Ariel Poem for Christmas 1954).

The Penny that Rolled Away, Putnam, N.Y., 1954. (Published by Faber in 1956 as *The Sixpence that Rolled Away*.)

Visitations, Faber, 1957, and O.U.P., N.Y., 1958.

Eighty-Five Poems, selected by the author, Faber and O.U.P., N.Y., 1959.

Solstices, Faber and O.U.P., N.Y., 1961.

The Burning Perch, Faber and O.U.P., N.Y., 1963.

The Mad Islands and *The Administrator: Two Radio Plays*, Faber, 1964.

Astrology, Doubleday, Garden City, N.Y.; Aldus Books, in association with W. H. Allen, London, 1964; re-issue by Spring Books, London, 1966.

The Strings are False, An Unfinished Autobiography, Faber, 1965.

Varieties of Parable, The Clark Lectures, 1963, C.U.P., 1965.

Collected Poems, ed. E. R. Dodds, Faber and O.U.P., N.Y., 1966.

One for the Grave, a modern morality play, Faber, 1968.

Persons from Porlock and Other Plays for Radio, Introd. by W. H. Auden, B.B.C. Publications, 1969.

II. SELECTED ARTICLES AND REVIEWS BY LOUIS MACNEICE

a. Articles
(including printed letters, discussions, etc.)

'Our God Bogus', in *Sir Galahad*, no. 2, 14 May 1929, Oxford.

'Reply to An Enquiry', in *New Verse*, no. 11, Oct. 1934, p. 7. (Enquiry on p. 2.)

'A Comment', in *New Verse*, no. 14, April 1935. (On Hopkins's versification.)

'Some Notes on Mr. Yeats' Plays', in *New Verse*, no. 18, Dec. 1935.

Essay on Poetry in *The Arts Today*, ed. with an Introduction by Geoffrey Grigson, John Lane, the Bodley Head, 1935, pp. 25–67.

Essay on Sir Thomas Malory in *The English Novelists, A survey of the novel by twenty contemporary novelists*, ed. Derek Verschoyle, Chatto and Windus, 1936, pp. 19–28.

Letter to *The Times*, on 12 Nov. 1936, in reply to a review of *Agamemnon*, 2 Nov; another to *Time and Tide*, 21 Nov. about review of *Agamemnon*, 7 Nov. (Reply from reviewer, 28 Nov.)

'A Dialogue on the Necessity for an Active Tradition and Experiment', between Louis MacNeice and Rupert Doone, Group Theatre Paper no. 6, Dec. 1936.

'Subject in Modern Poetry', in *Essays and Studies* by members of The English Association, vol. 22, Oxford, 1937, pp. 144–58.

'A Tripper's Commentary', in the *Listener*, 6 Oct. 1937 (abstract of *Minch*).

'Letter to W. H. Auden' in *New Verse*, nos. 26, 27 (Auden Double Number), Nov. 1937, pp. 11–13.

'In Defence of Vulgarity', in the *Listener*, 29 Dec. 1937.

Letter in *New Verse*, no. 28, Jan. 1938, in reply to an article by Kenneth Allott in the previous number on 'Auden and the Theatre'. (Holograph in Lockwood Memorial Library of the State University of N.Y., Buffalo.)

'A Statement' in *New Verse*, nos. 31 and 32, Autumn 1938 (in reply to a request that he commit himself about poetry).

'Today in Barcelona' in the *Spectator*, 20 Jan. 1939.

'Tendencies in Modern Poetry', a discussion between F. R. Higgins and Louis MacNeice, in the *Listener*, 27 July 1939.

'The Poet in England Today', in the *New Republic*, 25 March 1940.

'American Letter', to Stephen Spender, in *Horizon*, vol. 1, no. 7, July 1940, pp. 462, 464.

'Oxford in the Twenties', in *Partisan Review*, vol. 7, no. 6, Nov.–Dec. 1940, pp. 430–9 (substantially incorporated in *S.A.F.*, pp. 101 ff.).

'Traveller's Return', in *Horizon*, vol. 3, no. 14, Feb. 1941, pp. 110–17.

'Touching America', in *Horizon*, vol. 3, no. 15, March 1941, pp. 207–10.

'The Way We Live Now: IV', in *Penguin New Writing*, no. 5, April 1941, pp. 9–14.

Film reviewing in the *Spectator* during 1941: e.g. 'Freedom Radio', 31 Jan.; 'Tin Pan Alley', 'Arise My Love' and 'Arizona', 14 Feb.; 'Angels Over Broadway' and 'The Trail of the Vigilantes', 21 March.

Reply to Virginia Woolf's 'The Leaning Tower' (in Autumn 1940 issue), in *Folios of New Writing*, Spring 1941.

'L'Ecrivain britannique et la guerre', in *France Libre*, vol. 9, no. 62 Dec. 1945, pp. 103–9.

Introduction to *The Golden Ass of Apuleius, Translated out of the Latin by William Aldington, In the Year 1566*, John Lehmann, London, 1946.

'The English Literary Scene Today. A Return to Responsibility Features

Its Approach in the Present Crisis', in the *N.Y.T.B.R.*, 28 Sept. 1947.

'English Poetry Today', in the *Listener*, 2 Sept. 1948.

'An Alphabet of Literary Prejudices', in the *Windmill*, no. 9, 1948, pp. 38–42.

'Eliot and the Adolescent', in *T. S. Eliot, a symposium*, compiled by Richard Marsh and Tambimuttu, Editions Poetry, London, 1948, pp. 146–51.

'The Crash Landing', in *Botteghe Oscure*, no. 4, Rome, 1949, pp. 378–85. (Uses the same material as in the broadcast, *India at First Sight*.)

'Experiences with Images', in *Orpheus*, vol. 2, London, 1949, pp. 124–32.

'Poetry, the Public and the Critic', in the *N.S.N.*, vol. 38, July–Dec. 1949, pp. 380–1.

'Poetry Needs to Be Subtle and Tough', in the *N.Y.T.B.R.*, 9 Aug., 1953, pp. 7, 17.

A note on the mythopoeic use of his personal friends in *A.S.*, in the *London Magazine*, vol. 1, no. 1, Feb. 1954, p. 104.

Two appreciations of Dylan Thomas, in *Encounter*, vol. 2, no. 1, Jan. 1954, and the *London Magazine*, vol. 1, no. 3, April 1954.

Letter in the *London Magazine*, vol. 2, no. 9, Sept. 1955, in reply to a review of *A.S.* by J. C. Hall in the June issue.

'Lost Generations?', in the *London Magazine*, vol. 4, no. 4, April 1957, pp. 52–5.

Commentaries in *P.B.S.B.*, no. 14, May 1957, on *Visitations*; no. 28, Feb. 1961, on *Solstices*; no. 38, Sept. 1963, on *The Burning Perch*.

Essay on Dylan Thomas in *Dylan Thomas: The Legend and the Poet*, ed. E. W. Tedlock, Heinemann, 1960, pp. 85–7.

'When I Was Twenty-One', in *The Saturday Book 21*, ed. John Hatfield, Hutchinson, 1961, pp. 230–9.

Television reviewing in the *N.S.* in 1961, with obviously sound appreciation of technical problems—e.g. 'Godot on TV', vol. 62, July–Dec., 1961, pp. 27–8. Also in the *N.S.*, increasingly from 1961, some skilled journalism: e.g. 'That Chair of Poetry', vol. 61, Jan.–June 1961, pp. 210, 212; 'Nine New Caps' (largely a report of England versus Ireland at Twickenham), vol. 63, Jan.–June 1962, pp. 239–40; 'Under the Sugar Loaf' (on Dublin, the first contribution to a series 'Out of London'), vol. 63, etc., pp. 948–9; 'Gael Force at Wembley', vol. 65, Jan.–June 1963, p. 876; 'Great Summer Sale' (a description of President Kennedy's visit to Dublin), vol. 66, July–Dec. 1963, pp. 10, 12.

'Childhood Memories', in the *Listener*, 12 Dec. 1963.

b. Book Reviews by Louis MacNeice

Christopher Marlowe, by U.M. Ellis-Fermor (*Cherwell*, 19 Feb. 1927).

The Life of the Dead, by Laura Riding (*New Verse*, no. 6, Dec. 1933, pp. 18–19).

Variations on a Time Theme, by Edwin Muir (*New Verse*, no. 9, June 1934).

Poems, by William Empson (*New Verse*, no. 16, Aug.–Sept. 1935, pp. 17–18).

The Domain of Selfhood, by R. V. Feldman (*Criterion*, vol. 14, Oct. 1934–July 1935, pp. 161–2).

A Full Moon in March, by W. B. Yeats (*New Verse*, no. 19, Feb.–March 1936).

Dramatis Personae, by W. B. Yeats, and *The Notebooks and Papers of Gerard Manley Hopkins*, ed. Humphry House (*Criterion*, vol. 16, Oct. 1936–July 1937, pp. 120–2, and 698–700 respectively).

The Infernal Machine, by Jean Cocteau, trans. Carl Wildman (*London Mercury*, vol. 35, Feb.–April 1937, pp. 430–1).

The Collected Poems of A. E. Housman and *Last Poems and Plays*, by W. B. Yeats (*New Republic*, 29 April 1940, and 24 June 1940 respectively).

Some Memories of W. B. Yeats, by John Masefield, (*Spectator*, 7 Feb. 1941).

A Golden Treasury of Scottish Poetry, selected and arranged by Hugh MacDiarmid (*N.S.N.*, vol. 21, Jan.–June 1941, p. 66).

The Eclogues and the Georgics, trans. R. C. Trevelyan (*N.S.N.*, vol. 29, Jan.–June 1945, p. 293).

The New Testament, newly trans. into English by Ronald Knox (*Spectator*, 10 May 1946).

Pindar, by Gilbert Norwood (*N.S.N.*, vol. 31, Jan.–June 1946, p. 362).

Inishfallen, Fare Thee Well, by Sean O'Casey; *At Freedom's Door*, by Malcolm Lyall; *Fabled Shore*, by Rose Macaulay (*N.S.N.*, vol. 37, Jan.–June 1949, pp. 184, 334, and 618 respectively).

Chiaroscuro: Fragments of an Autobiography, by Augustus John (*N.S.N.*, vol. 43, Jan.–June 1952, p. 408).

Heroic Poetry, by C. M. Bowra, and *A Reading of George Herbert*, by Rosemond Tuve (*N.S.N.*, vol. 44, July–Dec. 1952, pp. 242 and 293–4 respectively).

Edward Lear's Indian Journal 1837–75, ed. Roy Murphy (*N.S.N.*, vol. 45, Jan.–June 1953, p. 402).

Two books on Ireland: *Mind You, I've Said Nothing!* by Honor Tracy, and *The Silent Traveller in Dublin*, by Chiang Yee; also *Teapots and Quails*, by Edward Lear (*N.S.N.*, vol. 46, July–Dec. 1953, pp. 570, 572, and 721 respectively).

The English Epic and its Background, by E. M. W. Tillyard (*N.S.N.*, vol. 47, Jan.–June 1954, p. 804).

The Letters of W. B. Yeats, ed. Allan Wade (*N.S.N.*, vol. 48, July–Dec. 1954, p. 398).

Two studies of George Herbert: by Margaret Bottrall and by Joseph H. Summers (*London Magazine*, vol. 1, no. 7, Aug. 1954, pp. 74–5).

The Poetry of Dylan Thomas, by Prof. Elder Olson (*London Magazine*, May 1955).

The Russet Coat, by Christina Keith (*London Magazine*, vol. 3, no. 8, Aug. 1956).

Dylan Thomas in America, by John Malcolm Brinnin (*N.S.N.*, vol. 51, Jan.–June 1956, pp. 423–4).

Leftover Life to Kill, by Caitlin Thomas (*N.S.N.*, vol. 53, Jan.–June 1957, p. 741).

The Variorum Edition of the Poems of W. B. Yeats, ed. Peter Allt and Russell K. Alspach (*London Magazine*, vol. 5, no. 12, Dec. 1958).

The Poetry of This Age, 1908–58, by J. M. Cohen (*Spectator*, 12 Feb. 1960, pp. 225–6).

Wilfred Owen, by D. S. R. Welland, and *Poems*, by George Seferis, trans. Rex Warner (*N.S.*, vol. 60, July–Dec. 1960, pp. 623–4 and 978–9 respectively).

The Odyssey, trans. Robert Fitzgerald, and *Patrocleia*, Book XVI of Homer's *Iliad*, adapted by Christopher Logue (*Listener*, 4 Oct. 1962).

A Preface to 'The Faerie Queene', by Graham Hough (*Listener*, 31 Jan. 1962).

Between the Lines, by Jon Stallworthy (a study of Yeats's textual alterations) (*Listener*, 21 March 1963).

The Saga of Gisli, trans. George Johnston (*Listener*, 27 June 1963).

The Poetry of Robert Frost, by Reuben Brower (*N.S.*, vol. 66, July–Dec. 1963, p. 46).

III. CRITICAL STUDIES ON LOUIS MACNEICE

'The Leaning Tower', by Virginia Woolf in *Folios of New Writing*, Autumn 1940. (MacNeice as a Leaning Tower writer, pp. 23–6.)

Chapter on Louis MacNeice, pp. 165–78 of *Sowing the Spring, studies in British poets from Hopkins to MacNeice*, by James G. Southworth, Blackwell, Oxford, 1940.

'Louis MacNeice: the Artist as Everyman', by Julian Symons, in *Poetry*, vol. 56, April–Sept. 1940, pp. 86–94.

'Louis MacNeice: Poetry and Commonsense', pp. 53–67 of *Auden and After. The Liberation of Poetry, 1930–1941*, by Francis Scarfe, Routledge, 1942.

'Some Poems of Louis MacNeice', by Stuart Gerry Brown, in *Sewanee Review*, vol. 51, Winter 1943, pp. 62–72.

'Mr. MacNeice and Miss Sitwell', by Richard Crowder in *Poetry*, Jan. 1944, pp. 218–22.

'Louis MacNeice: an Appreciation', by R. L. Cook, in *Poetry Review*, vol. 38, no 3, 1947, pp. 161–70.

'Louis MacNeice: A First Study', by Valentin Iremonger, in the *Bell*, vol. 14, no. 3, June 1947, pp. 67–79. (Stresses the neglect of MacNeice as a subject for lengthy critical study in periodicals.)

'Divided Loyalties in Northern Ireland' in a special issue of the *T.L.S.*, 16 Aug. 1957.

Chapter on Louis MacNeice, pp. 85–9 of *Contemporary English Poetry. An Introduction*, by Anthony Thwaite, Heinemann, 1959.

Chapter on Louis MacNeice, entitled 'Evasive Honesty. The Poetry of Louis MacNeice', pp. 179–92 of *Vision and Rhetoric. Studies in modern poetry*, by G. S. Fraser, Faber, 1959.

' "Snow", A Philosophical Poem. A Study in Critical Procedure', by R. C. Cragg, in *Essays in Criticism*, vol. 3, Oct. 1953, pp. 425–33. This evoked replies from M. A. M. Roberts, D. J. Enright, F. W. Bateson, and S. W. Dawson, in vol. 4. The matter was resumed by Marie Borroff in 'What a Poem is, for instance "Snow" ', in vol. 8, Oct. 1958, pp. 393–404, which evoked replies in vol. 9, pp. 209–11 and 450–1. The poem was also analysed by Sister M. Martin Barry, O.P., in 'MacNeice's "Snow" ', item 10 in *Explicator*, Nov. 1957.

'*Med Mitt Sinns Seks Sylindre. Lyrikeren Louis MacNeice*', by Ellinor Lervik in *Vinduet*, no. 1, 1961, Gyldendal, Oslo, pp. 227–32.

Obituary tributes: by T. S. Eliot in *The Times*, 5 Sept. 1963; Philip Hope Wallace and Julian Symons in the *Guardian* on, respectively, 4 and 5 Sept.; Philip Larkin in the *N.S.*, 6 Sept.; A. Alvarez in the *Observer*, 8 Sept.; Cyril Connolly in the *Sunday Times*, 8 Sept.;

John Boyd in the *Belfast Telegraph*, 7 Sept.; Walter Allen in the 'London Literary Letter' in *N.Y.T.B.R.*, 22 Sept.

'Louis MacNeice: A Memorial Address', by W. H. Auden, delivered at All Souls, Langham Place, 17 Oct. 1963. Privately printed for Faber and Faber. (Extracts in the *Listener*, 24 Oct. 1963.)

'Louis MacNeice: Memorial Impressions', by W. H. Auden, in *Encounter*, vol. 21, no. 5, Nov. 1963, pp. 48–9.

'The Legacy of Louis MacNeice', by Richard M. Ellmann, in *New Republic*, 26 Oct. 1963.

'Louis MacNeice', by Ian Hamilton, in the *London Magazine*, Nov. 1963, pp. 62–6.

'Louis MacNeice and Bernard Spencer', by John Betjeman, in the *London Magazine*, Dec. 1963, pp. 62–4.

Introduction by W. H. Auden to *Selected Poems of Louis MacNeice*, Faber Paperback, 1964.

'Modes of Control', by Thom Gunn in *Yale Review*, vol. 53, no. 3, March 1964 (ostensibly a review of *B.P.* but in effect an examination of MacNeice—on pp. 453–4—along with four other poets in terms suggested by the title), pp. 447–58.

'Louis MacNeice', by Douglas Sealey in the *Dubliner*, Spring 1964, pp. 4–13.

'Louis MacNeice', by Allen Curnow, in *Landfall*, vol. 18, 1964, pp. 58–62.

'Louis MacNeice and the Line of Least Resistance', by Stephen Wall, in the *Review*, no. 11/12 (a Special Number on the Thirties), undated [1964].

'Louis MacNeice', by John Press, Longmans, Green & Co. for the British Council, 1965.

' "The Dance Above the Dazzling Wave": The Poetry of Louis MacNeice (1907–1963)', by Desmond Pacey in *Proceedings and Transactions of the Royal Society of Canada*, vol. 3, ser. 4, June 1965, pp. 147–63.

'*Louis MacNeice, un poète pendant les années 30: un poète de la radio*', by Serge Faucherau, in *Critique*, vol. 22, no. 225, 1966, pp. 131–49.

'MacNeice as Critic', by John Wain, in *Encounter*, Nov. 1966, pp. 49–55.

'100 Years. Marlburian reflections.' Article in the Lent 1966 centenary edition of the *Marlburian* with much interesting material on the literary tradition at Marlborough, and on Louis MacNeice in particular.

'The Black Clock: The Poetic Achievement of Louis MacNeice', by W. J. Smith, in the *Hollins Critic*, vol. 4, no. 2, 1967, pp. 1–11.

' "A heart that leaps to a fife band": the Irish Poems of Louis MacNeice', by S. McMahon, in *Eire-Ireland*, vol. 2, no. 4, 1967, pp. 126–39.

'MacNeice's "Perseus" ', by J. I. Cope, in *Explicator*, vol. 26, 1968, item 48, p. 32.

'The Thirties Poets at Oxford', by A. T. Tolley, in the *University of Toronto Quarterly*, vol. 37, no. 4, July 1968, pp. 338–58.

'Louis MacNeice: The Last Decade', by Julian Gitzen, in *Twentieth Century Literature*, vol. 14, no. 3, Oct. 1968, pp. 133–41.

'A Demise of Poets', Chapter 10 of *Portrait of the Artist as a Professional Man*, by Rayner Heppenstall (Peter Owen, 1969), is a memoir of Louis MacNeice.

Many of the reviews of *C.P.D.* were retrospective assessments: e.g., 'The Brilliant Mr. MacNeice', by Stephen Spender, in *New Republic*, vol. 156, no. 4, Jan. 1967, pp. 32–4.

'MacNeice and Auden', by Graham Hough, in the *Critical Quarterly*, vol. 9, no. 1, Spring 1967; 'A Misrepresented Poet', by Michael Longley, in the *Dublin Magazine*, vol. 6, no. 1, Spring 1967; 'A Craftsman's Testament', by Sean Lucy, in the *Tablet*, 13 May 1967; 'The Cad with the Golden Tongue', by John Whitehead, in *Essays in Criticism*, vol. 19, no. 2, April 1969 (see also vol. 20, no. 1, Jan. 1970).

'Louis MacNeice', by Walter Allen, in *Essays by Divers Hands*, vol. 35, 1969, pp. 1–17.

'A Poet's Revisions: a Consideration of MacNeice's "Blind Fireworks" ', by Moya Brennan, in *Western Humanities Review*, vol. 23, no. 2, 1969, pp. 159–71.

'The Burning Perch. A Memoir of Louis MacNeice', by Robert Pocock, in *Encounter*, vol. 33, no. 5, 1969, pp. 70–4.

Several radio programmes, mainly recollections of MacNeice, also had critical assessments, notably: *Louis MacNeice: A Radio Portrait*, produced by Robert Pocock, and narrated by Goronwy Rees, Third Programme, 7 Sept. 1966; and *The World of Books*, produced by Jocelyn Ferguson, Home Service, 24 Jan. 1967 (where Goronwy Rees discussed *C.P.D.* with Bryan Robertson and Vernon Scannell).

NOTE

A much fuller Bibliography, by the same author, will be found in the *Bulletin of Bibliography and Magazine Notes*, vol. 27, nos. 2 and 3, 1970.

This has details of uncollected poems and prose fiction, including juvenilia, printed but uncollected; reviews of MacNeice's published work; location of unpublished works and drafts. Most of this last, outside the archives of the B.B.C., appears to be collected in four libraries in the United States: the Library of the University of Texas; the Lockwood Memorial Library of the State University of New York; the Butler Library of Columbia University; and the Berg Collection of English and American Literature in the New York Public Library. Details of the holdings in Texas and Columbia are contained in the following articles: 'The Louis MacNeice Collection', by F. G. Stoddard, in the *Library Chronicle of the University of Texas*, vol. 8, no. 4, Spring 1968, pp. 50–5; and in 'Recent Notable Purchases', by K. A. Lohf, in *Columbia Library Columns*, Nov. 1969, pp. 36 and 40.

(Any footnote reference to 'Bibliog.' not found in this abbreviated version will be found in the fuller Bibliography in the *Bulletin*.)

Index